The MultiGradeMultiLevel-Methodology and its Global Significance

Book series: Theory and Practice of School Pedagogy. Vol. 34

Thomas Müller, Ulrike Lichtinger, Ralf Girg

The MultiGradeMultiLevel-Methodology and its Global Significance

Ladders of Learning – Scientific Horizons –
Teacher Education

Prolog Verlag
Immenhausen near Kassel / Germany 2015

The German National Library registers this publication in
the German National Bibliography; details can be found on the internet on:
https://portal.dnb.de.

© 2015 by PROLOG-VERLAG Immenhausen near Kassel / Germany
https://prolog.budrich.de/

     ISBN   978-3-934575-87-5 (Paperback)
     eISBN 978-3-8474-1443-8 (eBook)

Jacket illustration: Bettina Lehfeldt, Kleinmachnow – www.lehfeldtgraphic.de

Books on Demand GmbH, Norderstedt

Preface

Can you imagine that we found excellent schools in a poor Indian village? Can you imagine that in this school the world's best education is practiced? Can you imagine that innovative schooling is inexpensively possible for all children in the world?

Our Research Team Integral at the Universities of Regensburg and Würzburg, Germany, has been most surprised when entering this village school near Rishi Valley, Madanapalle, India ten years ago: 40 children between four and eleven were sitting on the floor at different round tables over individual material and worked concentrated. The teacher was with some children at one of the tables. Some children were standing at the side of the room, writing on blackboards. Others were on their way to the back of the room where learning material was stored. Everybody in the room was deeply involved in his activities, contributing to an atmosphere of joy and mindful work. But – what was going on there? What kind of school was this?

First of all, it was even for well-trained school developers and researchers like us hardly possible to understand how the educational process was designed. It took several years of participatory action research to fully understand. This book is an attempt to introduce the pedagogy behind the shortly described situation above. It focuses on explicating learning with Ladders of Learning and teaching with the MultiGradeMultiLevel-Methodology (MGML). It is based on the in 2012 published book "Lernen mit Lernleitern", which for the first time presented the MGML-Methodology on a scientific basis in the German-speaking countries, showed variations in the German-speaking area and offered conclusions for teacher education. The present book is not only a translation, but represents a completely revised, updated, and expanded publication.

To do so, we would like to invite the reader into the world of Rishi Valley, India, where the impulses came from, and to the lives of Padmanabha Rao and Anumula Rama, the couple who invented MGML in the 1980s. The introduction will help the reader to find into this complex interesting educational cosmos and learn more about the Rao couple before chapter 1 tells more about MGML's history and design. Chapter 2 shows scientific traits. It offers the reader a fine grasp of how MGML is embedded in the 21st century's cultures of learning. Only through these aspects it can be made clear why the MGML-Methodology experiences such a strong demand and emanation worldwide. Without a doubt Ladders of Learning are an essential part of this methodology, but they are neither conceivable nor effective without an intensive examination with the underlying questions concerning the topic of learning in the beginning 21st century. Chapter 3 highlights international variations of working with MGML and opens out into chapter 4, outlining consequences and introducing existing projects. The main focus is on the arising and existing variations in Germany. From there chapter 5 discloses MGML's potentials of growth and flowering.

In pursuing the project of understanding the MGML-Methodology and publishing this book Research Team Integral has benefitted from action research in India. Of course, we have been particularly stimulated by the children and teachers at the schools and would like to thank them. Our learning has been inspired a lot by being with them, watching, joining in. Besides, many fruitful dialogues with Padmanabha Rao and Anumula Rama and their RIVER-team have taken place over the years and brought deep insights. Meanwhile, we also have become good friends and cooperation colleagues. Learning how MGML works and understanding its main principles has been such a fascinating endeavor, a joyful and meaningful activity. In this book we would like to share this experience with you.

Thomas Müller, Ulrike Lichtinger, Ralf Girg

Content

1 Introduction

Let us start our journey at the project's very beginning: In the 1980s a young married couple is holding an orange cloth bag in its hands. The two wander through a landscape plagued by drought in Southern India and arrive at a poor village. On the bag it says 'School in a Box'. They bring the school to the village. Thirty years later and with the development of the MultiGradeMultiLevel-Methodology and its Ladders of Learning the worldwide most effective school development movement has risen. 10.000.000 students learn with it. How did it come to this? And which fundamental ideas are to be found inside of the cloth bag?

This married couple has been working as the directors of RIVER (Rishi Valley Institute for Educational Resources) since the 1980s. Their names are Padmanabha Rao and Anumula Rama. Together with their team they have been establishing schools for the rural Indian population. In these schools every child is able to develop and pursue an individual, socially assisted and simultaneously structured path of learning on the basis of its cultural background.

At the beginning of Padmanabha Rao's and Anumula Rama's work stood an open, four-year long practical development that is characterized by them as 'action research'. The initial result of this development was a flexibly applicable learning set for individualized working by children called 'School in a Box'. Together with this learning material the couple organized the development and establishment of 12, today 10, rural schools. The so called 'Satellite Schools' are located in small villages of the rural population surrounding Rishi Valley School. Over the years RIVER has grown into a center of school development, teacher education and continuing education of teachers. In this position RIVER has been coordinating all national and international developments for quite some time. RIVER, in cooperation with experimental and model schools, supports school developments with fully individualized learning arrangements by means of corresponding designer workshops, seminars, courses, practical stays, and continued educations.

The goal has been and still is to provide educational processes in schools for children of all social classes and levels of aptitude, while at the same time making these processes manageable and shapeable for the teacher. This has been made and is possible through the development of the MultiGradeMultiLevel-Methodology (MGML).

The innovative effect of their commitment in India and beyond has been nationally and prestigiously rewarded internationally on several occasions. Hence, Padmanabha Rao and Anumula Rama were honored as directors of the RIVER-Team with the Global Development Award in 2005 that is sponsored by the Japanese government. In 2009 they won the 'Award for Indian Social Entrepreneur of the Year' by the Schwab-Foundation during the World Economic Forum. They gave a speech in Davos in 2010 and since 2012 RIVER is counted among the 100 best NGOs worldwide by The Global Journal. Furthermore, they also won the renowned Jindal-Prize for 'Education – with emphasis on moral upliftment' in 2012.

The most important European cooperation partners of RIVER are the authors of this book at the Chair for School Pedagogy at the University of Regensburg and the Chair for Pedagogy for Behavioral Disorders at the University of Würzburg. These European cooperation partners work together as 'Team Forschung Integral' (Research Team Integral). Both sides furthermore cultivate international contacts to further universities, educational institutions and school development initiatives.

Insights into the educational forms of MGML-Methodology design could be gathered through study and research stays since 2002. These initial contacts to RIVER developed into a continuing, scientific cooperation with the Indian colleagues. Since 2006 it is possible for teacher trainees and interested teachers to get involved with the meanwhile grown cooperation project and also to participate in its emanation. Practical development projects and variations of the MGML-Methodology have been established in the context of the international emanation at Bavarian schools since 2007. The participating schools range from special-needs schools to high schools. The interest of teachers and academics broadened nationally and internationally in 2012.

By visualizing the formation of the MGML-Methodology, a question remains: What exactly makes the effective power of Padmanabha Rao's and Anumula Rama's work?

How can it be that the initial work that has been literally been brought into the poorest villages amidst a landscape plagued by drought, villages to which not a single paved street leads and that have neither a sewerage nor running water, nor constant power supply, has developed into the worldwide most effective school development reforms ever?

Maybe it is the deeply-rooted trust in the life processes and the joy in education. The conviction of schooling is a society forming, supporting and changing power. Most certainly it is the freedom to let education and schooling grow with and by the people – far off from established expectations and administrative perceptions. Furthermore, to appreciate all people in the school environment with a strong awareness, regardless of age, life experience and profession, by perceiving, appreciating and validating that every one of them contributes something meaningful with his biography. From this future arises.

2 The MultiGradeMultiLevel-Methodology and its Ladders of Learning

Chapter 2 deals with the MultiGradeMultiLevel-Methodology's (MGML) development in Rishi Valley, southern India as well as with the description of MGML's major elements. Based on Jiddu Krishnamurti's philosophy on life and education it was the vision of MGML founders Padmanabha Rao and Anumula Rama to bring the best school to poor children of rural India. Within several years of action research a complex methodology was designed in the 1980s – MGML was born.

Within this methodology fully individualized and concreative learning is facilitated by systematic Ladders of Learning that are tied to an activity-oriented material pool. These allow children to work at their own pace, circulate through the classroom and feel encouraged to collaboration. Sophisticated evaluation tools show the learners' progress and free the teacher to new roles and tasks.

In several phases teachers are supported to internalize the possibilities of working with the MGML-Methodology. They are trained to create and use adequate MGML learning material, coordinate learning processes, observe, give support to children as well as reflect their attitude and actions.

2.1 History and Growth of the RIVER-Projects

Prior to taking a look at the development and progress of the Rishi Valley Institute for Educational Resources (RIVER) in recent years, it makes sense to illustrate the institute's content-related and educational embedding in the larger complex of Rishi Valley. Hence, the next couple of passages will serve to describe the regional location within India and to talk about the educational philosopher Jiddu Krishnamurti whose impulses lead to the establishment of the institute in Rishi Valley. Subsequently, the renowned Rishi Valley School's basic nature will be outlined.

2.1.1 Regional Location in India

Rishi Valley is located in southern India in the most southern part of the federal state of Andhra Pradesh near the city of Madanapalle in the Chittoor District. Rishi Valley is situated 800 meters above sea level at an average. This part of southern India belongs to the Karnataka Plateau and is well-known for its fascinating rock formations in its granite mountains. The scenery is cluttered with thin grass and bushes at higher altitudes. To the West and South-West Rishi Valley is bookended by the Rishi Konda and the nearby Hill-Station of Horsley Hills' mountain range that reaches up to 1400 meters above sea level.

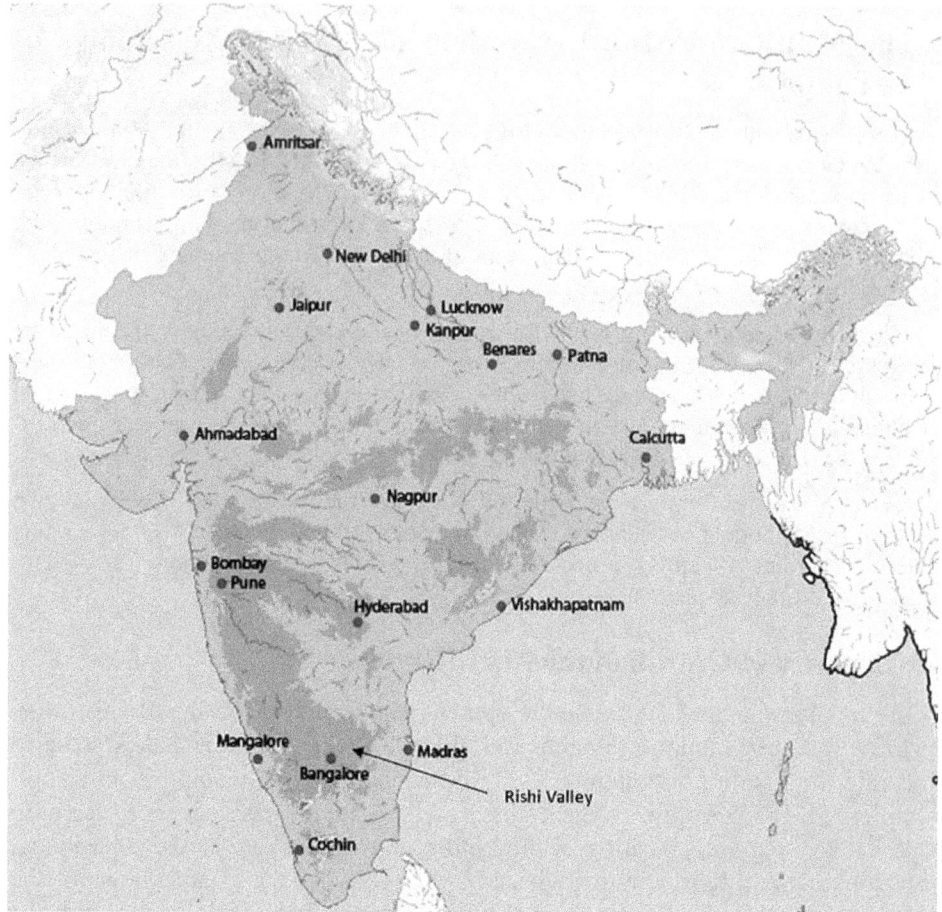

Fig.1: Rishi Valley, located in the south of India

The valley and the mountain plains that are being used as pastures have been civilized since the Neolithic Age. Shepherds and peasants have cultivated the area for centuries. Five smaller villages and one bigger place called Thettu are currently home to more than 5000 people. Thettu has a temple and a tradition of pilgrimage. The southern Indian language Telugu is spoken in the valley, as it is in the entire federal state of Andhra Pradesh. However, the vocabulary varies immensely in the various regions.

A new tarred road opens up the valley that is interspersed with little fields. The typical Indian buses run three times a day, move workers to the nearby city and pupils to secondary school. Today's transformations that under the name of global change have already been described in the introduction have found their way into the valley, especially in recent years. Two mobile transmission towers at the end of the valley are emblematic of this development.

The city of Madanapalle is about 14 km away from Rishi valley and has roughly 180 000 inhabitants. Madanapalle has seen a lot of building activity and is growing rapidly. On the way from Madanapalle to Rishi Valley one goes by several villages like Angalu that are changing into places with a small-town character due to the increase in population.

The eastern access into the otherwise quiet valley is tangent to a busy connecting road. Increasing truck and individual traffic, as well as a recently broadened four-lane bridge over a dried-out riverbed, have a presentiment of what is about to happen over the next ten years in the area. The dynamic developments of urban areas like Bangalore (120 km away) and Chennai (240 km away) with their industrial parks are arriving at the rural areas. Brisk building activity on the outskirts, new living and industrial areas, a new beltway that amply bypasses Madanapalle and the many new automobiles belonging to the Indian middle-class are witnesses of the quick transformations.

When climbing one of the big slabs of rock on the northern side of the valley a tree-lined green area several square kilometers in size stretches out at one's feet. This area covers the valley and is in stark contrast to the barren mountain plains. Granted sufficient precipitation per year, the green area sports an almost closed canopy of leaves. This oasis in the middle of an otherwise barren landscape is a result of decades of sustainable, ecological work done by the participants of Rishi Valley.

2.1.2 Educational Practice and Philosophy by Jiddu Krishnamurti

The green area just mentioned is home to the Rishi Valley Education Center that is the leading facility for all projects. The nucleus of these initiatives is the renowned Rishi Valley School. Its establishment traces back to the educational philosopher Jiddu Krishnamurti (1895 – 1986).

Jiddu Krishnamurti is counted among the most influential Indian philosophers of the 20th century in philosophical reference books, alongside Mahatma Gandhi, Ramana Maharshi, Rabindranath Tagore and Sri Aurobindo (Sequeira, 1996). The UNESCO listed him among the 100 hundred most important personages in the history of mankind regarding relevant statements considering the field of pedagogy (Thapan 2001, 273-275).

Jiddu Krishnamurti was born in the city of Madanapalle. He was proclaimed a 'world teacher' by members of the Indian section of the theosophical society in Adyar, Madras (nowadays Chennai) at the beginning of the last century. After parting with the theosophical society and also rejecting the projections of a 'world teacher', Jiddu Krishnamurti proceeded to offer and give impulses for all questions relevant in life. He held many lectures throughout the decades since the 1930s. Part of his actions and his work explicitly deals with the central questions concerning education. Amongst others, his books "Education and the Significance of Life", "The Whole Movement of Life is Learning" and "On Education" address the existential questions and phenomena one is confronted with in the field of education (Krishnamurti 1991; 2005; 2006a; 2006b).

From a scientific point of view that transcends a rational perception of Krishnamurti's extensive work, the philosopher provides central impulses for a non-dualistic sense of the world and a non-dualistic living culture by way of his teachings and scriptures. Both his actions and his opus, such as the numerous autobiographical documents like "Krishnamurti's Notebook" (Krishnamurti 2004), point to an altered consciousness that radically challenges the present conditioning of an individual's perspectival. Krishnamurti's seemingly multi-layered, transcendental-phenomenological analyses examine the conditionality of human action, the psychical sensitivities of human-beings and also their possibilities of perceptual consciousness. According to the authors of this book, he indicates to the possibility of abandoning one's own conditioning and instead being able to perceive the world with a non-dualistic consciousness. At the same time, he wants to enter into a real dialogue of collective perception and thought with the listener in his talks. Awareness of non-duality is able to appear within the flowing situation of the everlasting now.

Alongside further approaches of non-dual perception Research Team Integral places Jiddu Krishnamurti's pedagogical-philosophical assertions within the descriptions of an "integral consciousness" (Gottwald 2012) and for the field of education within a culture of integral educational activity cultures (Girg 2007; Müller / Girg 2007; Fuhr / Dauber 2002).

Jiddu Krishnamurti puts a special emphasis on learning within life in his statements. For him, life's connection to learning is a fundamental, primordial phenomenon: "Life is learning all the time." Learning takes place whenever it stays situated in the stream of life and the occurring situations are embraced as continuous reasons for learning. Everybody is a teacher and a student for himself all the time and therefore continuously stays a learner:

> "Life is a constant process of teaching and learning: To teach and to learn is not possible if there is a motive, and when we have a motive the state of learning is not possible. Now, watch this carefully: In the very nature of teaching and learning there is humility. You are the teacher and you are the taught. So there is no pupil and there is no teacher, no guru and no sisha, there is only teaching and learning which is going on with me. I am learning and I am also teaching myself; the whole process is one" (Krishnamurti 2006 / 1974, 149).

Hillary Rodrigues, a Canadian professor of anthropology and inter-religious studies, has delineated Krishnamurti's central statements concerning consciousness and its psychological, mental as well as emotional processes in a comprehensive analysis. Despite the danger of reduction when interpreting Krishnamurti, Hillary Rodrigues achieves to distinguish central, recurring sets of statements in Krishnamurti's teachings that she documented and systematized. Rodrigues finds the dissolution of an I-construction of the individual deemed necessary by Krishnamurti in a non-judgmental, non-dualistic perception of a "seeing what it is" that enables a "total insight". This total insight enables the individual to an immediate action, a "true action" that remains unimpaired by the perspective rationality of a conditioned 'I' (Rodrigues 2001, 117). If the individual stays in this flow of perception and action, a state will emerge that Krishnamurti calls "meditation". "The meditative mind is seeing, watching, listening, without the word, without comment, without opinion – attentive to the movement of life in all its relationship throughout the day" (Krishnamurti 1991, 18).

The scientific papers on Jiddu Krishnamurti by Ralf Girg further demonstrate the outstanding importance of Krishnamurti's statements on reality of life in the context of a non-dual pedagogy. These statements bring about a clearly deepened understanding of learning within life (Girg 2007, 142-44). What is more, this understanding bespeaks a diversified culture of action for teachers in school or lecturers at the university. Hence, teachers and lectures concede the decisive educational effect to the situative event as a concreative interaction within the educational processes over and over again, overriding all scheduling. Due to his contact with Indira Gandhi Jiddu Krishnamurti was also known and acknowledged in government circles during his lifetime.

Jiddu Krishnamurti's teachings that are available as books and video recordings in English are being published by the Krishnamurti Foundation India and international Krishnamurti foundations in the United States and Great Britain. The so called Study Centers, one of which is located in Krishnamurti's former tenement in Rishi Valley, offer a place for more sophisticated studies on the Indian philosopher.

2.1.3 The Rishi Valley School and the Rishi Valley Education Centre

Corresponding to the importance of education in Krishnamurti's teachings the establishment of schools ensued in India and later on also internationally. The first school that came to existence was the Rishi Valley School. A place not far from a gigantic banyan tree in Rishi Valley seemed to be the right spot for a school with a new culture of education. Nowadays there are eight schools all over the world that offer a culture of living and education nourished from Krishnamurti's impulses in their day-to-day practice. Six of these schools can be found in India, one in Ojai California and one in Brockwood Park School near London.

The Rishi Valley School as a residential school provides an integral education with a holistic understanding that in many ways follows Jiddu Krishnamurti's integral task description of a school in its everyday activities: "Surely a school is a place where one learns about the totality, the wholeness of life" (www.brockwood.org.uk/intentions.html).

The Rishi Valley School as an approved progressive school has been in existence for more than 80 years as an English Medium School, i.e. a school with English as its working language. Its diverse, culturally rich educational range offers graduations on the level of 'academic excellence.' The effort put in by the highly qualified staff to guarantee a comprehensive formation of personality and character makes available the best chances to get accepted by universities and furthermore enables successful professional developments and artistic ways of life. "If the teacher is of the right kind, he will not depend on a method, but will study each individual pupil" (Krishnamurti 1981, 27). The culture of collective learning and living on campus is emblematic of this holistic education with an integral culture of action. Throughout the daily job of education the goal is being considered that the educational processes in the Rishi Valley School, which are inspired by Jiddu Krishnamurti's teachings, far exceed strictly pragmatic prevocational or academic intentions. Questioning, open dialogue and collective learning within communal life are of major importance in the Rishi Valley School. Albeit also overloaded schedules in India, the people at Rishi Valley School take their time for various projects in order to indulge into the phenomena of nature, culture and the underlying life. The diversity of Indian culture is especially presented and preserved in Rishi Valley, for example, by the great number of artists from all genres and professions that on their visits to Rishi Valley School show off their skills or even stay for several years and work together with the adolescents in separate workshops.

The school is not based on competition and comparison. Instead, the uniqueness of every pupil in collective interaction is to be nurtured. This is the reason why initially no marks are assigned in this school. It is not until the higher grades that due to regulations by the Indian general education system even this private school needs to assign marks. The integral approach of educational work at the Rishi Valley School is formulated by Krishnamurti in the preface to his letters to his schools as such:

> "They are to be concerned with the cultivation of the total human being. These centers of education must help the student and education to flower naturally. The flowering is really very important; otherwise education becomes merely a mechanical process oriented to a career, to some kind of profession" (Krishnamurti 2006a, n.p.).

In order to support the flowering in the lives of children and adolescents Krishnamurti assigns comprehensive and undivided responsibility for the own as well as for the adolescents' educational processes to the teacher.

> "Education is not merely the teaching of various academic subjects; it is also the cultivation of total responsibility in the student. (...) You, the educator in these schools, need to have this deep concern and care of this total responsibility" (Krishnamurti 2006, 28-30).

In a sociological study that has been enhanced in a second edition in 2006, Meenakshi Thapan documents the underlying philosophies the teachers at Rishi Valley School choose to work with. This study clearly shows that while a large part of the staff relate to Krishnamurti in their actions and teaching activity, others have developed a distinct, profound, professional stance and still others interpret their job very pragmatically (Thapan 2006, 83-85).

Today Rishi Valley School is listed among the qualitatively leading educational institutions in all of India. It was awarded best 'Residential School' of India in 2014. Many parents attend interviews to be granted entrance to the school for their children. The high demand is being shown by the ratio of 1:10 for a spot in the school and the number of aspirants. Roughly 360 pupils spend about eight months, divided up into two terms, in Rishi Valley per year. They come from various cultural and linguistic regions all over India and are children from intellectually minded, often prosperous and wealthy families. Since the 'Right to Education Act', passed by the Indian parliament in 2009, the school is called on to also grant access to children from the surrounding region. Considering the awareness of cultural heterogeneity of its pupils and its school character, the Rishi Valley School would be labeled as an International School in Europe. In addition to school buildings for the Rishi Valley School campus also includes a big Assembly Hall, a Dance Hall, a facility for natural sciences and also a spacious area for arts including various workshops featuring materials and equipment for working with clay, wood, embroidering and doing batik. The pupils' dormitories, where they live with their house parents, are scattered all over the large campus. Further living units for teachers and staff not charged with 24h-care are located in other parts of the campus. A small hospital for seriously ill pupils that is run by a female doctor is situated in the proximity of the office building. A dining hall and a canteen kitchen are close by. They cater to everybody on Rishi Valley School campus in three double shifts. Solar-supported hot water batteries can be found on the roofs of the canteen kitchen and the dormitories. At night, the paths and roads are illuminated by recently installed solar lamps. A guest house for parents sponsored by alumni is located not far from the central office building. The central office building itself has a development department as well as facilities for teacher training. Parents are allowed to visit their children once every six months and to exchange views with the teachers on the progress and development of their children. All buildings are surrounded by large trees that alternate with open space which host colorful flowerbeds in the rather scarce rainy period. The own farm with cattle industry lies at some distance from the central area of the campus. Its biogas plant was established in 1984 and is thus testimony to a timely ecological and energy-conscious orientation. An adjacent area is home for fields for vegetable cultivation. The fruits and vegetables harvested from there are being delivered to the kitchen of the dining hall at Rishi Valley School all year long. Furthermore, sugarcane is being grown, pressed and processed to sucrose via traditional methods in the farming area.

The central coordinating institution in Rishi Valley is the Rishi Valley Education Centre. It coordinates all areas and departments that belong to the Rishi Valley School and the RIVER project with the Rural Education Centre, the rural school project with several own rural schools. Another organizational part of the Rishi Valley Education Centre is the Rural Health Centre, which is a big rural doctor station with three doctors. The rural doctor station is heavenly frequented by the surrounding population that comes from up to 90 km away. About 100 000 people are registered in the station's patients' files. At present 15 new people register on average each day.

An additional ecological project has been running for four years now. It is called 'Ecological Development Zone' and exceeds Rishi Valley Centre's own area. This project is executed in cooperation with the government of India and the regional district and encompasses the entire valley. Its goal is to secure the living situation of the rural population by means of sustainable, ecological development and thereby preventing migration into cities. The Rishi Valley Institute for Educational Resources, RIVER, has developed and grown with the task of 'Rural Education'. The initiatives of RIVER as well as the Rural Health Centre and the ecological project belong to the so called 'Outreach Programs' of Rishi Valley. Their goal is to approach the challenges in the valley in cooperation with the population, using the competencies and skills that arose from Rishi Valley.

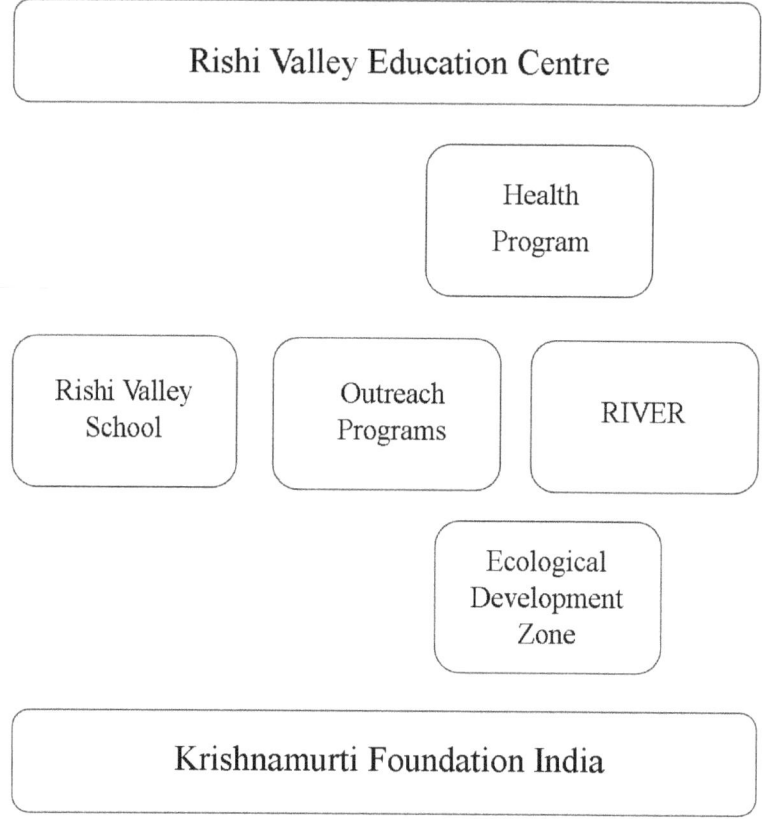

Fig. 2: The structure of Rishi Valley Education Centre

2.1.4 The Rishi Valley Institute for Educational Resources, RIVER

The Rishi Valley Institute for Educational Resources, RIVER, as explained above, is initially an organizational part of the Rishi Valley Education Centre, which itself is a self-governed part of the Krishnamurti Foundation India. The 'Outreach Program' for schooling in rural areas was initiated about 30 years ago. During his lifetime Jiddu Krishnamurti already pointed to the responsibility the team of the Rishi Valley Education Centre has for the education of the people and children in the villages and the surrounding settlements in the valley. A respective document can be found in a brochure that was recently compiled for internal purposes due to the 80-year existence of the Rishi Valley School on occasion of an alumni meeting:

> "First of all, I would get all the villagers together, and explain to them that we're going to have schools for their children. We'll see that we get enough money; we'll work for it. We'll say: 'We'll build; you help us to build'. That's one thing I would do: schools for them. And I would also see to the agriculture and all that side of it very clearly, definitely – expert work" (Krishnamurti Foundation India 2011, 1).

This clear task of enabling the rural population surrounding the Rishi Valley School to have access to educational processes thus is the basis for the activity of the Rishi Valley Institute for Educational Resources, RIVER. The current directors also play a vital part in this. Padmanabha Rao and Anumula Rama began teaching at Rishi Valley School as a young couple in the 1980's and immediately felt involved.

Fig. 3: Anumula Rama and Padmanabha Rao, RIVER directors

The RIVER-Team was prescient in recognizing the shortcomings and limitations of the traditional school system with its high quota of dropouts. Differentiated and nuanced analyses brought to the fore that the dominant textbooks that were centrally issued in the Indian federal states and the teacher-centered approach were the essence of the problem. Both resulted in the children's incomplete (learning-)progress that sooner or later lead to failure, especially in the rural areas with its fragile educational structures. The RIVER-Team sees the following central points of criticism and challenges as its tasks:

1. standardized lesson periods of 45 minutes, unmindful of the children's individual progress with all its negative repercussions
2. ignoring the families' cultural situations and everyday life in rural, small-town environments
3. rigid educational methods and corporal punishment
4. lack of support and assistance for slower learners
5. many and premature dropouts caused by a buildup of unbridgeable gaps in the learning progressive
6. demotivated teachers without an adequate education for groups with members of different ages
7. high absenteeism rate due to cultural customs and their destructive effects in the case of traditional lessons
8. educational alienation of the parents
9. content of textbooks being remote from real life and hence, content of textbooks not being compatible with the everyday experience and the everyday situations of the children

These general, critical aspects of education at school are getting worse in India's rural situation to this day. Teachers had to and have to be qualified to cope with and handle learning- groups that are heterogeneous, mixed in age and spanning several grades in remote villages. For this to be possible, a new, fundamental education has to be provided. At the same time, this new way of education is to be integrally and comprehensively developed considering the changing living situations in the villages. Even though the RIVER-Team does not explicitly refer to Jiddu Krishnamurti within the rural school project, his profound horizon is nevertheless present in the goals of the RIVER-Projects: "The highest function of education is to bring about an integrated individual who is capable of dealing with life as a whole" (Krishnamurti 1981 / 1953, 25). In an initial, brave step the RIVER-Team deconstructed the curricula and preexisting school books and developed learning material in the form of activity cards. These activity cards focus on the child's learning activity according to constructivist principles. These materials were then systematized by the way of diverse Ladders of Learning whilst taking into account numerous didactic and methodical principles. Over the course of a four-year long development progress under the direction of Padmanabha Rao and Anumula Rama, the first sets of material oriented on pupils' learning activities were created in cooperation with the RIVER-Team. The phases of testing and changing during those four years are described as 'action research', which is to be interpreted as a learning process within the project. The first set of material that was also easy-to-transport was called 'School in the Box'. The simple bags and pockets for the learning materials could be pinned or hung on any tree or house so that also remote villages with a high degree of illiteracy and prior a total lack of any education became approachable. The teachers, mostly young people from the region that began learning with the RIVER-Team initially went to the villages with their 'school bags'.

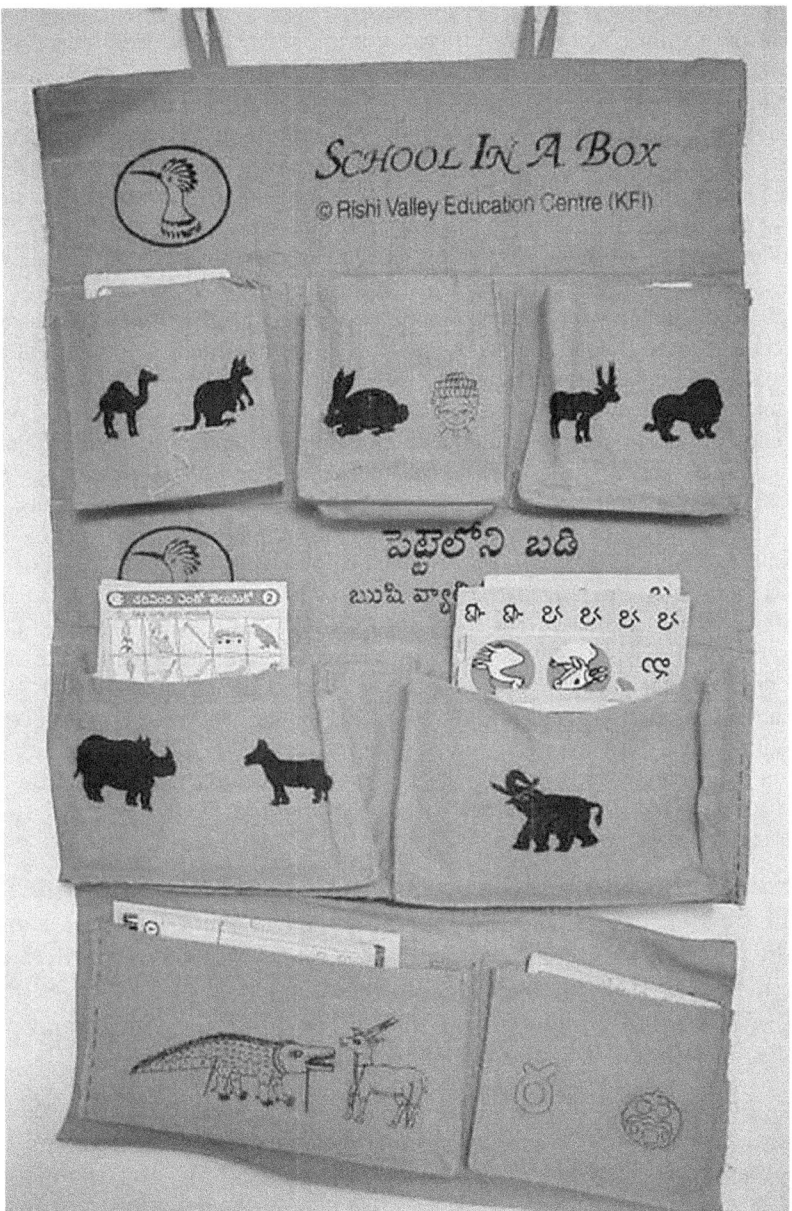

Fig. 4: School in a box

The first one-room school Valmikivanam in the small village of Eguvaboyapalli was built in 1986. Eguvaboyapalli is four kilometers away from Rishi Valley. The report on the first initiative of establishment is impressive:

"The first Satellite-School, Valmikivanam, the first of Rishi Valley's Satellite-Schools, opened on a high ridge about one kilometer off the Anantapur highway, in a village known as Eguvaboyapalli, the Upper Boya Village. The Boyas are settled woodsmen who claim descent from the poet Valmiki, himself a tribesman who lived as an outlaw before his compassionate transformation to an epic poet. Few of the two-hundred-and-fifty families in the village have their own land or animals. Some are sharecroppers; others are shepherds who tend animals belonging to people in a small town nearby. The majority are daily wage earners, with a reputation for shiftlessness. Valmikivanam was built on barren land donated by the Boyas for the school. With the help of students and local volunteers, the grounds were soon planted with fruit-bearing trees like jamun, tamarind, mango, papaya and guava. The entrance to the school is now brilliant with flowering bougainvillea and oleander, planted by the student community of Rishi Valley. A jasmine bower, marigolds, tabobias and roses turned up at the initiative of the village people, along with two clay horses that now stand guard at the entrance of the school. Initially there were thirty students at the one-room school, but in due course additional land was donated and now, perched on a small hill nearby, there is a nursery school for twenty younger children. Venugopal, a local village youth who had done a two-year stint in college and that went through RIVER's Training program, was initially nervous about teaching in his own village. But in the years he has been at Valmikivanam, he has gained confidence of the community. He now serves as an advisor to the village panchayat and participates actively in local decision making. Several batches of Venugopals students have now successfully passed the Andhra Pradesh State Education Board Class 5 Examinations. One of them is a teacher at the balwadi attached to Valmikivanam. All but three of them have gone on to further study at the local state school, and one is working towards a BA degree at a nearby college. In the evening Valmikivanam doubles as an Adult Education Centre. It has a small library and a wall-clock donated by members of the Adult Education class. The doors are never locked. The liquor vendor, who was once a prominent part of his village scene, has been banished. A village that was virtually illiterate a few years ago now has a 75% literacy rate. All adults under the age of thirty-four are now literate" (RIVER 2003, 16-17).

Several further Satellite-Schools were founded after the successful initial application of the new method in the valley and in the villages around Rishi Valley by the RIVER-Team and in cooperation with the respective village communities from 1988 to 1992. By 2014, ten schools belong to RIVER. Along with these is a small middle school from 6th to 7th grade with dormitories on RIVER-campus for the girls from the surrounding villages.

Due to the massive developments since the 1990s, continued education institutions for teachers as well as training facilities and project rooms for the RIVER-Team have been established as well. Today the RIVER-Team consists of the two directors alongside with further leading project members, a group of former Satellite-School teachers that participate for development and continued education and additional members of the team that take care of administrative tasks. The RIVER-Team, including all teachers from all Satellite-Schools and the teachers from the middle school, meets regularly to discuss current questions and issues in the schools or also to initiate new developments.

Especially noteworthy are the cultures of action that speak of the team's non-dualistic perception of the processes exercised by the RIVER-Team. The German-Indian cooperation reveals further typically integral forms of action by the RIVER-Team (Girg 2007, 239-41). The entire team seems to maintain an ongoing flow of action within which the team's individual activities permanently refer to the occurring situations and events within the project. The aforementioned action research thus becomes a principle that incessantly keeps the progress of learning open and available within the project's process. According to our perception this mostly happens without further pondering upon interpretations. The immediate action is in the foreground. On this basis all tasks are worked on highly efficiently, often also by way of the typical Indian seemingly unstructured processes.

Inquiries from the exterior, namely Indian as well as international educational establishments, are constantly and positively seized by the RIVER-Team which always aims at sustainable developments. These inquiries are then fleshed out to new emanating initiatives. Every member of the RIVER-Team is willing to give his or her all during the project process. This is especially true for the directors Padmanabha Rao and Anumula Rama. Commentaries or seemingly obstructive events during the working process are not looked upon judgmentally, but rather as another reason to learn within the team simultaneously. All processes are answered by acting since the learning character is being maintained. The RIVER-Team conveys the impression of a common, dialogue, progressing process that does not only allow the ownership of the respective partner but actively supports it throughout cooperation. This becomes evident when looking at the cooperation with the village population, as well as with national and international partners and contacts. The potential of each respective partner is actively requested, being incorporated and made available for the mutual projects.

This might as well be the reason why the MGML-Methodology and the RIVER-Team have both been early on inquired by Indian educational establishments and federal states. Although only being described here in a shortened version covering the intense development work for the school in the last 30 years, RIVER's documents showcase acute development and continued education work. In 1993 materials for the regional language Telugu for grades 1-5 and for Mathematics for grades 1-3 were tested for the first time and further refined throughout a five-year pilot phase. The creation of individual materials leads across several steps to a complete, holistic learning method that will be explained and closely deliberated later on in the book. The method is referred to as MultiGradeMultiLevel-Methodology or also RIVER-Methodology by now.

Already at this time did other Indian regions request RIVER's expertise in order to help forming and building up similar models in other federal states. The records on the development of the project show that numerous teams from other federal states have been trained by way of continued education for teachers and school development projects since 1994. Moreover, culturally and regionally modified versions of the MGML-Methodology have been developed. A small selection of the projects:

1993 – "School in a Box" - Through a series of designer's workshops and rigorous action research initiatives in the Rishi Valley satellite schools RIVER developed and published its innovative educational package "School in a Box". This first edition of school in a box in Telugu, consists of teaching learning aids, manuals for "Matric *Mela*" (a maths community festival), "Mothers stories" (adapting and using rural women oral traditions as reading programs for first generation learners) and a Ladder of Learning. During the R&D stage and after the publication, School in a Box was rigorously field-tested for five years in the Rishi Valley Satellite schools and this first successful experiment - Reduced dropout rate, improved learning outcomes, increased interest in academics and increased enrolment in class 6. The results were further substantiated when children from RIVER satellites schools passed the class 6 examination in the regular school method withv high percentages

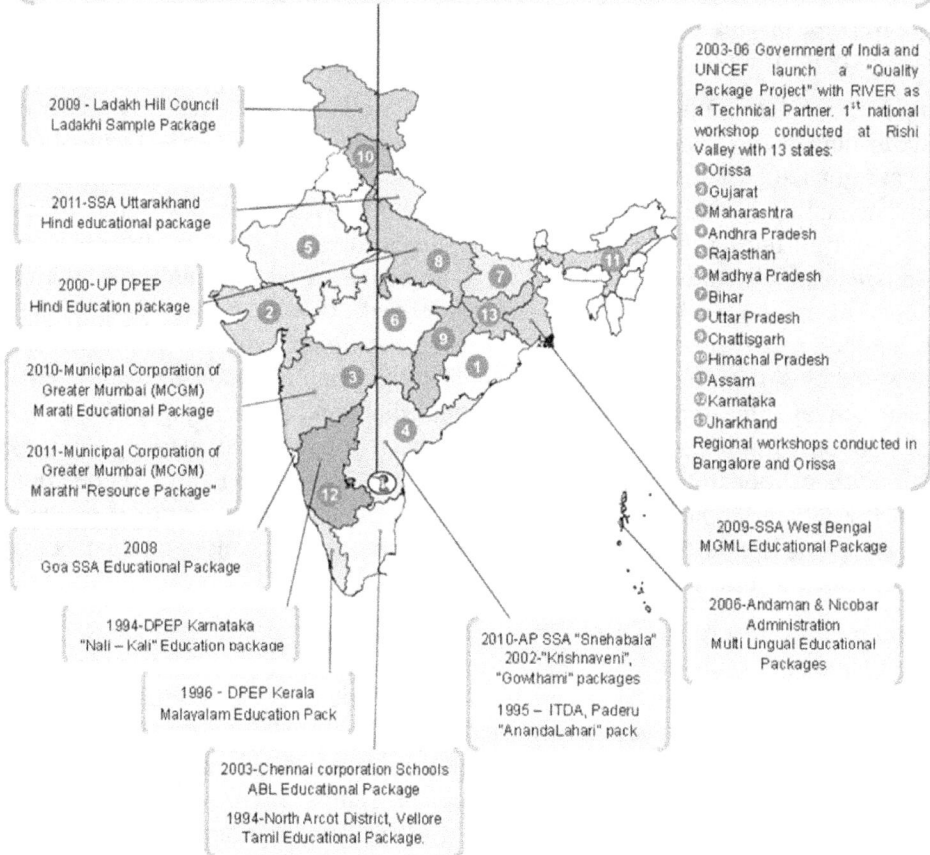

Fig. 5: Examples of project development by RIVER

RIVER permanently changed the Indian schools with their longstanding and numerous projects and contributed to a qualitatively more high-grade school development for primary education with a 'quiet revolution'.

Depending on the inquiry, RIVER provides the following arrangements to spreading the work:

1. initial information in terms of a one-day training on campus, for example for existing regional educational institutions for teachers (information)
2. two-day to three-day long informative workshops used for building up exemplary, initial skills in developing material (exploration workshop)
3. two-weeks to three-weeks long designer workshops on the RIVER-campus used for creating entire sets of material (designer workshop)
4. counseling of NGOs considering strategy formation for educational development processes
5. decentralized designer workshops in other federal states lasting several weeks
6. development of MGML-material sets in different regional languages
7. participation in the ecological model project 'Ecological Development Zone'
8. own one-year long training courses for teachers

The initiatives by RIVER are internationally known by now. Their long-term commitment and effort for the development of rural schools was repeatedly honored with national and international awards over the last couple of years. RIVER was bestowed the Global Development Award by the Global Development Network (GDN) that is sponsored by the Japanese government. The laudatory speech features a segment that praises RIVER as the 'Most Innovative Development Project'. This appreciation raised RIVER's international popularity once more. Another award for developmental commitment was the honor for '2009 Social Entrepreneur of the Year' in India at the hands of the Schwab Foundation. The directors of RIVER were also invited to the World Economic Forum in Davos in 2011 as an Indian NGO to due to their national and international connections. There they were able to present their projects in front of a selected international audience. In 2012 RIVER was listed among the world's 100 best NGOs by the worldwide magazine GLOBAL – The Global Journal. Among other things RIVER was praised as one of the most efficient and effective NGOs of the world.

The Indian colleagues of RIVER were also awarded the Jindal Prize in 2012. This Prize is a very-well-endowed prize for education by the prestigious Jindal Foundation in India. In the laudatory speech listed as the original text below, RIVER is especially - and with a reference to the MGML-Methodology - thanked for spreading their educational work in more than 100 000 Indian schools:

Rishi Valley Education Centre, Chittoor district, Andhra Pradesh has developed a Multi-Grade-Multi-Level Methodology (MGML) education program with Activity Based Learning (ABL) for primary education. In view of the widely acknowledged fact, that there is no co-relation between age and competency level in the majority of the schools in rural India, the MGML teaching methodology has been developed to address this core issue for educating students in rural schools.

Every classroom in this methodology represents a wide spectrum of achievement levels; the classroom virtually functions as a primary school in miniature with one teacher in attendance. The problem of non-uniform learning levels has been addressed by augmenting, and in certain cases even substituting the Language, Mathematics and Environmental Science textbooks with a series of graded cards and pictorial graphics called 'RIVER Ladders of Learning'. While students, working in groups and individually set their own pace for advancing through various levels of a subject, the teacher facilitates the learning process. MGML methodology of teaching has been implemented for example:

- Tamilnadu (ABL Program) – 37,500 schools, 200,000 Teachers
- Karnataka (NalliKalli Program) – 45,000 schools, 90,000 Teachers
- Andhra Pradesh (Snehabala Program) – 85,000 schools, 1,60,000 Teachers
- Chhattisgarh (Surjan Program) – 29,250 schools, 65,000 Teachers
- Madhya Pradesh – 5,000 schools, 10,000 Teachers

The demand for presentations and workshops by RIVER has risen since 2000, especially internationally. These tasks have increased since the RIVER-Team was given the 'Global Development Award' for the 'Most Innovative Development Project'.

Groups and Organizations from Ethiopia, Peru, France, Germany, Sierra Leone and Pakistan but also educational institutions from Thailand, Nepal, Spain, Bangladesh, the Maldives, Colombia, Cambodia and Bhutan have – although varying in intensity – contacted RIVER in order to get to know and study the developed 'RIVER-Model' or also to cooperate with the RIVER-Team in corresponding workshops for an extended amount of time. Since 2002 the cooperation with Research Team Integral, Germany, has also become part of the international teamwork.

2.2 Learning with Ladders of Learning

2.2.1 The MGML-Methodology as Initial Situation

The two directors, the married couple Anumula Rama and Padmanabha Rao, met at the University of Hyderabad when young. Towards the end of their studies both were looking for a professional challenge. They lived in a small village and dabbled in farming after their wedding. It quickly became obvious that they were not very successful. However, the time spent became the initial situation for the professional activity: the girls of the village regularly visited wishing to learn how to read and write. The young couple was shocked upon realizing that most villages did not have a school and if they did, access to schools strongly depended on the family's income. When the Rishi Valley Education Centre was looking for new teachers in the 1980s, the Rao's immediately reacted and started working at Rishi Valley.

The organization of Satellite-Schools began with a critical observation of textbook and teacher oriented lessons. This resulted in a complete rejection of this way of education. As opposed to this the couple tried to make the school a center of resources and heart of the village community instead of an isolated, anxiety-provoking and little transparent institution.

RIVER founded an educational network in order to prevent an isolation of each rural school and its teachers. Continued processes of exchange, advanced education and working contribute to steady renewal and development and obviate sluggish, hierarchical structures. By now there are ten Satellite-Schools in a circuit of 25 km around Rishi Valley. Each school has a teacher who mostly is from the village or one nearby. The schools facilitate education for 25 – 40 children of different performance levels.

Life in a region permanently threatened by drought forced the initiators to accomplish processes of revegetation by means of education. RIVER stimulates a sense of pride and appreciation for their school within the village population by actively involving them. Teachers become respected fellow citizens and the parents know that their children are in good hands. School is not an anxiety-provoking and 'intransparent' space anymore. In fact schools serve as a center of resources and a place for gatherings for the surrounding villages. A place where important changes can be discussed, for example: concerning the cultivation of land and power supply. Some Satellite-Schools are also open in the evening for adult education. Here, parents are taught simple mathematics and how to read and write.

After years of intense developing and testing RIVER was able to create a method that does justice to the regional and cultural contexts as well as the performance levels and prerequisites for learning of children at the simplest rural schools. The MGML-Methodology is a method that qualifies for children with different levels of performance and talent (MultiLevel) and of different age (MultiGrade). This enables classes that take place in group processes with pupils of different grades and age.

The MGML-Methodology is oriented on the governmental syllabus but does not work with the corresponding school books since these are not activity-oriented structured and hardly bear any resemblance to the pupils' environment. The academic part of the governmental syllabus was enhanced with a cultural part that was developed with the help and involvement of the local population and various artists. By doing this, the regional background and culturally rich traditions such as songs, stories, dances and customs were integrated into the education. There is also an ecologically oriented and aesthetic design of the schools.

The MGML-Methodology starts out from the natural heterogeneity of all children and acknowledges the singularity of their respective learning processes. This is not to be taken for granted in Indian context as it is in other countries: girls and boys are sitting apart from each other in public schools and do not really interact. Hence, they lack essential important experiences in terms of dialogue and cooperation with the other gender that would be meaningful for the social growth. Lessons in India are usually teacher-centered and often amount to nothing more than anxiously repeating proceedings that had been written on the blackboard. This conformity of Indian education translates into an ignorance of the singularity of individual learning processes in terms of how the individual pupil learns, how fast he learns and what performance level he is on. RIVER does not see the reality of different levels of learning and performance of children as a problem that needs to be pushed aside. Instead this is seen as a task and a chance that contains possibilities for each individual pupil but also for the class and even the teacher. The MGML-Methodology does not answer to the heterogeneous situation by trying to transform it into a homogeneous one. The MGML-Methodology rather consequently works on supporting the various individuals as well as collective learning processes.

The MGML-Methodology combines complex individualized educational methods and designs. Every child is able to adequately organize his own learning progress with his own pace and without any pressure to achieve and time pressure. By doing so the child receives a high level of stability and structure that gives orientation. If a child was to miss school for a certain amount of time due to harvesting or a religious or familiar festivity, it would irretrievably fall behind in the schedule at a different school. Within the MGML-Methodology the child is able to re-enter at the exact same spot of its learning process where it had exited. Depending on the region public schools in India feature very high dropout rates. Acknowledging a child's own learning pace does not only prevent unnecessary frustration but also manages to lower the dropout rate to 2-3%. Older sisters are usually obliged to watch over their smaller siblings which interferes with the older ones attending school regularly. Within the MGML-Methodology this is not an impediment anymore since the younger siblings are allowed to accompany their sisters to school. There they can play with other small children during classes.

The methodology offers learning that reaches across performance and age. All existing levels of performance are consciously incorporated within the MGML-Methodology. Social and regional circumstances as well as cultural characteristics are considered when creating the learning material, thereby making connotations to the pupils' environment. The heart of working with the MGML-Methodology lies in the initiative and activity of the learning child itself. This is not only mirrored within the methodology but in the entire organization of a day at school:

Upon arriving at school in the morning the children autonomously start cleaning the surrounding area. Garbage and leaves are disposed, plants are taken care of. Meanwhile a mother prepares breakfast that will be collectively consumed in the open. The children are also responsible for washing their own dishes. Prior to the lessons a small gathering is being held where a communal dance is performed or a game of pantomime is being played.

Before noon the children mainly work on the subjects of mathematics and language. A sequence roughly goes on for about one hour and 15 minutes but might be extended to as long as two hours. After every sequence there is a break. Lunch is also prepared by a mother. The expenses are being covered by the government's 'Mid-Day Meal-Program', as they are at public schools. In the afternoon the pupils work on the subject of 'Environmental Studies' (EVS). Additionally, songs are being sung, dances are practiced, or the class works with the traditional and locally rooted shadow puppet theater.

2.2.2 Material Pool for Learning Activities

The basis of the MGML-Methodology is the imagination and realization of activity-oriented, vivid lessons with unrestricted learning processes. The children conduct their own learning processes themselves with help from the MGML-Methodology and their Ladders of Learning, thereby also supporting their fellow pupils. This basis and the concrete procedure with and within the method is best expressed by the phrase 'The Child in the Driver's Seat.' The individual and collective learning in individual and content-wise meaningful and varying situations with partners, groups or in the collective of all pupils constantly interacts.

Fig. 6: Pool with activity material for Mathematics, Language and EVS

In the MGML-Methodology the learning and educational activities are induced by individual learning materials. The learning materials mostly come in the form of cards. The respective activities are explained on these cards. Each material is marked by a symbol and a number in order to be systematized. This provides goal-oriented and structured directions for the work. Each activity card offers tasks and is part of a systematized learning sequence, which in a so called Ladder of Learning is arranged in chronological order. The organization of the activity cards makes it easy for the children to find their way around in the material pool. Every card has a colored margin allotting it to a definite year-long Ladder of Learning. Pink cards belong to the Ladder of Learning for the first grade, green ones for second grade, golden ones for third grade and silver ones for fourth grade. Each card features an animal symbol and a number. Different birds signify mathematical tasks. Insects point to tasks in EVS while activities in language are distinguished by mammals. The number on the card corresponds with the respective milestone assigned to the activity and therefore also corresponds with the respective difficulty level.

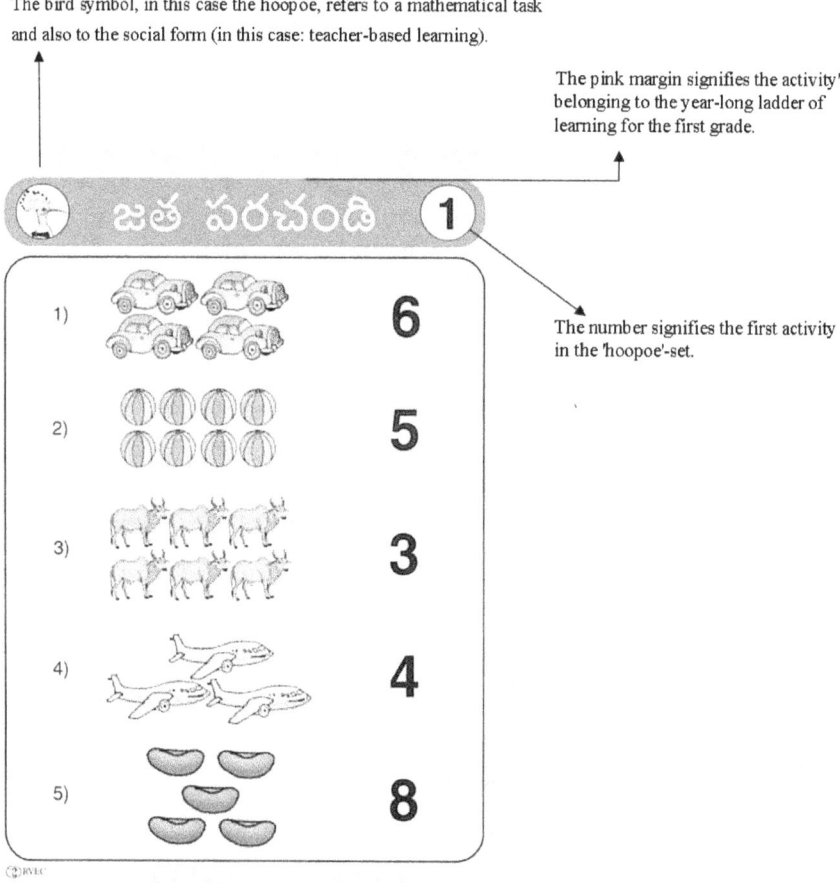

The bird symbol, in this case the hoopoe, refers to a mathematical task and also to the social form (in this case: teacher-based learning).

The pink margin signifies the activity's belonging to the year-long ladder of learning for the first grade.

The number signifies the first activity in the 'hoopoe'-set.

Fig. 7: Example of an activity card

All activities and their corresponding learning materials form a fully systematized material pool, which for grades 1-4 is organized for the subjects of Language, Mathematics and EVS. The material pool covers an entire wall of every classroom. The pool is divided into various departments on the shelves. Within these departments are boxes containing the activity cards. The entire material pool with its activity-oriented learning impulses corresponds to the valid Indian curriculum.

In the Indian context the materials are, with only few exceptions, made on print-basis in order to enable an inexpensive production. The printed material is being enhanced by newspapers and material from the direct surroundings such as bottle caps, seeds, legumes, stones and other natural materials. Content-wise more elaborate 3-D materials or material belonging the pedagogy of Montessori can be endorsed. The classrooms are starting to be supported technologically, so that the learning material is complemented by corresponding learning software and computer workstations.

2.2.3 'Milestones' – Systematized Learning Sequences

'Milestones' are detailed content-related and materially logical sequences that structure the Ladders of Learning. These milestones feature a systematized inert process structure that is designed as a five-step learning progress assurance. Each milestone commences with an introductory (1) that is most of the time being instructed by the teacher, or also by older pupils. Thereon various reinforcements (2) are built upon. Those are being handled in differing social forms. The reinforcements are finally succeeded by the evaluation (3), which should show if a pupil has understood the milestones' content and if the pupil can apply the content, respectively. In the case of insecurities and mistakes remedial work (4) offers intensification for working with the content. On the other hand enrichment activities (5) offer the possibility of consolidation. Each step can be supported by several activities. The levels of abstraction increase within the milestone from the very concrete up to the entirely abstract.

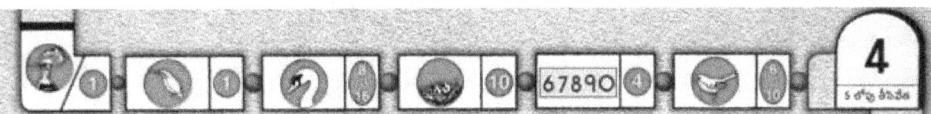

Fig. 8: Milestone in a Ladder of Learning

Using an integrated evaluation and offering adequate assistance of the learning processes, the milestones result in a qualitative assurance of free and at the same time highly structured forms of learning. Milestones work in individualizing and differentiating ways due to their set-up described above. This procedure largely prevents gaps in learning. The milestones are conceptualized considering methodical and subject-didactic characteristics, based on specific operations in mathematics, life-oriented stories in the subject of language or realistic situations and field research in EVS. Principally, milestones are only finished after a complete build-up of the processes of understanding. Potential gaps in knowledge and understanding that can occur due to the inadequate process of lessons not oriented on the child are thus being avoided. The destructive processes of children not being able to follow in class are thereby simultaneously being disposed.

2.2.4 Ladders of Learning and Their Variations

The Ladders of Learning for grades 1-4 can be looked upon as tools for structuring individual learning in subject-specific, free working processes. They enable a long-term control of learning processes that is being usually achieved by teacher-oriented lessons. In German-speaking countries they are incorporated in free unit studies.

The children commence their work along the Ladders of Learning with a preparation at the beginning of grade one. Hereby the children starting school learn the appropriate handling of the Ladders of Learning and train their fine motor skills in various exercises. Additionally, there are different basal tasks on colors, forms and symbols. This lowest part of the first year-long Ladder of Learning is laid out in a circuitry to enable the children to stay in it as long as necessary. It is not until then that they follow the linear course of the year-long Ladder of Learning. Some children starting school have already mastered dealing with Ladders of Learning when they start school due to their preschool phase and the contact with older siblings and pupils.

The guiding teachers are thus largely liberated from their common process-controlling task in teacher-centered education. The time gained can be used entirely for the complex work of giving advice and supporting throughout the learning process. Counseling, observing and supporting can also be accomplished in classes of more than 40 children.

The year-long Ladders of Learning guide all the way through the fully systematized material pool by means of the milestones that are being structured in learning sequences. The learning arrangement by Ladders of Learning hereby enables numerous and versatile learning activities with tasks of all kind in heterogeneous classes.

RIVER developed linearly structured Ladders of Learning for the subjects of mathematics and Language. A systemic learning progress is to be found in EVS: a learning board with interconnected topics and a heavily ecology-oriented alignment. RIVER considers the interconnected material structure of natural-scientific, social-scientific and humanistic topics.

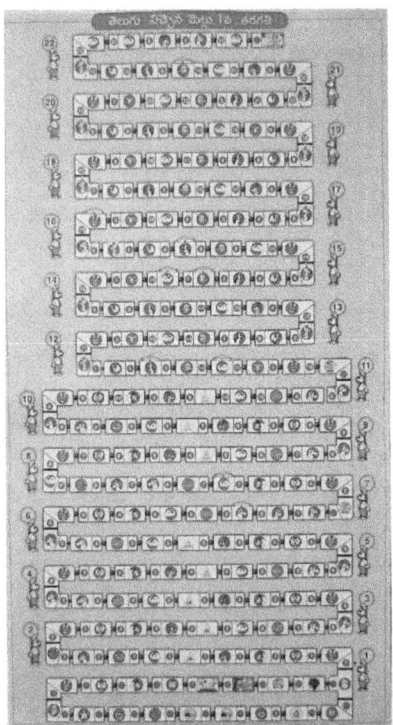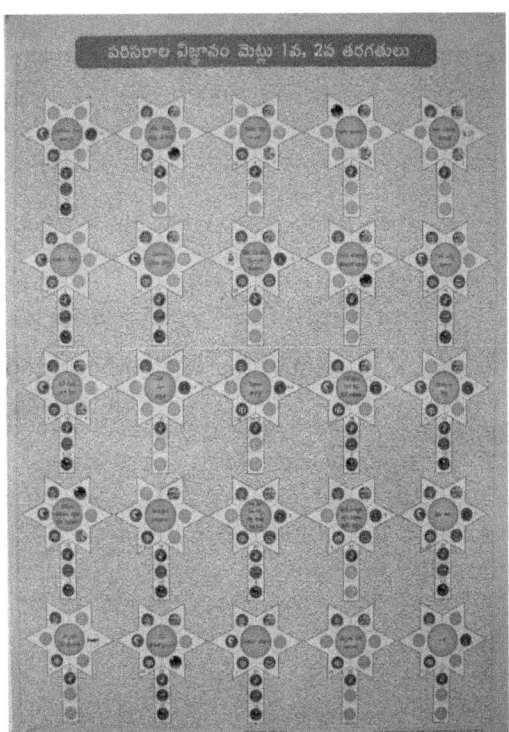

Fig. 9: Ladder of Learning for Language, linear (left) and Ladder of Learning for EVS, systemic (right)

Systemic Ladders of Learning are separated into small, interconnected units that represent epoch-like topics. Each topic is represented by an abstractly outlined flower. The 'stalks' provide introductory tasks concerning contemplation that transfer into mandatory and open activities in the individual 'petals'. It is the teacher's decision at which point in the year the topics will be worked on.

More Ladders of Learning have been developed in further Indian federal states according to necessary cultural adaption in various regional languages (see Chapter 3.1). By now Ladders of Learning have also successfully been employed in English. Societal and natural-scientific learning progressions were developed by splitting up the subject of EVS. Montessori material has partially and systematically been incorporated. The Ladders of Learning roughly coordinate two thirds of the study time. The remaining third is available at free disposal for theater, dance, music and arts.

2.2.5 Mixed-age Group Formation with an Integrated Support System

Diverse group formations further enrich the variations with learning of the MGML-Methodology. The methodology operates on varying group processes. Experiences in Indian schools exist with four to six cooperating groups. The respective variation is being picked according to the specific, regional situation. The following social learning arrangements can thus be found in a classroom:

- a group being guided by the teacher, especially when introducing a topic (teacher based)
- partially guided by the teacher, also supporting during exercises (partly teacher based)
- guided by a system of supporters regardless of age within the group, activity-based (peer group based)
- partially guided by a system of supporters within the group, oriented on communal topics and activities (partly peer group based)
- entirely autonomous working, process only guided by the material (individual)
- age 4-6, personal supervision (kindergarden)

All groups are conceptualized regardless of age. The composition of a group changes with the activity's characters that are signified by symbols for the materials. Integrated systems of supporters arise out of the differences in age and skill in the groups. These systems further strengthen the subject-specific free study units described above. The system of supporters is signified by special markers in the Ladders of Learning and additionally acknowledges the learning progresses of individual children. The following picture presents a graphical depiction of the grouping system for the subject of mathematics:

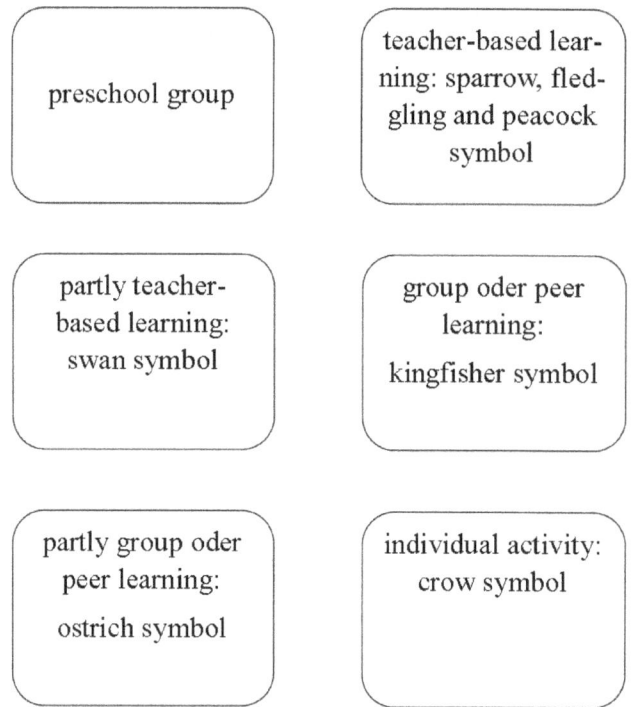

Fig.10: Possible forms of social supporting and working within a classroom

Working in the classroom – here in four social groups – looks like this for example:

Fig. 11: Children in various social systems of support

Mixed-age groups are common in Indian villages due to the size of the villages and thus are the starting point for the MGML-Methodology. However, also schools in Indian cities and urban areas that by now work with this methodology, have proceeded to change year-based classes to multigrade groups so as to reinstate the naturally given multigrade and multilevel learning group.

2.2.6 Evaluation of Progress and the Pupils' Success

The learning success immediately shows itself for the pupils in the progress on the Ladders of Learning. The successful buildup of knowledge and skills is being validated in the milestones via the afore-mentioned evaluative tasks. Bigger evaluations comprising several contents are scheduled within larger intervals of roughly two months. They provide information on the sustainability of what has been learned, on the adaptability of knowledge and the processes of understanding. Additionally, there are recurring occasions that are deliberately incorporated and that are achieved by every child. These are the markers (mouse symbol) where children become the 'king of learning' and get to wear a paper crown for one day. This way their individual performance is being esteemed. Simultaneously, an indirect form of evaluation is taking place. For the other classmates the 'king of learning' crown does not only signify his achieved performance level, but also identifies him as an 'expert' and 'adviser' for the respective skill. Being the expert of the day the 'king of learning' faces up to the classmates' questions and supports them with their tasks. This also reveals to the teachers if the child actually learned a skill and comprehended the content.

Fig. 12: The 'king of learning' is identifiable for all classmates by his crown

Teachers further document the learning progress of the children by so called 'assessment forms' within the MGML-Methodology. They write down the past activities within the milestones at that. The various ways of documenting the learning progress help the teachers to stay permanently oriented concerning the movement and progress of learning and performance of each individual pupil. These documents make the dynamics of learning and great advances in learning as well as a slowing down of developments individually perceptible. They further make these changes and transformations understandable for the parents. Consequently, teachers are able to specifically support children or provide them with individually tailored consolidations and extensions for a topic.

There is also the fact that the children themselves document what they have achieved on blackboards on the side of the. This self-conducted documenting of their learning enables the children to reflectively perceive their learning progress.

Fig. 13: Work on the individual blackboards on the side of the classrooms

Every child enters the government's state transfer examination of Andhra Pradesh after primary school years. The results are outstanding. More than 90% of the children succeed in transferring to a secondary school. Pupils of the Satellite-Schools belong to the best children of the entire administrative region again and again.

2.2.7 Spatial Structure of the One-Room School

The MGML-Methodology's preceding aspects point to the essential components that have to be provided for this form of cooperative learning by a correspondingly conceptualized spatial structure.

Elaborating on the room composition of the MGML-Methodology and a Satellite-School requires pointing out at least a small theoretical respective dependence on the integral perception of the learning space and a reflection on the historical evolution of the learning space design. These deliberations offer a background for interpretation that can adequately accompany the perception of the spatial structure within the MGML-Methodology.

When in a first line of thought asking oneself the question 'Where do processes of learning and education take place?' one has to assume the undividedness of learning spaces within an integral perception (Girg 2007, 279-80). The situation is the immediately present place of the learning and educational processes. The situation is outwardly open and extends into the world. The cosmos constitutes the widest dimension of the learning space. Natural and Cultural spaces that exist undivided since they are manifold interconnected in the cosmos, give occasion to an informal and formal life-long learning. They constitute the space of human life, the living environment that is microcosmically and macrocosmically interconnected and undivided. 'Everything' – even in the sense of Comenius – can be a starting point of learning. Everything is learning space and can be a place of learning and education. Wherever the learner might be at the moment, a place of learning presents itself.

The title of a film about the development of RIVER's rural school project by a French team is "School without Walls". This title exactly conveys the understanding of learning space described. The Satellite-Schools' learning place is tied back to the informal character of the lifeworld. Therefore the institutional learning space of the school remains unlimited and integrated at the same time. The space where educational processes take place is open but is centered by way of the spatial, materialized school with its area and facilities. Thus the learners are given a placing and a secured starting point.

This general, holistically-characterized understanding of learning space can be made out by looking at the first picture: a Satellite-School on the RIVER-campus. The unlimited character is recognizable. The informal learning space of nature encompasses the formal learning space of the small Satellite-School that is integrated into nature.

Fig. 14: Chandanavanam at Thettu - one of ten Satellite-Schools, integrated in the nature of Rishi Valley

The schools run by RIVER are usually located on an area at the outskirts of the village that is owned by the village community and that was previously unused. The community's connection to the place of education is thereby consciously supported; it is the school of the villagers, it is 'their' school. This ownership of the school assures its continued existence and guarantees for support with maintenance or small repairs.

The school premises of a Satellite-School are equipped with a main building that is laid out as a one-room school with a length of 10-12 m and width of 6-7 m. The main building is where the learning with Ladders of Learning for groups regardless of age takes place. Some Satellite-Schools are also equipped with a small store room of 4-5 square meters. The store room is accessible through a door at the side of the main building and is lockable.

The architectonic aspects of the one-room school reveal that the schools of the RIVER-Team are created in an inexpensive way with solid bricks. The bricks are compressed by hand as it is typical of the region and are burnt in a brickyard. If soil containing clay is in place, the bricks are often produced in the immediate surroundings. The rather small building is painted in a light-reflecting white color on the outside. Some Satellite-Schools also have colored paintings of large educational games on one of the big exterior walls. A painted map of India with all its federal states is also to be found on the wall. The room is bestridden with a simple, light roof construction out of metal. The corrugated iron roof and its overhangs provide the necessary shade during the summer heat and further serve as a shelter during the monsoon with its tropical rains – that seldom occur in this region. There are windows right under the roof for both of these reasons: during the heat they enable the necessary circulation of air in the room and they also provide protection against raindrops that might be blown in from the side. The canopy's supporting granite pillars are painted in red and white. Their colors resemble the pillars of the small rural temples nearby. The red-and-white pillars are an element that also indicates the atmospheric character of these schools. The educational philosopher Jiddu Krishnamurti, who has given the impulse for Rishi Valley's educational establishments, says about this:

> "First of all there has to be an atmosphere of immensity, the felling that I'm entering a temple. There must be beauty, space, quietness, dignity. There must be a sense of togetherness in the student and the teacher, a sense of flowering, a feeling of extraordinary sacredness. There must be truthfulness and fearlessness. The child must put his hands on the earth; there must be a quality of otherness" (Brochure Study Centre Rajghat).

There usually is a second, smaller building near-by. It is a rotunda with a diameter of 4-5 m with a palm-covered roof that is typical for the region of southern Andhra Pradesh. This room is used for instance for the pre-school group, for differentiating in various phases of education, for working on projects or phases of artistic design. The school area is complemented with a playground for the age-appropriate exercise-needs of children. A swing is hanging from one of the bigger trees. Additionally, there is a slide and seesaw. The entire area is enclosed by a natural hedge.

Despite the dryness, the effort and care for the outdoor facility is clearly discernible. Flowers are immediately planted during monsoon season. At the same time the small school garden is laid out. Only few flowers survive the several months long and more than 40 degrees hot droughts. Therefore the flowers and the school garden have to be laid out over and over again.

Higher trees guard the place and provide shade. In some of RIVER's 10 Satellite-Schools the paths are lined with whitewashed stones and the entrance to the school is painted with dried cow dung, which is the traditional regional way to keep vermin off. An ornament-like 'rangoli' out of rice flour is spread in front of the entrance door every day. This is both an old religious custom that protects the house and a sign of welcome for the people entering.

A simplistic 'kitchen', or better a roofed fireplace is located in the vicinity of the playground and the recess area. The kitchen holds place for one man or woman from the village, who prepares breakfast and lunch with the simplest means. As appears from the weekly menu, which is attached to the teacher board, rice is the most common staple food and is daily offered with diverse side dishes of vegetables.

The Satellite-Schools in the villages in and around Rishi Valley are consciously designed as publicly accessible places of education by the RIVER-Team. Since the Satellite-Schools are also being used as model schools for learning purposes during the continuing education for teachers, there are large open spaces with upstream benches out of stone on the fourth wall. If necessary, these are covered and shaded by additional palm mats in a marquee-fashion. As a guest one looks from the stone benches straight into the classroom. The seats at the side thus serve as an observation gallery providing the possibility of having an unassuming view into the learning processes.

On first entering the inside of a Satellite-School it becomes immediately apparent that it is a complex, many-linked spatial structure, which deals with the classical form of a one-room school in an innovative way and offensively interprets it. One-room schools themselves are not that unusual. They were also very common in small rural places in Germany until the 1960s and are internationally in many countries the starting point and place for education, too.

A historical digression seems appropriate at this point. Internationally one-room schools quintessentially point out the development and transformation of learning spaces. Initially, due to colonial influences continuous, justified and hierarchically organized rows of desks and benches were the rule. The different heights of the furniture bear the physical differences of the children in mind. They signify the grades and the growth. However, differences within one grade are not considered. The genders are separated to the left and right like in churches in the past.

Indian schools that have not yet adapted to a culture of education centered on the children's activities, still feature the characteristics mentioned above. In rural, Indian classrooms the children are seated on the ground as it is culturally typical. The small ones are in the front; the older ones are in the back. On the other hand, of course there are also schools that are equipped with chairs and desks. These have been introduced as a necessary standard for education since the British colonial rule. However, the furnishing does not tell anything about the quality of the education.

The rigid forms of interior spatial structure stated to dissolve over the decades of the 20th century in Europe. The children are allowed to sit on individual chairs instead of benches. The desks are no longer connected to the seating accommodation and the continuing benches disappear entirely. In their place three, four rows of desks are installed. The elevated pedestal of the teacher is lowered and adjusted to the level of the classroom's floor. The transformation of learning spaces that comes along with a transformation of understanding learning processes and education, is documented by what can be comprehensively iconographical described via image analyses. A central form has been preserved over the centuries, which focuses on the 'all-knowing' teacher in a frontal orientation and is still in use today. The way of teacher-centered education has been there since the time of monastery schools. The latter's pulpit of the monastery school has vanished by now. However, on a closer look the relics of this doctrine-centered situation are still present. The standing referent can still look down on the audience from an elevated position. The pulpit has its remnant in the high desk with the laptop. The pointer was replaced by laser pointer that is now used to explain the images from the projector. These have also replaced the theologically interpreted wall paintings of the monastery church. The school and its classrooms stand in the tradition of this usage of space and interpretation of learning space. Secondary schools and also universities find it very difficult to allow and participate in the transformation to a new culture of learning at their own institution.

The Indian educational system, too, is furthermore often hierarchical in this sense due to the British colonial rule and also its own culture. The spatial alignment reveals that. The traditional frontal, teacher-oriented way of teaching continues the teaching tradition that also exists in Europe, which speaks a definite spatial language. The afterimage shows this classic spatial situation. The teacher of this school is part of a team at a school in Chennai, Tamil Nadu that is in the process of dissolving the centering via an interactive model of the 'Active Learning Methodology', ALM.

As has been made clear in the preceding chapters, the RIVER-Team with its MGML-Methodology radically questions the teacher, who is standing in front at the blackboard, reciting the textbook. The RIVER-Team radically questions this teacher's appropriateness. The MGML-Methodology offers a changed interpretation of the learning space with a changed spatial arrangement. Hence, after the description of the exterior, the spatial order of a Satellite-School is to be considered closely in a second step. A starting point can be the perception and description of historically traditional relics.

There is a blackboard to be found in every Satellite-School. An area that is assigned to the teacher is here as well. The blackboard is located in the classroom as it is usual. What is different is that it does not seem to be the center. On the blackboard' top-right corner usually written is the date and the amount of pupils – separated into gender - that are present. Throughout numerous sitting in on classes and visits to the school it became apparent that the blackboard is only used sporadically by the teacher furthermore.

The meaning of blackboards with their seemingly dominating role within the yet existing teaching tradition is clearly put into perspective by additional elements of spatial design within the MGML-Methodology. There are more blackboard areas on the sides of the classroom as can be seen in the afterimage. These are divided by vertical lines according to the number of children of the mixed-age groups. Above every sub-segment there is a name. These large blackboards for the pupils leave a personal spot on the board for every child. This space on the blackboard can be used for practice, work, or creative design. The two sidewalls of the learning space are bigger than the teacher's blackboard regarding the square meters. This step in organizing the space, which considers the pupil's activity, clearly breaks up the dominance of the teacher's blackboard. The MGML-Methodology, being a prepared learning environment and a learning arrangement supporting cooperation, overrides an organization that is frontally focused on the blackboard. The methodology's characteristic of educational processes taking place consequently transforms the learning spaces within their interactive usage.

The material pool is located opposite of the teacher's board and covers the entire width of the classroom. The material pool contains all learning material that is necessary for the children's learning activities. It further serves as a powerful counterbalance to the teacher's board. From this perspective the material pool constitutes an anchor for the children's blackboard area. The brick-built system of shelves for the material pool with its numerous uniform segments structures the one-room school's rear wall. There is one segment each for materials used for language, mathematics and EVS, Environmental Studies. A fourth segment is flexibly used for a subject or a field of activity. The systematization of the MGML-Methodology that has been developed by the RIVER-Team is easily and obviously discernible in the room. The symbols denote the specialist learning activities in the segments of the shelves. Every activity has its designated spot, is organized in categories, distinguished by color and definitely identifiable by the children. Every material is located at a height that is reachable for every child. The working material is assorted in colored storage trays. The material pool and the blackboard on the side say way more about the learning of the children than the teaching of the teacher within the spatial language of a Satellite-School. The extensive pool of material, the children's blackboard space and the traditional blackboard form a didactically and methodically logically conceptualized ensemble and thus constitute logically the interior basic frame of the pedagogical space of the MGML-Methodology. From a quantitative point of view there is space ratio of three quarters to one quarter, if the areas of the room are attributed to the pupils and the teacher.

Fig. 15: Decentralized situation of learning space in a Satellite School

The rectangle formed by the four walls is mostly filled symmetrically. The children are seated on the ground when learning in a Satellite-School according to Indian culture in rural areas. The group areas discussed before are equipped with half-height group tables or connected tables for two people, depending on the Satellite-School. Colored mats that can easily be lay cover the floor around the tables. The children are seated on all sides of the tables. The group tables are next to the material pool. They are rather to be used for independent work or cooperation with a partner. The groups that work more teacher based or partly teacher based are situated closer to the small teacher's desk. The spatial localization of the social forms clearly ascribes itself to the spatial concept of the fundamental structure, hence and with logical consequence also filling the structure in the interior of the one-room school. This spatial structure and the children's various points of view immediately showcase the decentralized basic nature of the spatial use for the educational processes.

The small, rather unobtrusive teacher's desk before the blackboard is also low. Within the spatial language of the Satellite-School the teacher moves on the same level. His task is roaming the entire classroom and being in contact with the parents and the entire village also the communal environment, too. Within his assignment and within his spatial movement, he is a participating learner in the process of supporting and guiding the children. Sometimes the pupils approach his small desk in order to get some advice concerning further learning steps or to get their committed works revised. However, the teacher is mostly on the move around the classroom. He changes his perspective and circularly works all around the classroom in the occurring educational situations with its tasks. Like the children when learning, he has to adapt to new situations of learning again and again.

In addition to the spatial elements already mentioned the MGML-Methodology's controlling elements, the Ladders of Learning, are also discernible. They are loosely hung up in the shelf area. The children walk all over the classroom when changing their learning activities and thus orient themselves on their further tasks. The children regularly change their position in the room because of these activities and their progress on the Ladders of Learning. The children circulate between the different group tables according to their varying tasks. It is through these natural movements of learning that the children discover and use the entire learning space. In a way they appropriate their school, which is at their disposal in all areas. As a result, very precisely a change of perspective takes place spatially. This is one of the fundamental concerns of an integral educational practice, to not allow inner fixing or empty routines to develop. Dynamically engaging with further learning throughout life is thus intuitively learned by way of spatial use during educational processes.

On a second level above the side-blackboards and the material pool there is an exhibition area that goes around the classroom. The three walls of the classroom display the children's work from the artistic activities like drawings or illustrations to a story, excerpts from the newspaper on current topics, important knowledge modules or work results from the respective subjects. Likewise presented are documentaries, for example a long-term observation of the weather including sunshine duration, cloudiness, rainfall, wind movements and thermometer measurement.

Self-documented stories of the elder that have been orally passed on from one generation to the other are captioned 'Mother Stories'. These are often written down by the grandchildren and thus saved from being forgotten.

On visiting a Satellite-School the unusual usage of the ceiling is also striking. Sculptures out of paper or two-dimensional cuts from artistic projects dangle from numerous threads. Furthermore, there are English letterings in huge type. In this way the ceiling as a language space represents parts of the beginning basic vocabulary for the important lingua franca in India, which by way of its daily presence is brought into the children's focus. Thus, the ceiling has its effect throughout the school day, even when it is not directly worked on.

The floor is also used for further pedagogical activities. The corner of the classroom is shaped by a model version of the nearby village that had been explored during a class excursion, and is now fashioned as a model in small-scale. In this case the real external world is brought into the school. What has been determined and documented throughout corresponding excursions as 'village survey' is now brought to the interior of the Satellite-School and obtains its place. The educational effect of the exterior and the school's interior thus stay connected within the children's perception.

For the closing passage on the conceptualization of the learning space in the MGML-Methodology, we have to leave the learning space again that has just been described. As previously mentioned the MGML spatial design is a "School without Walls" that is situated in the environment. The educational work in India's MGML-schools is consciously connected to the surrounding nature and culture.

The school's close environment consciously becomes an additional learning space via the aforementioned environmental survey in the field of environmental studies and the ensuing field trips. The exploratory contact with the inhabitants enables learning in the own village. Parents and grandparents become experts in conversation on their agricultural and technical daily routines. The children have the opportunity to get an idea of life's wholeness – here of the village – into which they are endowed.

Nature observations in Rishi Valley help to develop a better understanding of the phenomena of ecological nexuses. The question which plants can be cultivated in the valley despite the missing rain then matters to children and parents. The closest villages or places like Angalu (not far from valley entrance), or Thettu (at the end of the Rishi Valley) are also being used as learning places. This is done in order to cause awareness for economic and societal changes or cultural traditions. The information gathered and gained in the respective researches is later on reflectively processed, systematized and saved in the Satellite-School.

The reference to culture and nature in the schools continues another historical line of development. This time it is an Indian and pre-colonial one. In these times the historical origins of education and classes are connected with the term 'Gurukul' in India. The highest social class and caste sent their sons to a guru for a considerable time. 'Gurukul' denotes the place where a guru as a spiritual master lived with his pupils. It was a school of life and for life that the guru taught.

The term 'guru' refers to this day to the sage who out of the depth of his own way of life existentially advanced into the art of living and the conduct of life. Complex knowledge and mystical immersion synchronously go hand in hand with dependence of the culture onto old, original knowledge on being and nature itself in India. This was often made accessible to the pupils in the master's often loving-harsh-affectionate way. The guru is often depicted beneath a tree teaching from the depth of being. The tree energetically offers the sheltering space of school. It is the most original form of education. The teacher's wisdom refers back to the symbol of the 'tree of life' and is inspired and protected by the unsurpassable wisdom of nature and cosmos.

Fig. 16: Class beneath the 'tree of life' - a 'School without Walls'

This former type of school as a means of culture that is sheltered and surrounded by nature is consciously upheld in the Satellite-Schools or created by new planting and cultivating school gardens. Therefore the village communities preferably locate the school area beneath or next to a strong and sheltering tree. Concluding the deliberations on the spatial conception of Satellite-Schools it can be assessed that the MGML-Methodology constitutes a clear and internationally important example of a contemporary understanding of pedagogical space. This understanding deconstructs the aged images of the school and transforms them into learning spaces that stay connected to the environment. The MGML-Methodology's conception of space lines up with internationally exemplary spatial arrangements for a premeditated learning environment. The space as a 'third pedagogue' signifies as a catchphrase. MGML's one-room school features all elements of interior design focused on the learning activity of the children. Moreover, it interprets the internationally requested 'new culture of learning' in its own idiosyncratic way; it interlocks the subcomponents of the spatial design in a consequently holistic way and relates all components and elements to another in a logical connection. The RIVER-Team has therefore not only transformed the aged tradition of teacher-oriented classes, but also put the paradigm of a 'premeditated learning environment' into an integral usage in resonance with the lived-in world.

From a German perspective the MGML-Methodology and its conception of space clearly indicate that commencing individual initiatives in Germany such as learning mosaics, learning desks or subject-specific learning areas in a classroom, have to be further developed towards 'flexible classrooms', 'learning workshops', 'learning offices' and 'learning houses'. If these pedagogical, methodical ideas, conceptions and cultures of action work together with a consequent spatial arrangement, schools will turn, on the basis of activity-oriented and interactivity enabling educational processes, into green pastures. Then schools will present themselves as "School without Walls" and act educationally as integral places of collective learning within life.

2.2.8 Time Structures in the MGML-Methodology

The question concerning time in the MGML-Methodology can only be answered by taking into account perceptions in the classroom, the methodology's design and spatial conception, and fundamental ideas on integral educational processes. The task of observing the MGML-Methodology's learning-processes concerning its temporal structure shows that also here the holistic set-up of the method with an integral culture of acting becomes operative. What is meaningful is what right now occurs to as a meaningful educational event. The set-up of the MGML-Methodology supports the concreative processes as a securing and structuring framework.

Previous criteria of temporal organization of time in the school are taken up again in the Satellite-Schools. However, these are further interpreted and designed and also stem from another basic orientation. At first it has to be stressed that the temporal structure of the MGML-Methodology follows the impulses of natural learning as it was introduced to pedagogy by Rousseau (Sting 1999, 100). 'Growing' of the child and 'allowing it to grow' is time-wise yielded precedence. Processes of self-education are welcome and are being supported. It is not hourly intervals or the teachers working hours that essentially structure time. Admittedly, the educational processes are guided by way of the year-long Ladders of Learning that interpret the respective Indian curriculum, which therefore preset a temporal horizon of goals. However, at the same time the educational processes are openly interpreted within themselves and are ultimately cleared towards the wide reach of lifelong learning.

Interestingly enough Rainer Maria Rilke already sent a reminder concerning this other usage of time in school more than 100 years ago when he talked about a school in Gothenburg called 'Samskola':

„[...] ganz leise nur, ohne Last, liegt das Netz des Stundenplanes über den Tagen. Es wird oft verschoben. Die Wochen gehen nicht mit der monotonen Eile eines Rosenkranzes durch die Finger. Jeder Tag fängt an als etwas Neues und bringt unerwartete, erwartete und völlig überraschende Dinge. Und für alles ist Zeit. [...] Es ist Zeit und Raum in dieser Schule" (Rilke in Winkel 1988, 315).

[rough translation: "[...] only very softly, without burden, does the schedule's net cover the day. Often it is deferred. The weeks do not rush through the hands with the monotonous haste of a rosary. Every day begins as something new and yields unexpected, expected and totally surprising things. And there is time for everything. [...] There is time and space in this school."]

The basic understanding Rilke offers here for the interpretation of time in a school also remains valid in the commencing 21st century (Girg 2007, 275-278). This is perceivable in the schools of the RIVER-projects on a daily basis. On observing learning in a Satellite-School it becomes immediately evident that the usage of time in this school is firstly provided and consistently used by the differentiated perception of the learning time of the individual children. 'Genuine learning time', which is based on the child's activity, as one of the quality criteria for lessons is here comprehensively accomplished. Like Padmanabha Rao and Anumula Rama, RIVER's directors, often address: the decisive and relevant question is not 'Is it taught?', but 'Is it learnt?' The time unit of the learning activity, which is provided via the material, is assigned an open and simultaneously radical basic criterion for the usage of time in the MGML-Methodology. It is the individual learning time, the actual time used for the individual learning activity, the time spent with the sustainable process of understanding that is needed by the child. The individual learning time is recognized and put into action by the MGML-Methodology as a school-educational time scale. The time structure of a school employing MGML is oriented on real-life events and not on a virtual notion of alleged learning processes. Hours for lessons and the progress are not subjected to dogmatic planning specifications like 45-minute periods. Temporal scheduling exists, but the scheduling remains an orienting, structuring and serving function for the learning process. The actual time needed by a child for its learning steps, for its learning process, for its understanding, its natural learning time is the starting point for the time frames offered within the MGML-Methodology.

This axiom of the respective individual learning time that occurs in the learning community proves to be a sustainable, stable factor of effectiveness for the processes of learning and education. The evaluations contained in the milestones and the Ladders of Learning constitute an example for this. The educational progresses can be comprehended via the quantitative temporal as well as qualitative documentations. The individual time for learning thus constitutes a free and liberating, obviously perceivable and by way of an 'assessment format' described and discernibly multi-variant and open criteria for the learning processes of individual children in the classroom. Emerging progresses, development boosts in accelerating processes or also redundant events of learning allow the child to be like it presents itself in the learning process with its individual learning pace at the moment. The fluctuations of intellectual, psycho-emotional or developmental factors are considered and given its space within this concept. The same is true for bio-rhythmical daily routines and often affecting climatic conditions. Therefore there is no standard that serves as backdrop for creating a difference, but there certainly are categories of goals that are represented by the Ladders of Learning. That way in the MGML-Methodology everybody is able to proceed to the next step whenever it is adequate according to his or her learning pace.

The phases and rhythms of learning enabled by the MGML-Methodology are designed and structured with the individual time as their starting point. At the same time they are collectively integrated. The Ladders of Learning provide a framework of standards that supports and relieves the teacher and grants him more time. The temporal duration of the progress, the time spent with the individual activities, the individual milestones up to the temporal extent of handling an entire year-long Ladder of Learning of the individual child and the entire class, are all not fixed. Class and education thus becomes a naturally developing event, instead of pulling and pushing, generating gaps in knowledge, creating a lack of understanding and being event oriented on a foreign standard. The deliberations on the various forms of groups in the MGML-Methodology show that the individual learning time can be put into action in various ways and is also incorporated in the periods of learning within the described groups in the class. Through this social implementation of the structure in learning, learning remains individually and collectively meaningful.

The learning time is created as a succession of individual activities structured by the Ladders of Learning on the one hand, but also by the structure of the day on the other hand. The learning time is readily comprehensible for the child due to the structuring milestones. Class is largely regulated by a flexible double period model for the subjects Language, Mathematics and Environmental Studies. Its essential character is that of a subject-specific individualized learning method that transgresses grades and school years. This regulation is to be found internationally in many reform-oriented schools that offer their pupils an individual learning schedule.

The learning time of class is integrated into further elements of the daily structure. The morning begins with 'Cleaning' or the so called 'Morning Jobs'. This demands a signal of co-responsibility for the entire school area from the first phase of the day on. Subsequently, a simple breakfast is provided. The following morning assembly can be fashioned with songs, stories, games or also small presentations by pupils or teachers. After this communal time with a strong social-cultural component the previously described individual, subject-oriented learning periods ensue. These are guided by the Ladders of Learning.

The following progress of the day is likewise interspersed with smaller breaks after the specific learning periods. A longer midday break, including lunch that is being cooked at the spot, interrupts the learning. Artistic-aesthetic corporal fields like dance, music, shadow-play and elements of artistic design are interspersed throughout the day, or are separately contributed in the afternoon. Also information technology learning in the central computer room on RIVER-campus enhances and enriches the proposition, guided by the Ladders of Learning, to spend the day. The children at a Satellite-School are able to get educated and educate themselves within a full-day of learning opportunities and propositions due to the combination with these further elements of the MGML-Methodology. The time structure thus follows a rhythmic daily routine that features clearly ritualized elements like the morning assembly at the beginning, the interspersed artistic elements and also the 'games' at the end of the day. Here is an exemplary daily routine of a Satellite-School:

08.00 – 08.30	Morning Jobs and Breakfast
08.30 – 09.00	Morning Assembly
09.00 – 10.15	Telugu (Language)
10.15 – 10.30	Break
10.30 – 11.45	Mathematics
11.45 – 13.30	Lunch Break
13.30 – 15.00	EVS (Environmental Studies)
15.00 – 15.10	Break
15.10 – 15.30	General
15.30 – 16.00	Games

Fig. 17: Daily routine of a Satellite-School

The daily schedule constitutes a basic matrix for the teacher of a Satellite-School. He or she can work with these time units freely, even flexibly change them according to current necessity. The schedule might vary for the different days of the week as can be seen on the photograph of a Satellite-School's weekly schedule below. Additionally, further activities outside of the school area are scheduled on different days like field trips or one-day 'environmental surveys'. The weekly schedule also clearly discloses the shorter periods in the afternoon. These are implemented in order not to demand too much of the children when their ability to concentrate is waning.

As has been mentioned concerning the conception of space, periods of learning on the school area are complemented with learning periods in the surrounding region. These 'environmental surveys' are exploratory walks and also field trips with specific issues. Class trips to different, religiously, culturally, geographically or ecologically interesting places with overnight stays are possible.

Culture-bound interruptions of the educational work occur for the entire school due to numerous regional and nationwide holidays and for individual children also due to family celebrations. These periods of celebration that are typical for India are shrewdly absorbed by the MGML-Methodology's temporal flexibility.

Of course, there are also respective celebrations and festivities in the schools throughout the year in India that are incorporated into the time budget of the Satellite-Schools. The periods of educational learning are thus mixed with periods of learning on special occasions or also with periods of learning outside the school area.

One of the highlights in the year is a three-day long sports festival that is conducted in the vein of the Olympic Games. All children from all Satellite-

Schools of the Rishi Valley Institute for Educational Resources and their parents come and meet on RIVER-campus on this occasion. The RIVER-campus has a sports ground of substantial size. There all the children compete in individual events or present scenically designed physical exercises in a group.

Fig. 18: Children from all Satellite-Schools at the yearly Olympic Games

The mathematical festivity 'Metric Mela' that goes on for an entire day in the village is another one of these pedagogical highlights of the year.

Apart from the perspective of the pupil's individual learning time, the teacher's perspective is also to be considered in the contemplations concerning the usage of time in the MGML-Methodology. While in a teacher-oriented, instruction-oriented education the methodically skillful presentation of the content and the classroom management absorbs the teacher's time, teachers working with the MGML-Methodology receive temporal open spaces due to the individually active pupils. Calm and quite working and learning in the classroom is made possible with the double period model that keeps the entire class on the same subject. It is easier to get considerable time budgets for guiding, counseling and supporting the children's individual learning processes as will be elaborated in the passage on the teacher's tasks in the MGML-Methodology.

The general questions concerning time management and usage are addressed in the RIVER-manual for the teacher training "Teacher Trainings Module I" in the chapter "Time Management in a MGML School". It is consciously designed to grant the teacher the most time possible for giving advice and support during the pupils' learning processes. The RIVER-Team phrases open questions in their impulses in order to point to a differentiated understanding of time management:

"What is the advantage if more than 45 minutes for each subject is allotted in an MGML School?" [...] "How does the 'grouping method' help the teachers to manage their time effectively in the MGML School?" "How can students and the community members help the teachers to utilize their time effectively" (RIVER 2003, 128)?

These and similar questions give an impression of how important it is to the colleagues of RIVER to effectively utilize the teacher's time that is pedagogically available and to make them available for the individual tasks of care and support during the children's learning processes. The included system of support by the king of learning also takes effect expeditiously. This time-wise relieves the teacher furthermore.

It becomes apparent as a principle that the teachers are first supposed to use their time in the MGML-Methodology to support individual learning. They should only invest their time in instruction-oriented phases of class if this was subject-wise inevitable or methodically necessary and is signalized by respective markers on the Ladders of Learning.

By implementing the MGML-Methodology two-thirds of the teacher's time are utilized for the care and support for individuals and smaller groups and only hardly one-third is necessary for instructions, group processes or also organizational things. This has been recognized and observed during the daily routines at a Satellite-School. The axiom of individual learning time is thus synchronously aligned with the quality-securing time of individual support and care on behalf of the teacher. Both elements work together in the educational situations and increase the respective effectiveness and quality of an 'activity based learning'. From a principal point of view the usage of time in the MGML-Methodology considers the "fertile moment in the educational process" (Copei 1969), as Copei has expressed it, to be a basic assumption. The children stay on subject the same as the teacher due to the mindful presence of the teacher and the mindful conduct of learning processes in concreative situations (Kaltwasser 2010). There is another gain in time for the teacher. Since the curriculum via the MGML-Methodology as a premeditated learning environment already exists as a lasting preparation for lessons, the teachers are equally lasting relieved in the planning of class. The time budget of the teacher increases once more for the task of individualized preparations, for contemplations on care and support, the documentation of the children's learning processes, but also for the cooperation with colleagues and contact to the parents. The reduced time that is necessary for the preparation of class lends more time for contemplating, but also for the phases of regeneration and rest from the school day.

2.2.9 Cultural Components of Design

Considering the MGML-Methodology in its wholeness as 'merely' a method would be a reduction of its comprehensive conception. As a holistic educational concept for an integral educational practice it is based on the previously shown material pool with its system of Ladders of Learning. At the same time the MGML-Methodology contains further important cultural aspects, which support these methodical arrangements. The RIVER-Team is also concerned with preserving old regional traditions as cultural assets for the schools.

Mother Stories. In order to preserve the abundance of stories passed down orally the RIVER-Team together with the children of the Satellite-Schools organizes meetings with mothers and grandmothers. In these meetings the elderly women of the respective village are being asked to tell stories that they had been told by their parents. These are registered by the RIVER-Team via various media and written forms of documentation. The obtained rich material of regional oral history provides the Team with holistic language situations for the creation of the 'Telugu' language material. These are starting points for further linguistic tasks. Furthermore, the older pupils of the Satellite-Schools were and still are asked to document old stories that are being told in their families. All stories are illustrated and collected in a book. They become part of the reading material in the classroom. These storybooks are very motivational for all children since they come from people and authors they know and are related to. From a cultural point of view the Mother Stories consistently preserve oral cultural assets threatened with extinction.

Fig. 19: The Mother Stories connect three generations

Mothers' Committee. Beyond this special occasion of documenting the Mother Stories the mothers of the school children do also regularly meet in the Satellite-Schools for the Mothers' Committee. This assembly of mothers in the school entrusts them with a particular responsibility concerning the educational processes of their children. At the same time these gatherings acknowledge and appreciate their educational work within the family. Moreover, these meetings also further the growth of a sense of shared-responsibility for the school in the village. Some Satellite-Schools grant responsibility for the preparation of breakfast to the mothers. At the same time the Mothers' Committee is a forum that strengthens the often difficult role of the woman in the village since according to Indian tradition she changed from her original family to her husband's family.

The issues and topics of the meetings vary. Questions of daily routine at school can be addressed together with the teachers. Assistance measures for children can be sorted out in cooperation with the mothers who offer corresponding support and assistance. Further topics are concerned with questions of health, nutrition, hygiene or also with medical first measures on treating illnesses. They focus on old repertoire of regional household remedies from the own herbal garden. Cultural evenings with literary events are also organized. In the beginnings of the RIVER initiatives evening classes on adult literacy enhanced the education at a Satellite-School. RIVER's documents speak of the successful actions for mothers:

> "Lilavati has been at night school for six month. In that short time, she has finished Class 2, an achievement that puts her ahead of Bharati, her daughter, who has just entered Class 2 in the day school. She has overtaken her husband, who joined night school with her but dropped out because he found it awkward to be the only man in the class. Lilavati is nonetheless determined that her husband, who can only sign his name, will learn how to read and to count properly. She borrows material from school and, time permitting, supervises both her husband's and daughter's work at home" (Rishi Valley Education Centre n.y., 20-21).

These tasks of adult literacy in the village have all but vanished for RIVER in recent years thanks to the pleasingly fast acquired basic knowledge of cultural techniques by the village population. By now there are pupils in the schools whose mothers could already successfully learn in a Satellite-School. However, the school still remains a place for adult education. The Mothers' Committee also collects the low school fees, administers it at the bank and decides which families do not have to pay for tuition due to their poverty.

The highlight of the collective work with the Mothers' Committee is the Mothers' Tour: an excursion with a cultural program in other regions of India that lasts several days. The women of all twelve villages that host a Satellite-School embark on the journey in big buses alongside with the RIVER-Team. Thereby the women transcend the horizon of their own families and their villages and open themselves up for new perspectives due to the communal study trip. Sometimes the workings of the Mothers' Committee also lead to the foundation of women's cooperatives. These women's cooperatives establish field of employment and sufficient means to earn a living in order to secure the basic income of the family.

Puppet Show. The Puppet Show is also of high cultural importance within the MGML-Methodology. This ancient art of Shadow Theater that is typical for the region is on the brink of extinction in India. Every Satellite-School owns a large set of figures and a transparent canvas behind which the delicate figures on a stick are being played. The figures are designed and created by the teachers together with the children. The skill and technique of Shadow Theater is part of the continuing education of teachers and is content-wise and technically differentiated and explained as well as practically put to the test (RIVER 2004, 52).

The entire class is involved in developing the story. Some function as narrators, some as operators of the figures and the others play the part of noisemakers. The noisemakers acoustically support the events of the story with self-created instruments or claves. All other classes enjoy the show as audience, often joining in narrating the gripping stories. The plays are mostly fables, but sometimes also plays with a religious or mythological Indian background.

Children and teaching staff can also practice with the big shadow theater figures on RIVER-campus, with whom the Puppet Show players used to travel from village to village. The huge puppets are made out of transparent and dyed animal skins. They are fixed to several sticks or rods and are moved with a sophisticated technique. The Satellite-Schools of RIVER participated in school competitions for Puppet Shows at a supra-regional level and successfully came first several times. Alongside the Puppet Show the children also learn numerous regional songs and dances over the course of their five years in school. They know all the lyrics and choreographies by heart and are able to perform them without any guidance.

Newspaper in the School. A separate period of time within the subjects of a Satellite-School is dedicated to the current regional, national and international events. The 3rd to 5th graders of the multigrade study groups are asked to choose topics from newspapers or journals. They develop competence and knowledge on the events of the day alone or in the group. The older children of the Satellite-School school create theme books that consist of cut-out images, own texts or also commentaries.

By means of these activities the Satellite-School educate and develop the children's autonomy concerning the acquisition and gathering of information, the deduction of information and the processing of information. Since the children also give small presentations as experts, they nurture their ability to communicate and exercise giving presentations from an early stage on. At the same time this procedure encourages the entire learning group to engage with new questions time and again. The existing material that is represented by the Ladders of Learning is being enhanced by the arising topics and issues with information on current events. These skills become even more important regarding the Indian 'Right to Information Act' from 2005, since these competencies lead to socially participatory abilities. This rule of law guarantees that every Indian is able to be informed about all processes of administrative bodies and has the right to quick disclosure. The required communicative and methodical competence to gather and acquire information for oneself is a prerequisite for this. An analysis on the range of topics in the subject EVS of the MGML-Methodology that Research Team Integral conducted for the 'Hanns-Seidel-Stiftung' New Delhi showed that the MGML-Methodology sustainably incorporates the intentions of Civic Education as well as Global Education concerning the content and the applied methods. These intentions are also proclaimed as goals by the EU in Europe.

Metric Mela. The tradition of celebrations and festivities in India is also consciously acknowledged in the Satellite-Schools. Next to the festivities of the ordinary time and the Rishi Valley Olympic Games the so called Metric Mela takes on an important role.

The Metric Mela is a mathematical festival that has been especially developed by the RIVER-Team with the joy of celebrating as its concept. The festivity is organized by the school for the entire village and also nearby schools. By including mathematical phenomena from the living environment and playfully incorporating them into the celebration, a positive attitude for lastingly dealing with mathematical problems and questions is established instead of building up fear from mathematical tasks. The experiential implementation creates a general, realistic mathematical understanding that optimally supports the systematized learning opportunities of the mathematical Ladders of Learning.

Special arrangements are met by the school for a Metric Mela. The entrance of the school and the entire school area are transformed into a market place by festive banners, the typical banana trees to the left and right of the entrance, festoons of flowers, flags as well as strewn ornaments on the ground. Everybody is dressed in colorful garments. The golden borders of the girl's and women's saris are glittering in the sunlight and foster the powerful atmospheric impression.

The RIVER-Team again pursues a holistic educational strategy with the Metric Mela that consciously incorporates the entire village community. In this process ten objectives and effects were drafted that RIVER explicitly names in its documents:

1. Members of the village community are consciously involved in the activities of the school.
2. Members of the village community realize the value and importance of school and education.
3. The implementation of this attractive festivity shall prevent the danger of premature dropouts from school.
4. Mathematical concepts learned in class are being connected to reality.
5. An awareness concerning health and hygiene shall be mediated to the villagers.
6. The children are becoming aware of the main aspects of communication:

speaking, understanding what is being explained, and accurate reading. These potentials shall be supported.

7. The children are becoming aware of mathematical concepts that are useful for everyday life, like addition, subtraction, positional notation, fractions and methods of measurement.
8. Hidden talents shall be detected and emphasized in the course of the event.
9. An awareness of cultural programs and folk art 'indigenous art' is being generated.
10. Scientific and logical thinking shall be mediated to the children.

The Metric Mela is set-up with 18 stations across the school area. Two children of the Satellite-School supervise each station. Every participant is handed a ticket at the entrance of the Metric Mela that serves as a control slip. All stations of the Metric Mela are recorded on the ticket.

Every participant enters his name and age at the headpiece. All kinds of mathematical challenges await the participants. Some stations are about measurement: height, waist circumference, the span of the arms, length of the feet, even the length of the nose and the weight are being determined. All measurements are being recorded in charts. Therefore after the Metric Mela it is possible to compile statistic data concerning the village and its inhabitants.

A second group of stations is concerned with recognizing geometrical forms. Others are about guessing weights, lengths or durations. Further tasks on the school area require calculations of small amounts of money, matching exercises, or the right arrangement of little card sets that make up an entire mathematical operation. Games of skill drawing on fine motor as well as gross motor skills complement the course.

The participants' results are registered in either category A or B at every station, signifying if the tasks was or was not successfully executed. In the end points are given out that in adding up provide information on the quality of accomplishments.

Fig. 20: A station of the Metric Mela

An international visitor of RIVER describes his impressions at a Metric Mela as such:

> "As we walked past the entrance, on both sides children between the ages of seven and ten were taking charge of their stalls. One could buy hot dosas, vadas, sundal, sweets and watermelons or have one's weight or height measured! Colored ribbons were strung across to one to guess the length and poles struck into the ground to guess height. At the end of the row one could time oneself and see how many peoples could be transferred from one box to another box in a matter of sixty seconds. [...] We left after a couple of hours but the mela continued. We were told on the next day the names of the villagers who guessed the height and weight correctly would be announced and the prize they collect is a colored photograph of themselves! There are also announcements as to whom is the tallest, the shortest and heaviest in the village" (Rishi Valley Education Centre n.y., 10).

Up to 500 participants are registered at a Metric Mela in the villages. Every one of them enjoys the happy festivity. Parents are proud to point to their children who are running a station. The children baffle some adults with the mathematical riddles at the stations that quickly touch on the ignorance of the adults. However, nobody is being embarrassed. Everybody is granted a second chance or is being helped by the supervising children with adequate assistance.

Mothers offer food and beverages at another part of the school campus. In the meantime a dance or a song is performed. The festivities take place once a year on average in every village that hosts a Satellite-School. The celebration of mathematics has thus become a permanent feature of the village culture and the schools with their teachers and children are hosts for the village community on this day.

2.2.10 Ecological Components of Design

In addition to the MGML-Methodology's cultural components of design, the ecological aspects touch upon another level of the RIVER-projects. The generally holistic approach of the MGML-Methodology in form of a non-dualistic educational practice comprises the surrounding and cultural environment. The ladders are our beings foundation and in the times of ecological changes become even more important. Drawing on the fundamental concept of 'Oikos' as the communal house of the earth in which we all live, the MGML-Methodology deliberately does not separate the natural and the cultural environment. The MGML-Methodology processes this fact – among others – by way of the interdisciplinary subject called 'Environmental Studies' (EVS). EVS is beyond the scope of the subjects 'Local History and General Knowledge' or 'Communal Lessons' that is common in Germany.

As previously mentioned, Ladders of Learning with systemically connected topic areas are available. The star or blossom shaped topic areas serve as a basis for further learning, which ensues from the child's natural and cultural learning environment. The educational processes in EVS can be looked upon as sophisticated perceiving and studying of environment and 'social world'. Its goal is to recognize and realize the intricacy of the already existing holistic complexity of the individual and the community within the wholeness of nature and culture. Out of this arises a feeling and realization of the symbiotic cooperation of the factors. Nature in its rhythms, progresses and effects is quintessentially conceived in the Environmental Studies. The child's natural environment is the starting point in the MGML-Methodology, which becomes a learning situation with all its phenomena, plants, animals, weathers, or also rhythms in nature. The teachers of the Satellite-Schools refer back to the experiences of the children when they commence a new ecological topic.

Holistic impulses of images and pictures on central themes of live are methodically used as a starting point in EVS in the MGML-Methodology. The teachers initialize an ensuing open dialogue with the help of the images' impulses. The dialogue generates questions for the factual conversation on the topic. It is followed up by sophisticated working steps. The formations of hypotheses, which are a result of the working steps, develop a researching and exploring attitude towards natural phenomena in the children together with the teacher. The EVS' set of picture cards deliberately leaves natural and cultural situations unseparated, as to draw attention to respective dependencies and effects of nature and culture.

All together there are 27 topic areas at hand for the first and second grade. About half of them deal with explicitly ecological issues. Each topic in turn is assigned activity cards that are as in the subjects of Mathematics and German organized in different categories of activity. All of them are distinguished by symbols. The sets of cards are available in the material pool under the section for EVS.

The initiators of the MGML-Methodology draw on an old principle that is also popular in Germany. It has been referred to as 'Original Encounter' by Heinrich Roth in the 1960s (see Roth 1976). The point is to let the thing or phenomenon talk to oneself at the immediate encounter with the thing in culture and nature. Insights are being gained through the perception via a process of contemplation. The immediate, original encounter enables the children to relate to the phenomena of nature. Put holistically, the pre-existing ecological relationships are realized and become aware to the children via the collective work in the learning process: the involvement of the human-being in the ecological context becomes transparent.

In addition to the sets of material developed for the Environmental Studies and the systemic arrangement of the Ladders of Learning, learning locations outside the school are introduced to class. Environmental Surveys and Field trips are mainly used for this purpose.

Environmental Surveys are in metaphoric and concrete sense surveys of the environment. They are a matter of explorations that offer the possibility to ask questions but also to find answers (Dühlmeier 2008). In the process the researched field that is approached by children of the across age learning group is examined from multiple perspectives and investigated on numerous aspects. Environmental Surveys often take place in the surrounding region, frequently in nearby villages, which is in hike-distance from the Satellite-School. However, sometimes jeeps are also available to explore the environment at a greater distance.

The attentive and sophisticated perception of the phenomena is what is most important during the explorations. All phenomena, be it a fallen tree, a birds nest in great heights, the burnt grass on the edge of a field, an empty cistern, a limping cow or the unusual formation of clouds in the sky, as content can become the starting point for further questions and learning. Environmental Studies therefore are exploratory researches and surveys that are followed up by small and open research propositions whose content only reveals itself in the process. The perceptions lead to questions that can entail further activities at the learning places outside the school. The children start to collect information throughout these explorations and document their gained insights. Their illustrations might likely end up becoming another theme book, which further enhances the material pool in the classroom. The preparation of small exhibitions concerning the topics is also a part of the creative activities. The collected exhibits are labeled and appealingly arranged by the pupils. In the role of experts they then proceed to explain their work on the subject to other pupils.

Very concrete Field Trips on specific subjects are the second variation of learning in nature. Field Trips are further developed activities outside the school area. These are conducted with specific questions and an elaborated goal.

The joyful activities for the children during the Field Trips and in Environmental Studies are in the focus as they are in the entire MGML-Methodology. Considering, observing, collecting objects, making drawings, conducting interviews and so forth are activities that are introduced and guided by the supervising teachers. Furthermore, the children learn how to structure their collected information: compiling charts, drawing maps, or evaluating the content of an interview. Long-term observations like the daily observation of the weather are also performed.

As is the case in all other departments, the sections of Environmental Studies are diligently prepared and arranged in the MGML-education of the teachers: the teachers are faced with the central questions of the methodology considering the Environmental Surveys. Some of them are:

- What is the challenge for the teacher when the children are to conduct an exploration and a survey autonomously and the teacher should not give them direct information?
- In what ways can the village community and its resources be used for the trip and the survey?
- How can the collected information be used in the classroom later on?
- Which further sources of information can be used for the field of environment and social world in addition to the trips and surveys?

The ecological building blocks of the MGML-Methodology make a contribution to the preservation of the livelihoods and the living situation in the villages, as does the entire educational conception of the MGML-Methodology.

As for material, work with images is used. For example, two images are testimony to the urgency for differentiated ecological action and thinking in India and also in Rishi Valley. The images, functioning as comparative recordings, provide situations from 2006 to 2012 that are to be ecologically interpreted. Both show a groundwater reservoir in Rishi Valley in a filled and the now dried-out state. That which becomes frighteningly apparent by the images is not only the task of the adults in the major ecological project of Rishi Valley, but also the collective task of the school. It prepares the children to deal with existential ecological questions that definitely lie ahead of them. This demands a learning that supports the ability via open questions to be open for different ways of acting and living throughout the transformation of the ecological and thus also the economic situation.

The sophisticated culture of acting that poses ecological questions can be made clear to the children by means of this or similar material of images. The entire learning group and the teacher deduce general ecological questions from the perceivable processes of change and transformation in the immediate surroundings of the children. The content is prepared according to their age but also in demanding fashion. The school area is also available for the study of flora and fauna as has been mentioned in chapter 2.2.8. The created school gardens, herb gardens and fields of flowers are diligently cared for by the pupils during the rains. A corresponding distribution of tasks assigns the pupils their responsibility. In their intention the ecological components of design of the MGML-Methodology clearly go beyond this narrow horizon. They are geared towards the sensitive perception of all events of life in nature and culture and also promote the corresponding competence to handle these events and processes. All ecological questions and also the ecological building blocks of the MGML-Methodology at the Satellite-Schools are also connected to the major ecological regional project that has been established as an Indian model project in Rishi Valley in 2009.

The ecological project 'Rishi Valley Special Development Area', RVDA, encompasses the entire Valley with all its villages and has the goal of a sustainable ecological development. The RVDA has been executed by the Rishi Valley Education Centre in cooperation with governmental agencies and regional as well as ecological oriented NGOs since 2009. 'Women and Livestock', 'Traditional Livelihoods', 'Natural Resource Management, NRM, and Horticulture', 'Education and Employment of Youth', and 'Health and Nutrition' are the five fields of work of the project. The educational realm of the RIVER-initiatives is involved in this important Indian model project with the Satellite-Schools and all other schools in the valley. An important contribution to preserve the living environment in the valley is therefore made.

The MGML-Methodology, with its holistic methodical approach and also its specific contents of ecological learning, facilitates education for sustainable development as it is aimed for by the UNESCO worldwide.

2.3 Teaching in the MGML-Methodology

2.3.1 Being a Teacher in India

The MGML-Methodology, with its possibilities of design extending to a fully individualized common school, starts out in an integral sense from the permanent flow of processes of learning and education of the learners. Organizing and structuring these processes and giving advice and support throughout them can be seen as the teacher's core task in the MGML-Methodology.

This changes the image of the teacher enormously by Indian standards. The image of the strict teacher who stands in front of the class he teaches, disciplines and – if necessary – metes out punishment, has prevailed for many Indians from the times of British colonization up to this day. The separation of children and educators into two frontiers is already visible in the classroom itself. The desks are aligned facing the blackboard in the front. The children sit at these desks, clad in their uniforms and shall listen to the teacher that is speaking in the front. The contents are taken from textbooks that have been centrally designed for the entire country in India. Subsequently, many of these contents hardly bear any relevance for the everyday life of children that live in villages far away from the capital Delhi. Hence, going to school is often associated with feelings of avoidance or even anxiety and fear. In many schools this fear is also used to establish discipline and order in class. Children are verbally intimidated and put under pressure. Even the cane is indeed in use these days.

The lessons' missing connection to the reality of life leads to a rather diminished interest in school, especially within the rural population. One of the consequences is that hardly any young people are becoming teachers in these areas. There is a lack of teachers, positions remain vacant and schools are orphaned. Children are not schooled at all, or only by casual teachers that are not at all or hardly trained and qualified and thus feel overstrained in their role as teachers with its demands and occurrences at school.

As has previously been mentioned, it was the task of the founders of RIVER to react to this situation and to create an educational model that considers the individual children's learning processes, but also those of the teachers. The option to rely on experienced and professional teachers that are skilled in progressive teaching did not exist.

Fig. 21: Working in a class at a Satellite-School

On the contrary, a possibility for not at all trained teachers to quickly and efficiently acquire new methods and ways of working had to be established. This possibility should further enable the aspiring teachers to adapt and adjust these methods to their own possibilities and local realities. The teachers' awareness for their changed challenges and new roles had to be raised. In addition to that the teachers had to be shortly and intensely prepared for the realization of these tasks.

2.3.2 The Roles and Tasks of Teachers in the MGML-Methodology

The MGML-Methodology, as an open form of education, needs a teacher that is able to act accordingly in the previously extensively described learning situations. It rests on the teacher to take responsibility for all processes and to adequately act out of a fundamental understanding. The teacher has to realize that the classical role of lecturing fades into the background for the benefit of other roles.

The teacher rather has to prepare the learning environment and become the interpreter, the initiator, the counselor and helper of the children. He has to successively reflect on and further his own processes – assuming every position is crucial for the success of the work with Ladders of Learning. Only if the teacher professionally provides all necessary parameters and learning possibilities, is it possible to achieve a high quality individualized working of the pupils with the support of the teacher in across-the-ages and mixed abilities classes.

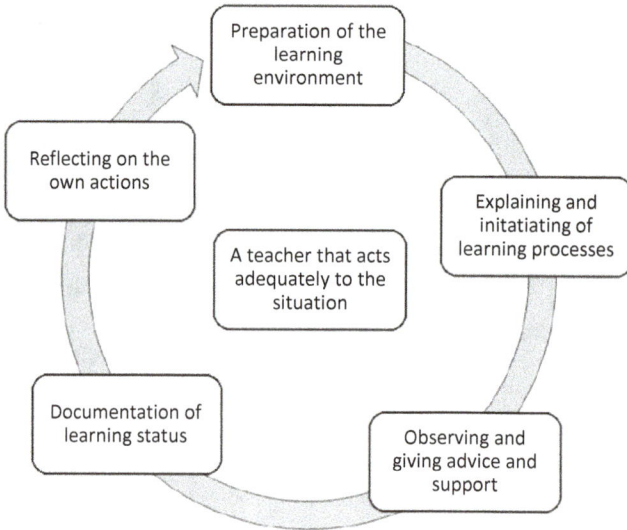

Fig. 22: Tasks of the teacher

The Ladders of Learning guide every pupil through class individually. Everybody designs the working process for himself. The teacher is released from the obligation to control the process in the immediate events of class. Instead, he is free to engage in other tasks such as giving advice and support.

Teachers used to teacher-centered teaching are forced to rethink and let go of accustomed patterns of action. The focus of their tasks switches from 'standing in front of the class' to working and engaging in small groups or with individual pupils. This is also mirrored in the teacher's position in the room. He does not stand singled-out opposite the pupils within the social events of learning, but rather actively and immediately participates in various roles. Therefore the teacher is seated at a designated spot – like the pupils. He introduces children that are sitting at his table to new topics or gives out further explanations, if demanded. He is not as present for the children seated at other tables. In this case the teacher obtains the role of a silent observer.

This seemingly 'minor' change of position already radically affects the entire system. The classical oppositions of teacher-centered teaching disappear. There are no two sides. Working with Ladders of Learning is a living cooperation and a meeting of adults and children that see eye to eye in direct contact. This also changes the spatial distance between teachers and pupils in in-class situations. The public 'lecture-distance' of a teacher-centered education becomes a personal distance and closeness to the pupil, respectively, which enables a more familiar conduct. In addition to working with contents the child also perceives and recognizes a non-verbal interest in its persona via the form of direct communication: You are so important that I will only tend to you or this small group for the next couple of minutes.

As is known from the numerous progressive teaching approaches, the duties of the teacher are to be found within a 'prepared learning environment'. Hence, another one of the teacher's duties is to create the learning arrangements and/or skillfully use the provided learning arrangements and to interestingly refine them. The sophisticated learning evaluations provide the teacher in full with the educational processes of the pupils and thus enable him to share these documents with the parents. An ongoing process of reflecting, supports the own actions and serves as a basis for the further development of the own competences.

2.3.3 Preparing the Learning Environment

The purposeful design of the learning environment is a prerequisite for a successful teaching process. It is an absolute peculiarity in traditional Indian schools to switch from a frontal arrangement of the desks to round, big group tables – as is common in the learning room at RIVER-schools (see 2.2.7). Children and teacher working together at low tables while sitting on the ground, is another example that strikingly differentiates the RIVER-schools from conventional schools in India. In doing so RIVER takes the fact into account that this model of schools captures and represents the national and regional characteristics. School is being lived as a representation of cultural tradition. If children discover a school design that is close to their homely environment, this resemblance creates security and trust.

The teachers, who mostly hail from the region and are familiar with the regional circumstances and the village community, have the task to establish schools according to these standards and to include cultural specifics from the village and the environment. This also becomes apparent in the design and structuring of the materials for the Ladders of Learning and beyond that in the further education. Stories and narratives are collected and documented together with the local women in the previously mentioned 'Mother Committees', on the basis of which the children work on grammatical phenomena in language acquisition, for example. It is the teacher's task to create appropriate material for the Ladders of Learning from these and to deploy them in his school. This ensures a double 'ownership'. The 'ownership' of the teacher, who rediscovers himself in the classroom and in the work with the children by means of the entirely individually developed material on the one hand and the 'ownership' of the village population that lies in the collective collection and selection of texts on the other hand. The content of class also makes the school really their school. The people of the village gain significance. Their stories are so valuable that these are being used for studies by the following generation in school. Everyday life and life at school are tightly interwoven through the tasks of the teacher; the teacher is not only the contact person for the children, but also a reference person for the entire village. In case the teacher is absent, he is self-evidently replaced by members of the village community – mostly mothers. The school thus is an important integrative part of life in the village. Another important department in the learning room is scheduled for the presentation of working results. The teacher pays attention that the documentations are exhibited in a timely manner and are accessible for all children. Furthermore, the results are exhibited for a certain time in order to be replaced by new ones. The teacher requires skills in the design of learning environments for the preparation of learning environments. Next to the correspondence between the school environment and the living environment of the children, these skills ideally encompass profound knowledge on fitting possibilities of mobilization. Components of flexible design of learning spaces and fractal structures respectively, are discussed and applied these days in Europe. References to distance zones and the consideration of fields of work for various social forms and forms of working that take into account the cultural frame of reference among other things, are also factored in (Lichtinger 2014). The low tables that are typical in India are an example of these deliberations. The integration of a sofa or maybe a bunk bed for reading could be possible in Western Cultures.

2.3.4 Observing and Giving Advice and Support

Accompanying the pupils throughout their doings is central to the process of learning and teaching. This might sound easy but often turns out to be the most difficult task of all. It is not so much about predetermining, presenting and showing, but the more about letting the child grow throughout all processes. The teacher is not in the center – also not spatially, but stays in the background and at the sides respectively. He is alert and open for everything that happens. A nuanced and comprehensive perception and confiding waiting and seeing demands a humble attitude from the teacher towards to the child, as well as indulgence with one's own impatience. In some instances it is almost unbearable if a child fails to retrieve some material immediately or is not able to implement a practice the way the teacher had in mind. However, these exploratory phases are extremely important for the children. The senses of achievement, after everything finally worked out and the task could have been solved, are vital for the delight in learning and are a positive starting point for the next working step. Processes of observation on the part of the teacher are very complex, but usually happen so fast that the individual steps can't be isolated and perceived individually and often also cannot be brought to mind. Nevertheless decidedly that is which is necessary. At first, the situation is perceived by one or more sensory organs. The situation encompasses objects, people and processes. Whatever actually gets registered from the complex situation is only a part of what happens in the situation. The registration of phenomena is usually immediately connected to judgment – the comparison of the impression with previously made experiences already constitutes a subjective valuation (Jäger 2007, 54). However, this subjective valuation has to be realized again and again and has to be put to the test. For RIVER the training of observation already possesses a central dimension in the education of new teachers. Not only is the practical implementation of the necessary requirements pointed out to the teachers in observational phases at model schools that span several months, but also their own ability to observe that is so important for their future workings, is being trained. This is done by means of prefabricated observation papers on which observational categories are noted and allocated to central spheres of activity. The categories comprise general statements such as "Students are neatly dressed." or "The teacher does not sit in a chair while teaching." up to "The children help one another when the do an activity" (RIVER 2003, 206-218).

Observation Points in a MGML School (3 months)

Activities	Yes	No
Methodology		
• Grouping charts have been prepared.		
Language		
• The teachers narrate stories from the 'Bull' logo cards with actions; as they finish, they hang the 'Bull' logo cards on the clothes-line / wire one by one.		
• Alphabets are taught by using words as a base.		
• Find out what is being done for Telugu. The format contains the activities achieved by students according to their learning level.		
• Students play the game of asha.		
Maths		
• The local resources are utilized in teaching mathematics.		
• All the activities given in the "Bird nest" logo cards are taking place.		
EVS		
• Students fill in the weather index every day.		
General		
• Students are neatly dressed.		
• The teacher has taught the children short stories and "action songs".		
• Students have learnt a minimum of ten assembly songs.		

Fig. 23: Observational tasks while sitting in classes

The observations and documentations are followed up by the teacher reflecting his own actions. It is seen as the teacher's task to understand and refine the quality of 'his' school. This progression is immediately related to the teacher's self-innovation. This is also defined as a central task by RIVER (RIVER 2003, 138-39). Giving advice and support to the children while fully considering the respective learning and living situation takes top priority. Essentially, the teacher has to find adequate solutions for all processes, whether it is the structuring of learning at a model school, providing learning opportunities for children with special needs, or the elaboration of teaching material for children who cannot attend class because, for example, they have to work (RIVER 2003, 192-93 and 197-98).

2.3.5 Documenting and Reflecting

The documentation of the learning progresses of all pupils via documentation overviews of the so called 'Assessment Formats' (see Chapter 2.2.6) are important for the teacher for several reasons. For one thing they serve as an occasion to meet and talk about the current state of learning for the teacher, the pupils and possibly also the parents. This does not only enable everyone involved to discern the contemporary process, but also offers the possibility to describe and evaluate the process from different perspectives and to make sense of resulting similarities and differences. For another thing these documentations enable the child to evaluate itself – also in comparison to other children – without this evaluation being tied to a grading. The documentations simultaneously provide information as well as an understanding and a sense of self-classification. For this reason the teacher does not come to the fore as a controller or administrator of learning processes. He continues to accompany the pupils: he does not dictate but rather recommends, he does not know for certain, but rather assumes.

The inert aspect of encouragement in this approach reveals itself also in other forms of the documentations. The crowning of 'King of Learners' constitutes a ritualized act, which delegates a heightened position in the overall system to the children for a certain amount of time. They become co-teachers can assume tasks of the teachers like explaining, initiating learning processes or giving advice and support to fellow pupils.

On top of that it is the teacher's task to use the documentations of the learning processes as an opportunity to contemplate him and to reexamine his actions in terms of meaningfulness and competence (RIVER 2003, 206-218).

2.3.6 Attitude

Such a conception of the role of the teacher and its connected tasks – as has been delineated in the precursory chapters – are linked to a certain idea of education and its fundamental cultures. From a scientific point of view this idea is nurtured by an encompassing understanding of learning as an integral phenomenon (see

Chapter 3.3). However, this is not explicitly and thoroughly approached in the training by RIVER. It is rather implicitly imparted via the training instructors as role models as well as metaphorical principles.

'The Child is in the Driver's Seat' shows that the child is in control of its own processes, educates itself and takes full advantage of the provided possibilities. This picture leaves space for the teacher as the co-driver at the most. He can sit next to the child, counsel and accompany it from the side and witness its development. This metaphor also enables the possibility to view the teacher as the driving instructor. The driving instructor could support the pupil with indications and information, show the way or give a lead concerning the learning method and the analysis of the issue respectively. This role foregrounds the part of explaining or also initiating, whereas the role of the co-driver sees the teacher more as a pure observer and companion. A third option would be that the teacher is not inside the car at all, but rather is located outside in the role of guide that points the children in the right direction if necessary.

Whichever of the different roles the teacher is currently embracing, the embodiment is always underlain by an attitude shaped by inner humility, as the philosopher and teacher Krishnamurti says. This attitude is carried by integral fundamental cultures that find expressions in an integral culture of action (Girg 2007, 239-241). Some of them are:

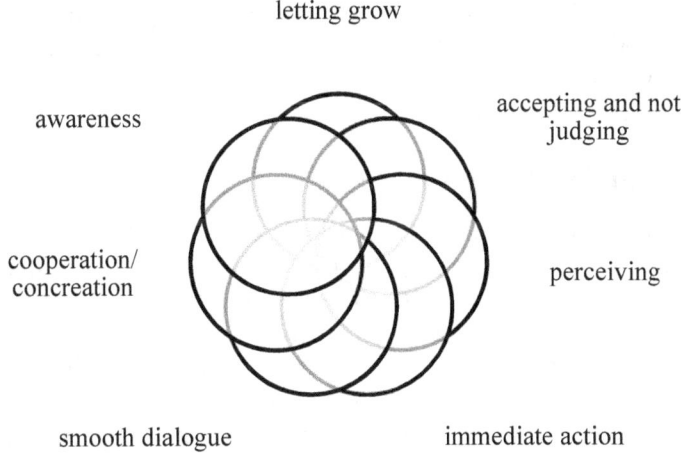

Fig. 24: Integral cultures of action

These dimensions become obvious in the questions or categories of observation in RIVER's training manual. The teachers in training are invited to reside cautiously and unobtrusively in the learning room so that the processes of the children are not disturbed (RIVER 2003, 229). At the same time it is of pivotal importance for every teacher in training to become aware of the respective unique and singular situation. They carefully need to get themselves into the situation and diligently act with and within it. Krishnamurti speaks of "Awareness" (2005, 73), an attitude and a corresponding state of consciousness that originates from an undividedness of all phenomena of life. The teacher in school that is often riddled with schedules and preliminary considerations sees it as a permanent task to come back to the current moment again and again and to be ready and prepared for any new events (Thich Nhat Hanh 1999, 68). By letting go of previous images and experiences, the so called 'conditioning' (see Krishnamurti), and truly and fully seeing what is, the teacher is able to be open for the new. The question of the girl, the conversation within the group, the picture of a boy – all of these events become the inducement for a new situation out of which unforeseen possibilities arise that find its collective, special and unique expression through the act of getting involved. The situation thus shapes itself in a certain way, becomes unique and can never be repeated in this exact same way. To bethink of this and to consciously imbibe this singularity of every moment turns every progress and movement of life – also those at school – into a new, valuable and unique (living) opportunity again and again.

This direct experience of perceiving the tangible example in class enables the new teacher, who might be an observer in the learning room, to an active engagement with the topic and also leads him to the next immediate step. Perceiving is about a first acceptance and non-judgment of what has been experienced. However, this does not mean that the teacher should not have an opinion on the event or develop a stance towards it. It is requested to undertake own reflections and to develop questions in order for a smooth dialogue with colleagues and training instructors to be possible. This smooth dialogue is a space in which every issue – also oppositions – can be addressed and collective solutions for the children can be sought.

2.4 Teacher Training with RIVER

The RIVER-Team developed teacher training and further teacher training modules parallel to the methodology itself in order to support learning, to apply the MGML-Methodology and its linked work with Ladders of Learning. Teachers and also larger project teams that are interested are being educated in this program. They are taught the educational conceptions underlying the MGML-Methodology and are enabled to get to know fundamental attitudes and methodical approaches as well as discovering and exploring an access to working with Ladders of Learning for themselves.

The basic principle of 'The Child in the Driver's Seat' is transferred to the teachers: all learning possibilities are scheduled to cater to the respective teachers' needs. What is interesting is that RIVER therefore hardly makes use of workbooks and manuals in the classical European sense. Instead there are materials with questions to which the new teacher should attend to when he intends on working with Ladders of Learning. The questions are at the center of the individual modules and serve to find the answers together. The respective perspective of the teacher is as much considered as the necessities that come along with the implementation of the MGML-Methodology in one's own lessons. The teachers understand and get to know working with Ladders of Learning by means of films, presentations and sitting in on classes in specific examples at school in order to figure out which aspects they have to include in and consider for the new composition of their classes. This should lead the teachers to learn to develop own milestones and Ladders of Learning that fit their own needs and implement them in their classroom. The teacher training takes place in several phases with the goal of internalizing the possibilities of working with the MGML-Methodology. The process' starting point is the desire of the teachers to employ the method in their own schools and classes themselves. A practical, efficient implementation is the goal of the time-wise limited project:

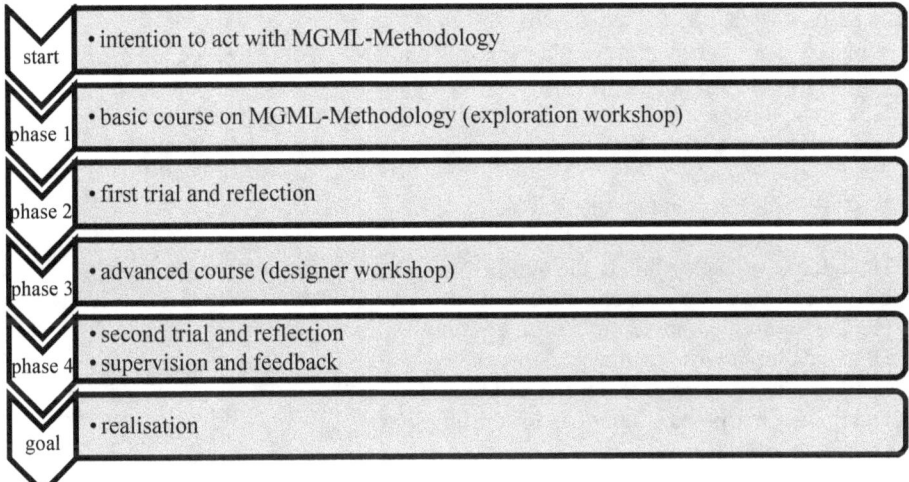

Fig. 25: Steps of the teacher training

2.4.1 Exploration Workshop

At first the interested teachers complete a five to nine days long introduction into working with Ladders of Learning, usually as a team of an entire school district or federal state. For that reason they come to Rishi Valley and participate in an Exploration Workshop. In classes at the local Satellite Schools RIVER consciously schedules this workshop at their own continuation school since the teachers can sit on. Experiencing this working with Ladders of Learning is crucial for the following training steps. The goal of sitting in classes is among other things to open up a change of perspectives within the teachers and at the same time making them realize that education is also possible in a different form. The visit at the Satellite School is backed by observational tasks in which RIVER directs the teachers' attention to specific subcomponents of the MGML-Methodology. Thus the work pad that is given to the teachers for the Exploration Workshop starts with almost 40 questions and tasks on sitting in on classes. The so called 'A Model School Observation Format' requests on top of comments on school or lecturing teacher also notes on:

1. In which way and where are the children sitting in the learning room?
2. How many working groups are there? How are they organized?
Name of a boy/girl in the first group:
Designation of the task card and activity
Name of a boy/girl in the second group:
Designation of the task card and activity
Name of a boy/girl in the third group:
Designation of the task card and activity
Name of a boy/girl in the fourth group:
Designation of the task card and activity
Name of a boy/girl in the sixth group:
Designation of the task card and activity
3. Which works of art with thematic emphasis on the subject Language are exhibited?
       1   2   3   4   5
4. How many boxes with material on the subject Language are there?
5. Are stories contributed by the parents visibly exhibited in the classroom?
       1   2   3   4   5
6. What does the environment look like?
7. What does the classroom look like?
8. How does the teacher talk to the pupils?
9. Do the children look neat and clean?
10. How many shelves are there in the classroom?
11. Do the children write on the black board?
12. What do the exercise books of the children look like?
13. Did the teacher prepare activities for the children?
14. Do the children wear crowns?
          Name: Learning card:
15. Are there any books of stories designed by the children?
16. Did the children perform any observable activities?
17. How do the children sing?
18. Which learning cards are available that considers regional material?
19. Is there a cane in the classroom?
20. Do the children move around the learning room during class?
21. How do the faster learners help the slower ones?
22. Total number of pupils: Boys: Girls:
23. Total number of pupils present: Boys: Girls:
24. Which activities do pre-school children perform?
25. Which materials were co-created by members of the village?
26. Did you observe the teachers' position during class? Does he stay at one spot, or is he moving around to help the children?
27. How many boxes with learning material are there?
28. At which point throughout the day is language being taught?
29. Which logos are used for language cards?
30. Why do pupils learn from text books?
31. Does mutually helping each other play an important role in the classroom?

Fig. 26: A model school observation format

By the use of these questions the teachers are enticed to contemplate their previous teaching experience. The questions turn the attention from the educational atmosphere and the work with the individual children to the overall design of the learning room as well as the design of the learning material again and again. The MGML-Methodology is employed in different school districts for different motivational reasons. However, the administration of schools and the teachers are connected by certain fundamental concerns, such as:

- creating access to education for everyone (Sarva Shiksha Abhiyan, Indian initiative for education for all)
- recognizing and using the skills and possibilities of the teachers at hand
- enable joyful learning for the children without the use of a cane
- including the village community in designing the school
- qualifying teachers to implement a highly complex system within a short amount of time

Already the Exploration Workshop is very practically orientated. The evaluation of sitting in on classes is immediately followed by the creation of an own milestone in small groups. It is through learning by doing that the teachers come across further questions concerning the implementation, which are consequently collectively answered in small theoretical building bricks as well as the showing of the educational film A Freedom to Learn. The encountered questions are furthermore adequately interpreted concerning the needs of the respective teacher teams and their milestones. The instructors of RIVER pay very close attention to teachers' getting to know and learning to implement the original and central components of the Ladders of Learning. Components of content are usually always the structure of the entire Ladder of Learning, the conception of a milestone, the description of the individual learning steps in form of a concrete example from the field of language, as well as criteria necessary for a successful component.

On top of that the teachers receive further information on the genesis and the current situation of RIVER as well as ongoing projects in small presentations. The workshop concludes with a presentation of and contemplation on the created milestones, which the teachers take home and forthwith implement at their own schools.

2.4.2 First Testing and Contemplation

Following the introduction into the MGML-Methodology with the creation of own milestones up to an entire year-long Ladder of Learning for one field, is the implementation of what has just been learned. The teachers incorporate their milestones in their work with the children and offer those to them. In order to do so not only the use of the materials but also the new interpretation of the learning room according to the system of group tables is necessary. This means that upon returning from Rishi Valley the teachers re-organize their classrooms, present the learning material on shelves and commence working with Ladders of Learning.

For the purpose of a process that is fruitful and preferably devoid of disturbances, establishing certain rules as well as exercising the new learning conduct is an important prerequisite. During the period of the testing phase, which demands a real changeover from the teacher as well as the pupils, the teachers are able to receive help and support from their colleagues or RIVER, ask pressing questions and mutually help each other. The testing phase is always linked to a contemplation which the teachers regularly undertake and document. Questions on which to reflect by RIVER guide this process. In a first step all aspects of the new work should be made visible for the teacher by means of a diary for scheduling and contemplation. The teachers should be put in a position to identify their own needs considering the scheduling and structuring of the learning environment. RIVER offers a personalized plan of actions for the vocationally-oriented further education. Planning steps and deliberations can be noted down, re-read, reflected on and further developed by the teachers in this tabular overview. Their documentations as well as experiences throughout the weeks of testing the Ladders of Learning serve as the basis for the Designer Workshop.

2.4.3 Designer Workshop

Designer Workshops are mostly organized and fashioned by the RIVER-Team and project groups that hail from other federal states in India. The teams might be from the educational field or from NGOs that run scholastic educational initiatives. Everybody has already qualified in a first step in the MGML-Methodology via the previously described five to nine days long Exploration Workshop.

The Designer Workshop is being offered with three central goals:

- An entire set of material for one grade should be created by this pilot group with help from the project team.
- A first team of teachers is to be qualified for the practical usage of the MGML-Methodology.
- At least three model schools in this federal state are named and established for the implementation of the MGML-Methodology.

These approaches by RIVER proved to be successful for reasons of sustainability. Tasks concerning the respective cultural characteristics of the federal state or district are incorporated in the fundamental aspects of the MGML-Methodology in the Designer Workshops. For that the respective valid state curriculum needs to be taken into account content-wise and activity-oriented.

RIVER shapes the respective project groups around a broadened circle of roughly 30 to 35 people with different profiles of skills in order to guarantee these intentions. Aside from experienced teachers and directors of schools also members of the supervision of schools, experts on curricula, members of teacher training facilities, artists and writers, domain experts, but also media designers participate in the workshops. Regional employees of UNICEF or UNESCO and financially supported NGOs who are active in the region are also invited. The project groups splits up into small teams that work on complete Ladders of Learning as well as creation and design of all materials for Mathematics, Language and Environmental Studies. Throughout the Designer Workshop the mixed project group is instructed and guided by the RIVER-Team. If these workshops do not take place in Rishi Valley but externally in a different federal state, the developed material are after the initial process of creation immediately put to the test during the ongoing workshop in the model schools. Experienced teachers cooperate with the first teacher pilots on the spot in order to directly include the practical expertise of the RIVER-Team. Necessary modifications of the material are thus immediately recognized in the process of creation and can be transformed into improved conceptions or other forms of design.

The RIVER-Team developed a special strategy of procedure for the process of the Designer Workshop. Following the Exploration Workshop the project group is asked to extensively collect material on the targeted field of learning. Meanwhile the project groups bring along all statements to the current valid curriculum and the already existing school books too. This forms a collection of incitements that can be methodically and didactically dissected. Deconstructing these materials into the smallest learning units constitutes the material base for process of constructing the Ladders of Learning. Congruent to the shown systematics of Ladders of Learning with its milestones as well as the various categories of learning activities, this pieces together the newly conceptualized learning material.

The teachers are trained for the refinement and profound contemplation on this new teaching culture by the RIVER-Team throughout the Designer Workshop. All theoretical elements continue to be reasoned out by practical questions. Besides, the basic structures of activities, milestones and Ladders of Learning, sub-topics and their implementation are clarified together again. These tasks include questions such as:

- time management at an MGML-Methodology school
- initial problems
- testing of pupils evaluation of pupils' progress
- year-long schedules for MGML-schools
- range of variation in the classroom
- inclusion of the village community
- games and joyful activities
- usage of local resources
- education of mothers via the children
- girls-boys issues
- puppet show
- production of simple musical instruments
- appealing exhibition of pupils' works

2.4.4 Second Testing through Supervision

The deepened knowledge and the newly acquired additional skills are immediately put to work with the children at school. A second testing follows. Since the Designer Workshop takes place on location at the school as mentioned above, this can be connected with the additional phase of testing and supervision. Instructors from RIVER sit in on classes and immediately give the teachers individual feedback concerning their work with MGML Ladders of Learning. Key topics are furthermore collected and discussed with all colleagues. Goal is the optimization of one's own work as well as the ability to give each other qualified feedback.

2.4.5 References

Copei, F. (1969). *Der fruchtbare Moment im Bildungsprozess* (9th ed.). Heidelberg: Quelle & Meyer.

Dühlmeier, B. (Ed.) (2008). *Mehr Außerschulische Lernorte in der Grundschule: Neun Beispiele für den fachübergreifenden Sachunterricht*. Baltmannsweiler: Schneider Verlag Hohengehren.

Fuhr, R., & Dauber, H. (Eds.) (2002). *Praxisentwicklung im Bildungsbereich - ein integraler Forschungsansatz*. Schriftenreihe zur humanistischen Pädagogik und Psychologie. Bad Heilbrunn: Klinkhardt.

Girg, R. (2007). *Die integrale Schule des Menschen: Praxis und Horizonte der Integralpädagogik*. Regensburg: Roderer.

Gottwald, P. (2012). *Integrales Bewusstsein: Wie es zur Sprache - und zur Welt – bringen?*. Frankfurt/Main: Peter Lang.

Jäger, R. S. (2007). *Beobachten, beurteilen und fördern! Lehrbuch für die Aus-, Fort- und Weiterbildung*. Erziehungswissenschaft 21. Landau: Verlag Empirische Pädagogik.

Kaltwasser, V. (2010). *Persönlichkeit und Präsenz: Achtsamkeit im Lehrerberuf*. Weinheim: Beltz.

Krishnamurti, J. (1953/1981). *Education and the significance of life*. San Francisco: Harper & Row.

---. (1991). *The second Krishnamurti Reader*. London: Penguin Books.

---. (2004). *Krishnamurti's notebook*. Ojai: Krishnamurti Publications of America.

---. (2005). *This light in oneself: True meditation*. Boston: Shambhala.

---. (1974/2006a). *On Education*. Chennai: Krishnamurti Foundation India.

---. (1981/2006b). *Letters to the Schools, Vol. 1*. Chennai: Krishnamurti Foundation India.

---. (n.d.). The Intent of the Krishnamurti Schools. https://www.brockwood.org.uk/intentions.html. Accessed 9 December 2014.

Krishnamurti, J., & McCoy, R. (2006). *The whole movement of life is learning: J. Krishnamurti's letters to his schools*. Bramdean: Krishnamurti Foundation India.

Krishnamurti Foundation India. (2011). Rishi Valley School: 80 years. Chennai: Krishnamurti Foundation India.

Müller, T., & Girg, R. (Eds.) (2007). *Integralpädagogik: Wahrnehmungen im lernenden Leben*. Regensburg: Roderer.

Rilke, R. M. (1988). Samskola– Wie Schule sein könnte. In D. Lenzen, & R. Winkel, *Pädagogische Epochen: Von der Antike bis zur Gegenwart*. Düsseldorf: Schwann.

Rishi Valley Institute for Educational Resources (RIVER). (2003). *A multigrade trainers's resource pack: Background document-I.* Chennai: Krishnamurti Foundation India.

Rodrigues, H., & Krishnamurti, J. (2001). Krishnamurti's insight: An examination of his teachings on the nature of mind and religion. Varanasi, India: Pilgrims Publishing.

Roth, H. (1976). Die „originale Begegnung" als methodisches Prinzip. In H. Roth, *Pädagogische Psychologie des Lehrens und Lernens.* Hannover: Schroedel.

Thapan, M. (2001). J. Krishnamurti: (1895-1986). *Prospects: the quarterly review of comparative education,* 31(2), 273-86.

---. (2006). *Life at school: An ethnographic study* (2nd ed.). New Delhi: Oxford University Press.

Thich, N. H. (2004). *Das Herz von Buddhas Lehre: Leiden verwandeln - die Praxis des glücklichen Lebens.* Freiburg: Herder.

3 Cultures of Learning in the 21st Century

Chapter 3 shows scientific traits. It offers the reader a fine grasp of how MGML is embedded in the 21st century's cultures of learning. Only through these aspects it can be made clear why the MGML-Methodology experiences such a strong demand and emanation worldwide. Without a doubt Ladders of Learning are an essential part of this methodology, but they are neither conceivable nor effective without an intensive examination with the underlying questions concerning the topic of learning in the beginning 21st century. The methodology is embedded in a holistic perception and understanding of an integral world. We are all one living community in one world which also has effects on our implicit and explicit learnings. Consequently, learning in school has to be thought globally - interconnected with the developments in the societies. Trends of exclusion, loss of identity, global issues of education have to be considered. This global and even cosmic understanding of life and world leads to what we call integral pedagogy. It is introduced in its foundations leading to the cultures of acting and learning that are essential for using the MultiGradeMultiLevel-Methodology.

Chapter 2 served as an introduction to understand RIVER's motivation for inventing the MultiGradeMultiLevel-Methodology. Their mission of bringing the best school to the poorest children drove them to elaborate a complex methodology that allows children to individually learn and develop. At the same time it guarantees the teachers a manageability of the educational processes. Diverse elements of designing learning materials and structuring educational processes have been combined to the MultiGradeMultiLevel-Methodology in a highly sophisticated way.

However, it has to be taken into account that the MultiGradeMultiLevel-Methodology is more than material, more than structures, more than a simple method. The methodology is embedded in a holistic perception and understanding of an integral world. We are all one living community in one world which also has effects on our implicit and explicit learnings. Consequently, we have to think about school globally - rebound to the developments in the societies. Trends of exclusion, loss of identity, global issues of education have to be considered. This global and even cosmic understanding of life and world leads to what we call integral pedagogy. It is introduced here in its foundations leading to the cultures of acting and learning that are essential for using the MultiGradeMultiLevel-Methodology.

3.1 Schooling in the Context of Global Developments

Advancing globalization and its corresponding processes, developments and changes heavily influence the forms of societal structures in many parts of the world. Rapid transformations create new tasks and immense challenges in all fields of societal coexistence. Furthermore, these transformations lead to new problems concerning education and learning in the 21st century.

Cultural spaces and their adjacent forms of living clash melt and expand under the pressure and speed of global changes. The issues of lifestyle, exclusion and inclusion, as well as global and cultural identity become the attention´s center of a necessary discussion within these processes, while continuously fading into an uncertain complexity.

The MultiGradeMultiLevel-Methodology and its Ladders of Learning offer pupils and teachers a stable framework that enables them to incorporate and culturally as well as regionally elaborate on these changes. The pressing issue of cultural, social and personal identity as a hallmark of belonging within these global processes can sufficiently be answered by this methodology. The MultiGradeMultiLevel-Methodology is therefore to be seen as way more than a shrewdly assembled teaching tool. Education science (pedagogy) can considerably be conductive to gain a diversified point of view on the developing and altering lifestyles and globalization itself: in this age of globalization many families all over the world – in the metropolises of the western world as well as in the rural communities of emerging markets and third world countries – place their hopes for a brighter future on their children's education. Ideally, their well-equipped children should flexibly and successfully roam this globalized world. The hopes and fears and expectations of parents in the beginning 21st century seem understandable, nevertheless, it is worth reflecting on the task for pedagogy, education and school to successfully communicate that globalization is not merely the realization of these desires and demands, but also brings along the challenge to stay in touch with oneself, surrounding persons and one´s own culture and to develop lastingly sensible tasks for the individual as well as the community.

Additionally, one wonders how to convey the pressure created by these apparently individualizing ways of living to children and adolescents, especially since economic interests capitalize on these lifestyles and not the people. This increasing individualization would mean the loss of a cultural 'We' and the ensuing decline of cultural and therefore also personal identity:

> "When everybody wants to be different from everybody else, the 'We' disappear. 'We' – that is always the others. Market economy and branding do not generate a common identity but moral temporary employment without any attachment to a milieu. Being able to choose an identity also means to no longer have one and to not gain one. [...] The label of our time is the negative identity, the staged non-membership as an evidence of individuality. We are not citizens anymore but investment bankers of ourselves. Once things go wrong, the investment banker withdraws his capital of attention, work force and trust. The paradoxical equation of our radicalized individuality means to stay true to oneself. Hence, the equation is: the more individuality the less identity" (Precht 38/2009, 47).

Before explicating the MultiGradeMultiLevel-Methodology and its Ladders of Learning as an exemplary sustainable and at the same time meaningful framework considering these contexts at length in the following chapters, we will have a close look at the ongoing changes and their adherent challenges education and learning are facing in the recently begun 21st century.

Defining globalization is not a simple task. Depending on the context and point of view globalization can signify and be associated in highly differing ways. However, seven fundamental characteristics can be outlined as such:

1. Globalization takes place on a communicative level: human-beings interact and learn about each other faster and more frequently via communications media. Subsequently, changes in pace of communication and reaction affect experience and action.
2. Globalization takes place on a transitive level: more and more people are able to change locations fast and easily. Commodities can more and more rapidly be shipped and transported. Simultaneously, more people are forced to commute between different locations or leave their home entirely and follow the flows of goods and economy and hence the possibility of employment.
3. Globalization takes place on a fiscal level: the first two characteristics progressively bring about a transgressive exchange of commodities and especially money.
4. Globalization takes place on a regional level: faster communication and transport results in the use of specific regions according to their specific potentials. On the one hand this offers chances of development for many regions on the other hand it also carries along the danger of failure and collapse, in case the specific potentials of one region are being replaced by those of another.
5. Globalization takes place on a dynamic level: the dynamics portrayed in (1) and (4) demand a higher level of flexibility and adaptability from the people. This necessity offers the possibility to develop individual potentials for many. Where this degree of flexibility cannot be achieved due to individual, social or cultural circumstances globalization brings about the exclusion of human-beings.
6. Globalization takes place on a complex level: the dynamics of globalization inevitably give rise to more diverse and more complex systems and networks. An almost inscrutable specialization as well as dependencies and displeasure are the results.
7. Globalization takes place on a self-sufficient level: global developments often 'obey' own laws and can hardly be controlled. These global dynamics partially or fully elude national and political regulation and surveillance. This holds chances for development as well as dangers of losing control and falling into chaos: "No political entity considers itself responsible for assuring the sufficient reproduction of collective goods like the protection of water, air and biodiversity, peace, fairness and social balance. [...] National politics has become too big for life's small problems and way too small for the big problems of the world" (Seitz 2002, n.p.).

Most aspects listed above are initiated, regulated and more or less accounted for by certain groups of adults living in the so called 'First World' or emerging markets. Nevertheless, the repercussions of these dynamics affect people and especially children and adolescents who do not live in these emerging economies and the First World. The saying of the 'Global Village' is subsequently wrong since it - "this densification of the social, economic and cultural networks primarily focuses on the globalized middle class in the North and South, East and West, while two thirds of the human beings, those that neither have a bank account nor a telephone connection, nor a postal address, remain excluded. However, this does obviously not mean that they are exempt of the stresses and strains of globalization. One just has to think of the effects of the turmoil at the financial markets and the debt crisis for the poor, or the ramifications of climate change that effect those in Bangladesh or on small insular states the most who fewest of all are responsible for its emergence" (Seitz 2002, n.p.).

This shows that particularly those people who did not or only marginally cause the negative effects of a globalizing world are the ones mostly suffering from the repercussions. This results in more and more forms of social exclusion that to an exceedingly high degree affects children and adolescents worldwide.

3.1.1 Exclusion – a globally multifaceted process

More and more people leading their lives in socially pressurized or exclusionary ways constitute a manifest moment of global change. This is among other things attributed to the developments called the "challenge to the clarity of the world" (Bauman 2006, 77): over the course of several years many societies have emerged to portray no clarity concerning ways and conditions of living, collectively binding values and landmarks as well as social order and biographies. In contrast to that some societies still adhere rigidly to said clarity thereby constraining developments and making it impossible to catch up with global transformations.

It appears to be blatantly obvious that people ceased to continuously move forward in hermetic ways. In the process of life movements man needs to become aware of his social contexts' self-realization. "There is no positioning of humans anymore, humans have to position themselves" (Meyers-Wolters, 19). This positioning makes it hard to limit or even taboo the individualization of lifestyles and the formation and configuration of habitat. Meanwhile more and more people are denied access to these individual liberties. Anything goes, yet often little is possible.

The absence of clarity and dissolving of individual and social points of reference result in a lack of firm, solid and binding landmarks for the people to adhere to. Thus Bauman refers to this time children and youth growing up nowadays as "the brave new liquid modern world" (2005, 9): life in consumer societies where human relations are mostly determined by indulgence and the pleasure principle (Freudian term), respectively; a civilization of excess and superfluousness, of waste and its disposal. Superfluous are the ones that do not have access to the consumption and possibilities of pluralized lifestyles. This exclusion has a particularly harsh effect on children and adolescents growing up in these environments.

"Our planet is full." (Bauman 2005, 4) Bauman coined this simple but essential statement to characterize the global and societal status quo. He goes on: "Each order casts some parts of the extant population as 'out of place', 'unfit' or 'undesirable'" (5). Bauman even goes a step further by referring to those excluded from the machinery of globalization as "human waste" (5), as people that become useless for society. By any means, he is not using this harsh terminology to discriminate certain people but to reveal how societies treat groups of their members.

Additionally, these lifestyles that globalization creates root human-beings up worldwide. Globalization deprives these people „of their heretofore adequate ways and means of survival in both the biological and social/cultural sense of that notion (Bauman 2005, 7). From a market economy perspective they are worthless. They cannot and must not take responsibility for themselves or the society they live in - they are aimlessly drifting in fluid modernity. Even worse, according to Bauman they become 'super-fluous': "To be ‚redundant' means to be supernumerary, unneeded, of no use" (Bauman 2005, 12). Considering this, people, who become superfluous for a society pose, are a financial problem since they need to be taken care of. "People declared 'redundant' (…) need to be 'provided for' – that is fed, shod and sheltered. They would not survive on their own" (Bauman 2005, 14).

At the same time Bauman points out that merely surviving does not qualify anyone to be 're-authorized' into society and its ways of life and therefore not be seen as superfluous anymore:

> "These men and women lose not only their jobs, their projects, their orientation points, the confidence of being in control of their lives; they also find themselves stripped of their dignity as workers, of self-esteem, of the feeling of being useful and having a social place of their own" (Bauman 2005, 13).

This illustrates the almost impossible task for children and adolescents, who are at the mercy of global developments way more than adults, to not lose sight of the possibilities of physical survival, maybe having to fight for it day in day out, while at the same time being stripped of "the self-confidence and self-esteem needed to sustain their social surviving" (Bauman 2005, 40).

> "In an average modern society, vulnerability and insecurity of existence and the necessity of pursuing life purposes under conditions of acute an unredeemable uncertainty are assured by the exposure of life pursuits to market forces" (Bauman 2005, 50).

The market is spoiled by success and hardly knows societal or even moral laws. Hence, children, youth and their families who exist on the very edges of market developments fall out of the market, first via school later on in the world of employment; or they never even get any access to them events in the first place. Instead, the material desires of marginalized people are being abused by the market's strategies of seduction. What little these people have is being used to feed the glutton that is consumerism. This behavior inevitably leads to new (pseudo-)needs that ultimately culminate in bigger encumbrance. Simultaneously these children and adolescents are often growing up in families that are not able to assure their livelihood anymore, because their traditional way of making ends meet has been taken away. They "have [...] been earmarked for destruction, [...] assigned to disposable waste (and) cannot be choosers (Bauman 2005, 59). Thus they can barely fulfill material needs in an environment that does not offer manifold ways to structure daily life and where one especially cannot be picky. This can happen to the children of an American or German skilled labor the same way as it could to those of a Chinese migrant worker or an Indian peon. "Bereaved of trust, saturated with suspicion, life is shot through with antinomies and ambiguities it cannot resolve" (Bauman 2005, 93).

The increasing speed of transformation, alongside with the growing possibilities and requirements of global processes and situations, brings about that everything which just now seemed desirable and necessary becomes worthless and "marking it from the start as the waste of tomorrow, whereas the fear of one's own wastage that oozes from the life experience of the dizzying pace of change prompts desires to be more avid and change to be more quickly desired" (Bauman 2005, 109).

The so called superfluous drop out of social systems, do not find a way back in or grow up outside of these systems and their ways of communication in the first place. Witnessing these processes, realizing that the amount of people that are considered superfluous, that are not needed, steadily increases, and nourishes the fear of being excluded oneself.

"What we all seem to fear, whether suffering from 'dependent depression' or not, whether in the full light of the day or harassed by nocturnal hallucinations, is abandonment, exclusion, being rejected, blackballed, disowned, dropped, stripped of what we are, being refused what we wish to be. We fear being left alone, helpless and hapless. Barred company, loving hearts and helping hands! We fear to be dumped – our turn for the scrapyard. What we miss most badly is the certainty that all that won't happen – not to us. We miss exemption – from the universal and ubiquitous threat of exemption" (Bauman 2005, 128).

How do society and the government treat those whom they declared as waste, as superfluous? Bauman supposes that the task of providing for members of society, that are not capable of providing for them, will be executed less and less in the future. Instead, the tasks will redeploy:

"Having rescued or severely curtailed its past programmatic interference with market-produced insecurity, having proclaimed the perpetuation and intensification of that insecurity to be, on the contrary, the prime purpose and a duty of all political power dedicated to the well-being of its subjects, the contemporary state must seek other, non-economic varieties of vulnerability and uncertainty on which to rest its legitimacy. That alternative seems to have been recently located [...] in the issue of personal safety: threats and fears to human bodies, possessions and habitats arising from criminal activities, the anti-social conduct of the 'underclass' and, most recently, global terrorism" (Bauman 2005, 52).

The term 'social exclusion' is not only acknowledged sociologically but also becomes more relevant politically. This development is emphasized by the European Commission's definition of social exclusion as a process "by which certain people are pushed to the fringes of society and hindered from fully participating due to poverty, insufficient basic skills, missing offerings for lifelong learning or discrimination" (European Commission 2004, 12).

It is not easy to answer the question how the processes of 'social exclusion' come about and how to explain them as phenomena of modern forms of society. Without wanting to go further into the current controversial debate between theorists of globalization and theorists of exclusion, two essential aspects can be delineated:

1. For instance, processes of globalization and their effects on unemployment rates, organization of social services and social well-being cannot simply be used as an explanatory scheme. John Goldthorpe emphasized this in his empiric study on "Globalization and social classes" in 2003. Additionally, "all social structures show a high macro stability of conditions that is not only to be conciliated with people's perception which again is determined by the experience of escalating micro turbulences" (Bude / Willisch 2006, 11). This should not abstract away from the possibility that a micro turbulence, as declared as such by an analysis of the social structure, can in the case of the individual child or youth indeed constitute and individual as well as social macrocosm and is also experienced in its full force.

2. On the other hand processes of globalization involve the risks of impoverishment, exclusion and discrimination. These are "contrary to the assumptions of boundaries dissolution by theorists globalization still conventionally, unevenly distributed. Unemployed, migrants, single-parents and families with many children are especially affected. It is not a big surprise that low credentials, which in any case increases the threat of impoverishment, join in. Furthermore, poverty despite having a job is underestimated" (Bude / Willisch 2006, 10).

Two phenomena that are deeply intertwined with the superfluousness as well as the processes of exclusion are the "social vulnerability" (Castel 2000b, n.p.) and the "precarious wealth" (Hübinger 1999). Both phenomena are concerned with societal groups that did not yet end up on society's 'garbage dump', but nevertheless have something to lose and are therefore very much endangered. Modernity's absence of clarity and tenseness, everything that Robert Castel summarizes under the term "negative individualism", brings about family, social and professional constellations that are extremely fragile.

> "The category of social vulnerability can consequently be defined as a social relationship situated between two poles: between the probability of being confronted with certain economic, social or symbolic risks and the ability to avoid these risks or to mobilize resources against them" (Vogel 2006, 344).

Whereas the phenomenon of the 'precarious wealth' points however to social positions in which people find themselves in a financial, social and emotional balancing act between poverty and a safe and sound existence. Families living in so called emergent countries are especially concerned.

> "Those who live in this zone of society must avoid any drawbacks in their social and professional everyday life – such as losing their job, chronic illnesses, divorces or other family problems, or unexpected financial demands and burdens (Vogel 2006, 346).

Both phenomena and their corresponding societal groups have in common that they are just not yet excluded. However, they are well aware of the threat and the conditions of a possible exclusion. They are subjected to heightened inner, emotional pressure since they find themselves living in a kind of double ambiguity: on the one hand the ambiguity that comes along with modern developments of society and on the other hand the ambiguity inherent to each specific, individual as well as social, emotional and professional situation caught between security and instability. Treading a new path in life runs the great risk of becoming an outcast as well as spinning out of personal stability into emotional distress (Müller 2008, n.p.).

This statement can even be expanded from a pedagogical point of view. Society does not merely discard children and adolescents and their families by deeming them superfluous, it even contributes to the constitution of fragile and broken identities that oscillate between consumerism and waste, between conditions of life and desires and between integration and deprivation.

The 'liquid modernity' features two fundamentally contrary needs of mankind: for one thing the desire of having a 'safe haven' that prevents one from drifting into a social 'no-mans-land'. For another thing human-beings want to be as independent and free as possible, possess enough scope and thus live preferably self-determined lives. However, this also implies to be the 'captain' and hence take responsibility for the chosen 'course'.

> "The fundamental thought of modernity is the idea of constructability of both lifestyle and identity as individual accomplishment. Only the conditions of modernity enable, or expect, almost all members of society to take over control of their own lives. Modernity does not only mean more openness for conditions of acting and the orientation towards a biographical principle. It simultaneously stands for the necessity to individually carry out certain goods and services that formerly were predetermined by traditions and binding rules of conduct. These could be and had to be adapted without question" (Behringer 1998, 22).

Most notably children and adolescents, hailing from families struck by poverty and social discrimination as a result of global yet specific processes of exclusion do hardly get the opportunity to take responsibility in manifold ways and to experience them as efficient for and in society.

> In addition to the poor countries, a new poverty arises in the rich countries hearts. [...] The difference is not the financial situation but the access to knowledge and education. Already now these factors decide over the access to a dignified life" (Böhmer 2006, 103-104).

In order to comprehend these developments and transformations it seems reasonable to take a look at the past as well as to consider social developments while at the same time paying attention to the transformation of childhood.

3.1.2 Historical Transformations and their Impact on Today's Children and Youth

Traditional societies are structurally characterized by offering orientation, security and stability which are nurtured by factors such as religion, tradition and clear-cut family structures. At the same time traditional societies were running the risk of imposing heteronomy, constraints and limitations on individual as well as communal developments. As many forms of society developed, the structures and forms of organization towards modern forms of society. The possibilities changed contingent to the Enlightenment, sparked off by the belief in progress during the industrialization, but also as a result of rising democratizing and globalizing developments: individualization, change in values and pluralism became the 'new' trademarks. Space and time, but especially place and situation usually coincide in pre-modern societies. Sociologically this is characteristically termed as presences. Modernity's advent marked the turning point for this. Space is more and more distinguished from place. Places can politically, economically and socially be influenced even across great distances. Presences cease to be a necessary element of formation for places. According to Giddens the dynamics of modernity and in consequence the separation of space and time is characterized on the one hand by a disembedding of the social systems and on the other hand by a reflexive regulation and realignment of social relationships. These form in consequence to newly discovered understandings and their effects on culture in relation to action of individuals and groups (see Giddens 1995). It needs to be stated that this is a doubled dynamic at the least: firstly, the separation of space and time leads to increased mechanisms of disembedding. Secondly, this very separation and its inherent disentanglement from localized and situational constraints mark a prerequisite of multifaceted transformation in the first place. Modern enterprises constitute valuable examples in ways that were impossible traditional societies by connecting the local with the global combine forms of processes, production and trade. Admittedly, trade and commercial routes all over the globe, like the Silk Road or crossing the Alps, had been used for centuries. These trade routes, however, were linear connections based on exchange, not on networked production processes with effects on a social, local and global stage.

"Once mankind realized that it was able to change and mold the world according to their ideas it was only a matter of time until the old image of world order created and carried a creator spirit would be replaced by a new one – one that saw them themselves as discoverer and designer of the world. This transformation in perception took place unbelievably fast in the Western world. It only took a few generations since the Enlightenment and the advent of industrialization. By now, only remains of the old, stabilizing matrix are still there. Its former assurance-lending, orientation-offering, organizing and structuring function has all but vanished for the most part of the population in the high-technology industrialized countries. However, the new image of the human-being as the creator and order assurer could not achieve what the old image still was able to do. The new image might have certainly offered many people a certain support, but essentially only as long as they were successful, and thus were able to confirm and fortify this self-image. In order to not lose their support, these people have to be successful" (Hüther 2006, 38).

Uprooting, instability and disorientation can emerge as repercussions of transforming systems and lifestyles. Those who find themselves on the 'waste dumps' of society are the ones that are secluded from the pool of individualization in terms of a high degree of freedom of choice that is concerned with the ability to construct and plan one's own life. Those people fail to keep up the pace of progress (any longer) or over the course of these processes are simply left behind. According to Bauman their life is one that is "wasted" (2005) and without boundaries. Furthermore, the belief in progress gets rocked heavily over and over again: by climate issues, natural disasters, economic changes, familial and personal failure and last but not least due to the multiple financial crises. Those who are neither needed nor personally wanted are the victims.

The step towards a modern society by means of dissolution of heavily patriarchal regulations was significant for the development of family structures and the pluralization of lifestyles. On the one hand this led to liberalization, opportunities of self-fulfillment and the chance to part ways with relations that were not sustainable anymore. On the other hand these emerging forms of living lack certain capabilities, especially in socially pressed circumstances and the lower social strata, when it comes to cultural as well as emotional competencies that are required in order to maintain and sustain this 'new life'.

Childhood itself and how we look at this phase of human life has not remained unaffected from these developments and changes either. This has long been proven by respective studies (Fölling-Albers, 2001). The organization of everyday life and lifestyles has changed just like growing up as a child and its experience has done as well. The so called discovery of childhood as well as the progressive teaching movement at the beginning of the 20th century played vital parts in that. However, the big differences in the experience of childhood according to the varying living situations must not be forgotten – and now. Kränzl-Nagel and Mierendorff for example address this in the context of the

Western world, considering the dynamics of growing up in different social classes:

> "Therefore, childhood could turn out very differently for children that lived during the same epoch. Hence, the trend towards pedagogization and towards viewing children as beings that can be molded by education, had different effects on children from varying social backgrounds: while children from the upper classes of society had access to education, but they were forced down by a repressive pedagogy that is referred to as 'black pedagogy' in hindsight. Economic changes in the 17th and 18th century lead to new forms of childhood for children from the lower classes" (2007, 10-11).

In the end new dependencies and power relations developed between children and adults and have continued to do so. Even though many things changed in these developments in the 20th century, such as a different perspective on children, compulsory schooling and the privatization of childhood, similar differences and tensions (conflicting priorities) still prevail worldwide: children do not go to school at all because they cannot or are not allowed to. Or else, they attend expensive private schools and the best educational establishments available. Children do not have to work at all, are heavy consumers and form a market-based quota itself or they labor in stone pits, factories or waste dumps without any rights whatsoever. Youngsters either would like to go to school, are curious, motivated and passionate, or they lost any interest in learning, deny attending classes, or even suffer from the pressure executed by the educational system.

Giddens chooses the picture of the Dschagganath-Wagon as an emblem for modernity. The Dschagganath-Wagon is an old hinduistic wagon of monstrous size that is used in processions: the vehicle is maneuverable up until a certain degree. When this degree is exceeded the wagon takes on a life of its own and crushes everything in its path. On the one hand the vehicle is an absolute object of worship; on the other hand it constitutes a potential machinery of destruction. This demands a permanent border management that is bound to various conditions. Depending on individual and social skills, powers and societal potential and possibilities this border management might be successful. The results may vary, though, ensuing in both strengthening and convincing self-efficacy or in collapse, depression and failure.

In this context Dahrendorf provides a concept by adding ligatures, social affiliations and bonds, as a necessary prerequisite to one dimension of the options, namely the social as well as individual opportunities and liberties. This should broaden the opportunities in life (Dahrendorf 1979) for everyone. Dahrendorf sees options as the given level of choices in a social structure that are significant for acting and enabling as well as heightening chances of autonomy. He describes ligatures as meaningful affiliations that form the foundation of any acting. Opportunities in life are hence to be understood as some kind of 'correlation' between both options and ligatures.

Dahrendorf assumes that ligatures need to be solved enabling people to seize the opportunities of modern society (58). Reduction and finally destruction of relations multiplies the options but only to a certain degree (58). Whenever a postmodern society and its lifestyles and prerequisites for life throw options and ligatures off balance, the opportunities in life reduce. Dahrendorf elaborates on this in three moments:

1. If individuals are cut off from society's options then this is due to deep cultural attachments, namely the ligatures, which enable the people to find their ways in a world of operations (58). They either lost or were deprived of the orientation designated to help them with their decisions on why it would make sense to pick this over that option (58).
2. The progressively accelerating decrease and "destruction of relations in important parts of some societies" (58) within modernity in a process of assimilation ultimately has the effect to "reduce complexity, which again results in a reduction of opportunities in life: the options themselves that the postmodern society should offer vanish" (58-59). Simultaneously the complexity in some parts of society proliferates while individual choices decrease. This results in an inner and outer 'paralyzation' that reduces options as ligatures and therefore also opportunities in life.
3. A societal or globally enforced discontinuation of ligatures might "ultimately endanger the social contract itself and announce the return of a dog-eat-dog war [...] The destruction of ligatures reduced human opportunities of life up to a point that again threatens the chances of survival" (59-60).

Further evidence that the balance between options and ligatures has long been upset is provided by Schulze's studies (1992). While describing the de-standardization of lifestyles on the one hand, he is able to locate a communal characteristic in members of such societies: "it is the design idea of a beautiful, interesting life that is subjectively perceived as valuable" (Schulze 1992, 36). Yet the freedom of choice in respect to these lifestyle-related decisions is fictional – a permanent mirage at the horizon. Whoever lacks the inner strength or concrete opportunities to identify these mirror images as deceptions over and over again will inevitably be victimized and find him- or herself as the "waste of globalization" (Bauman 2005, 63).

A somewhat different approach, however not too far away from Dahrendorf's thinking, is provided by the Indian Nobel Prize winner for economy Amartya Sen: the 'Capability-Approach', an approach concerned with the opportunities for self-realization. He takes the position that capabilities constitute the freedom of an individual to realize very specific life plans.

> "To these belong, for example, the possibility to be exempt of avoidable illnesses, to be equipped with sufficient skills for all essential areas of life, to pursue individual goals in the working life, to participate in the social life, to practice a religion, or to openly show oneself without shame" (Arndt / Volkert 2006, 9).

According to Sen the amount of capabilities comprises a hub of possibilities of actually feasible life plans. For example, one (usually) can choose to practice a certain religion or choose not to, while the chances to participate in societal life are not automatically a question of one's own decision. In his explanations Sen criticizes equation of income and well-being often seen in debates on social justice that are lead in a utilitarian way. According to his critics low income would also entail a lower level of well-being. This can easily be confuted: "Single parents are satisfied once their children are developing nicely, even if they did only achieve this through enormous personal sacrifices" (Arndt / Volkert 2006, 10). What is really important is to which extent an individual has the possibility to convert income into well-being. These so called 'societal conversion factors' have been especially considered by John Rawls in his outline of a theory of justice (1988). Going by Sen this possibility of conversion does not really suffice to truly be able to estimate how a 'self' manages his or her own situation or moves and acts within it. For Sen, in addition to the societal conversion factors the personal conversion factors are decisive (2002, 109). The possibility for the self – to either end up on the societal 'waste dump' or not – diverges according to age, sex, education, impairment and health even though the social opportunities seem equal.

3.1.3 Identity within the Term of Global Change

Pedagogy plays an important part: depending on how successfully children and adolescents are supported in order to understand themselves and their environment will they be able to gain strength and orientation from this understanding. Depending on how pedagogy succeeds in providing opportunities for children and youth to constructively cope with themselves and their environment will they be able to 'control' and navigate their lives in the best way possible. Last but not least, depending on how pedagogy manages to develop a multifaceted perceptive of understanding themselves and the 'world' will make their lives a meaningful and purposeful one.

The transforming lifestyles all over the globe derive from the subjective as well as collective challenges and constraints of human experience. In the process the loss of cultural and regional traditions alongside their (re-)cultivation plays a significant role. The modern individual runs the risk of becoming a plant that cut off its own roots and is now forced to position itself in a fragile and fluid network. Rootlessness is perhaps one of the characteristic notions for mankind's existential situation.

> "Identity formation is exacerbated because the identity-securing environments and milieus lose their reliability. They are replaced by a complex, ongoing process of self-controlling and self-ensurance concerning biographically relevant proceedings" (Behringer 1998, 23).

Which social requirements are therefore necessary in order for children and adolescents to acquire a stable identity in the 21th century? A sustainable identity needs a cultural horizon or at least a structure of social conditions that provides people with a context and orientation for their self-conception and interpretation. Such horizons include normative and ethical orientation as well as the possibility of an autonomous human existence. A social as well as individual identity can therefore evolve from the interplay of this relation. The issue of identity formation and stabilization is essentially a pedagogical one. However, considering the challenges and effects of globalization on the dealings with education on a worldwide scale, this issue cannot be answered simplistically.

3.1.4 Education as a Global Issue

Education has increasingly become a global issue over the last decade. This development can clearly be demonstrated by looking at several aspects. The international comparative education performance studies make this especially evident, alongside the biennial published UNESCO World Education Report. A further aspect is the propelled progress and expansion of schools in its worldwide institutions. While national and regional differences exist, it is notable that the phase of elementary school years is similarly structured and construed worldwide. Secondary schools distinguish themselves by their increasing complexity and specialization of teaching and learning content. Additionally, various media platforms broaden the access to knowledge and enrich the collective library. Lenhart points at global semantics of education:

> "Not only do we get a hold of it in our globally cited 'Four Pillars of Education' which the Delors Commission declared in their report 'Learning – the Treasure within' (1996) on behalf of the UNESCO (…) But it also surfaces in the empathic emphasis on the human right to education as stated in the World Education Conference Dakar 200 report 'Education for all 2000 Assessment'" (Lenhart 2007, 811).

Due to these and other global developments the pedagogic challenges are very manifold. Changing social parameters and lifestyles and the ascent of education towards a global value affect situations of education worldwide. This does not only apply to the importance ascribed to education and apprenticeship, but also to the fact that regional situations of education are affected by global influences.

> "Nowadays every educational measure has to stay abreast of the fact that – apart from family, peer group and schools – further entities of socialization emerge; they virtually act from afar. Among these entities are mass media, a global youth culture, but also the fears and worries of children concerning global crises, environmental disasters and wars" (Seitz 2002, n.p.).

Whenever something global affects something regional it becomes more than ever necessary to deal with difference and the diversity both resulting from them. From a pedagogical point of view this simultaneously poses the task to know and understand the own persona and their circumstances.

Pedagogy is not only faced with problems immediately concerned with children and adolescents. Education as commodity and subsequently as servicing business becomes increasingly more interesting. This becomes apparent while looking at the rising numbers of newly established elite and private schools. The challenge mostly entails preventing the formation of two-class society and providing the highest quality of schooling, education and training places in New York, Berlin and Shanghai as well as in the plateaus of South America, in rural India or the deserts of Africa. All this needs to happen based on pedagogical concerns and beliefs and not on sniffing a chance of a promising business in an area that is not yet conquered.

In the context of globalization and education so called key competencies are mentioned all over the world. These should help gaining access to a global world and secured lifestyle. Here again pedagogy is faced with the challenge of not letting itself get instrumentalized by apparent contents and economic interests. Dealing with new media and modern communications is not as important for a proper, lasting handling of life's duties in the 21st century as are questions of social learning, responsibility for one´s own life movements and learning processes as well as ecological awareness and peace education. However, all these aspects are rarely addressed on a global scale when talking about key competencies.

Education worldwide is faced with enormous challenges and enormously contradicts itself.

> "More than 110 million children between the age of 6 to 11 are excluded from attending school. This is one fifth of this age bracket. Pedagogy inevitably has to deal with the social gap that globalization, which also includes a pedagogical globalization, obviously accelerates. [...] The more the level of education becomes decisive for social and individual possibilities of development, the more the risk grows that insufficient educational possibilities lead to biographical failure and societal exclusion" (Seitz 2002, n.p.).

Children and adolescents get in contact with the repercussions of all these changes and movements, transformations and developments within their families and their daily lives. Schooling hereby takes a central position. Every part and aspect of a classroom, not only the education programs, contains moments that are culturally meaningful and pertinent to identity. The education of children and therefore also their self-conception and self-efficacy are shaped by all these aspects: how and by whom classes are organized, which materials and means are used, where it takes place and where it leads to. If schools are seen and designed as an identity-establishing passage in life, they can help children and youth to manage and mold their own and collective processes of cultural and global orientation. For this to happen, pupils need to become aware that within their individual movements of learning and life they are part of a collective cultural identity at the same time. Furthermore, they need to become aware that their communities likewise have a part in their respective identity formation.

Considering the contexts above and in order to bring the MGML Methodology and these nexuses together, it seems important to put some essential questions first:

1. Are we aware that the ongoing global and societal developments are the result of our individually as well as collectively occurring decisions and actions?
2. Are we capable of becoming aware that pedagogy has to and can strike new paths if it does not want to simply mirror global processes, but instead sustainably offer individually as well as collectively meaningful developments for and with children and adolescents?

Based on these superordinate questions and considering having children and adolescents in view the following questions arise:

1. How is it possible for us to begin acknowledging and (educationally) appreciating the singularity of every child's or adolescent's life and learning movements?
2. How can we achieve meaningfully to be 'awake and alert' understanding that it is always us who are at all times actively involved and effective in regional as well as in global contexts?
3. Are we are aware that we do not live in a changing world, but that we are this changing world?

3.2 Life in the Horizon of an Integral Educational Practice

From a sociological point of view the above firstly points to the vehement contexts of the global development, in which the individual, the communities, societal manifestations and cultural transformations move in changes. They constitute a scenario, an unseparated, in which every human being is differently and at the same time inescapably woven into. 'Liquid Modernity' arrogates humans in ambivalent variations of life, offers rooting and uprooting, inclusion and exclusion, material and intellectual wealth or poverty, isolation or community experience.

Nobody is able to evade the globalism phenomenon, not even in niches of life or in remote places. This applies to rural areas in Germany and India also. The dynamics of transition and transformation is sensible and perceptible everywhere. They have an impact on people's living conditions indifferent to social or societal situation, or cultural placing. The world itself is 'liquid', a self-organized, dynamic phenomenon. The world a few a seconds ago is never the same world as just now or the same world as in a few seconds. Every human being, every child, and every teenager the same as all other agents are interwoven with this world. They contribute to their ever changing gestalt in new ways over and over again. The educational assignment of the individual and the communities, which is woven into the global horizon, turns out to be multifactorial and multidimensional. The educational assignment is uniquely individual and collective at the same time. Every participant, every child, every adolescent and every adult of the world process contributes with his or her own way of seeing and understanding the world as well as his or her own potential for action and transformation. The multidimensional world is interpreted and screened from multiple perspectives by the contributing people.

The world itself in its dynamic transition proves to be an unseparated phenomenon. Within itself the multidimensional, multifactorial and the multiperspectivity can be found in situations. We as human beings form the situation in this course that is affluent (see Müller 2007, 35). The transitioning life that takes place within this situation is the actual school that is being offered. It is the school of life in which everybody is a learner. The school of life, the school of dynamic transition in this world in its infinitely multidimensional complexity thus virtually constitutes a 'MultiGradeMultiLevel-Methodology' in which everybody works educationally with himself or herself and everybody else. Informal, formal and even unfathomable processes of what happens are combined within.

How does one handle the complexity of a vibrant life in which everybody participates? Is finding one's way the current central question of the educational remit?

Some argue the educational remit is the ability to record and capture the world's phenomena. The craze of taking pictures with digital cameras at mesmerizing touristic sights forms a valid example. Regardless of the amount of different documented perspectives, at the end of the day it is only a tiniest section of the events that is covered. What is behind and underneath all this is left in the dark. The spectator is being excluded, he is not in the picture, though, and he is perspectively represented. Filming and recording does not really help either. What is happening is always bigger than any perspective, transcends perspectives, is a-perspective. Scholars share the same problems when it comes to research processes despite variety of methods and adequate triangulation.

Whoever takes the phenomenon of unseparated lifeworld as a starting point leans to deduct ideas of the context of the wholeness of life and the world from fragmentary pictures. However, the ignorance of the wholeness ultimately remains. Will learning from and with the pre-liminarity of one's own stand; one's own perspective and the ongoing acceptance of new facets become the new educational remit of our days? What is to be done when controlling the ever regenerating phenomena of the world's dynamics cannot be the goal? What is to be done when instead adequate answers are required? Do human beings have to acquire a certain 'liquid' understandings of themselves and the world? Are change and the willingness to change the means for a new understanding of education?

Contributing amidst the transformation of the stream of life, which is an event in the unseparated wholeness of the undivided universe (Bohm / Hiley 1993) can be referred to as integral beyond any perspective. The school of transformation is an integral school of life. It refers to all aspects of being. In every occurring event with its actions the integral school of humanity points beyond the individual to the universal wholeness.

In combination with the character of global transformations described above one nowadays has to speak of a cosmic responsibility and accept it as the educational horizon. Everybody is cosmically called upon. And this does not only reflect within the global questions with its regional and local implications. This can be elucidated by a historic recourse to Maria Montessori. The world-renowned educator whose educational influence remains beyond her death up to this day talks about the individual's unique cosmic task in her remarks on cosmic theory. Here educating one stands for the human being's task to rediscover his internal secret of cosmic existence over and over again. Unfolding his or her own (growing) potentiality in the context of humanity and the things of the world shapes to be a continuous process of search and identification (Eckert 2001; Ludwig 2008).

The former president of the UNESCO's European agency for culture, Edgar Morin, seizes this thought now when talks about "cosmic condition" of mankind. As a participant he is woven in the dynamics of a vivid self-organization between micro- and macrocosm (Morin 2001, 61). Theodor Ballauff supports this from a pedagogical point of view:

> "The principle of universality constitutes the independence of thinking ahead as a task to give in to the knowledge of the wholeness in its immeasurable vastness, its immeasurable depth. It will be the art of every educational method to answer to this universality in all its ways, neither offering simplifications nor abbreviations. It will be the challenge to discover the wholeness in its context and abundance within everyone" (Ballauff 2000, 120).

The expression 'Duality in Unity' delineates this simultaneous phenomenon in eastern characteristic. Everyone is actively involved in the phenomenon while seemingly being each other's counterpart. Being woven in the cosmic existence and its change is constitutive and presets the 'liquid' horizon as educational remit, as a preconditioned reality (Fischer 1975, 111).

People generate preliminary perspectives of world affairs by subjectivity. However, these perspectives can be modified or expanded by any other perspective. Perspectives operate complementary, they enhance each other or they override each other in a dynamic, cyclic connection. Ultimately multiperspectivity coincides in oneself, if one recognizes and accepts the possible perspectives of perceiving and interpreting the world as fact.

Do the integral school of life and the institutionalized models of school really deal with acknowledging the others' preliminary perspectives and making them become more transparent together with the multifacetedness of existing perspectives of perceiving the world?

The shift in consciousness from a rational perspective to the integral wholeness can lead to a holistic perspective (see Chapter 3.2.3). Jean Gebser was one of the first to point this out in his work "origin and present" (Gebser 1999, 174).

Does realizing the a-perspectivity or even an integral consciousness constitute the current educational goal? Integral educational practice leaves phenomena in their global-universal contexts liquid, undivided and bound to the wholeness. The global participants prove to be changing and learning entities in the progressing conduct of life.

We as Research Team Integral take as a reasoned starting point that the MultiGradeMultiLevel-Methodology with its holistically designed layout is adapted for sustainably supporting integral educational practice in learning life. The variations of the MGML-Methodology, which will be discussed later on, show that they can flexibly expand beyond their Indian foundation into further variations which also seem to feature the inert response towards education from the stream of life.

The fact that the project staff understands itself as a permanently learning and developing team does certainly contribute to this, too. The team of the Rishi Valley Institute for Educational Resources, RIVER, describes this way of developing methods out of the stream of life as continuous, sustainable "action research".

3.2.1 Collectively Living in Uncertainty

The manageability of challenges and inquiries in global society hardly seem to be constituted for the individual with the most diverse variations of crises. Some things seem to be overwhelming and overcharging. In the global home the ancient question 'What should I do?' nowadays also generates feelings of uncertainty and helplessness next to the search for meaning and identity. Next to an exaggerated want for safety there is irrational risk-taking, next to intended synergistic cooperation there is distinction and isolation. By combining risk and prospect (Warwitz 2001) it is attempted to transgress everything previous. Often this happens without reassuring and acknowledging the quality of the transformation.

How should a child in Germany, in India or elsewhere in the world learn to cope with this challenge? Is it even possible to preparatory live radical transformations? Should the confidence and willingness to take the next step be provided? Are educational processes learning experiences that explore life? Are they expeditions into and out of the depth of one's own development? Is it a journey that has the now in today as its only certainty? Is it the job of school itself to perceive what this now in today offers as a next step? When working with children and adolescents is it the case that one should initiate the next educational step oneself in order to redefine where to get to next and how to get there? Furthermore, where are accessible – viable – paths to be found? Last but not least should this also be looked upon existentially (instead of merely contemplated) and, acted out epistemologically-constructivistically?

Celestin Freinet introduced the interesting term of tentative trying in his pedagogy. Yes, learning this progress might be an answer. Step by step new ways can be discovered that lead to the respective next one just like a blind person with a white stick that is simultaneously multi-sensory supremely mindful and aware of what's happening in front of him or her.

The willingness to get involved in the unknown new opens up the proposition of learning and preliminary finding. Certainty and uncertainty, searching and finding, order and chaos can seamlessly blend into each other or do often get entangled in the stream of life. The educational process creates itself as an again opened up, many-faceted event. It continues expected processes with unexpected surprises and new constellations, thus remaining linked with learning. The UNESCO entitles its educational concept for the 21th century (Delors 1996).

"The emergence of the new cannot be foretold; otherwise it would not be new. The emergence of something creative cannot be known beforehand; otherwise it would not be something creative" (Morin 2001, 99). It is our task to learningly turn towards the new.

The question 'What should I do' itself seems to be easily re-locatable, if an isolated 'I' is hardly recognizable. Instead many contributors that apparently exist next to each other, but actually work together, a constantly take an active part in life. Ambiguity, doubtfulness, shocking or threatening anything previous could now unilaterally be allocated to uncertainty. From the point of view of persisting and less preserving conservatives this would be quite understandable, since they cling to the status quo by halting. However, learning collectively bursts this open. The uncertainty always stems from the respective other, from the individual's environment, from participates in nature, culture and society. The other, the strange, everything that by differentiation is not us induces these impressions and sensitivities.

Albeit, uncertainty is not only an expression of the individual's external, it is also an indicator when facing inwards: inert discomfort or pleasant well-being reminds us of the complex interplay of e.g. psycho-immunological, neuropsychological or body-mind-and-soul powers. Human beings are hardly able to rationally comprehend what is going on on a microcosmic level inside them. Only in sensitively perceiving and in a careful, intuitive mindfulness can be fathomed what it actually is being kept in balance. Although so much research has been done on the issue it still remains mysterious. In another passage Edgar Morin states that inner and outer uncertainties and imponderables have to be considered as necessary factors of our time. In his remarks he points to an uncertain world. In this world we feel the uncertainty of reality which incorporates any multiperspectivity previously mentioned. The uncertainty of cognition highlights the permanent preliminarily of our cognition. Considering the linkage between the uncertainty and the ecology of action as well as the limitations of individual acting, we realize that every action is already integrated into a sea of actions where it works or declines (Morin 2001, 97-98).

However, the possibility of learning remains and it offers a consistency of going along. What was initially regarded as strange, the other, is seen as a collective task and challenge in learning and can be classified with the own development of potential.

What happens on a day-to-day basis, in encounters and events of communal and individual acting and structuring, can give orientation on how natural learning and natural processes of learning take place. By actively turning towards this uncertainty of potential the encounters and events become part of the transformation and enable their own growth. Jiddu Krishnamurti uses the gentle yet powerful term of "flowering" (Krishnamurti 2006a, n.p). Learning becomes a transformative power. It lets people leave the old behind and yield new things. People are able to generate different ways of acting that offer different and new perceptions and qualities of life.

At the same time nescience remains. Maybe even to the extent of the old 'docta ignorantia', which in being aware of the nescience, almost comfortingly combined the awareness of singularity of any moment, person and the collective being (Girg 2007, 53).

Is school about supporting enjoying the new, the unfamiliar, the previously unknown, in order to continually grow globally and universally?

3.2.2 Concreation – Integral Participation within the Interconnection of the Single in the Whole

The global, the universal is nowadays commonly perceived and described as the hologram-type interconnection of the detail with the whole. Every single represents the whole, literally as the total centering of the whole in the detail. This shows "an interdependent, interactive and inter-retroactive tissue made out of the object of cognition and its context, the parts and the whole, the whole and the parts and among the parts themselves" (Morin 2001, 47).

This concept follows the integral basic assumption that all of life's situations which are a reason to learn are cosmically complete and woven in the whole. The inherent meaning of life in sharing the experience of learning with the shared situations can be deciphered by everyone in his or her own way and become part of the educational process. Heinrich Rombach terms this the phenomenon of concreation. Concreation is the interaction of everybody in everything that is happening. Rombach treats concreation as pivotal in his ontological remarks on situation. It is the interaction of all agents in every situation that has always existed which offers a "concreative encounter for the release of the powers to overcome oneself" (Rombach 1993, 128).

Is synergy in this sense therefore as a central element of lessons preferentially to be consolidated and expanded?

Even though the developers of the MultiGradeMultiLevel-Methodology do not analytically-theoretically describe it this way, Research Team Integral sees it as a central point for effectiveness.

As an integral phenomenon the transforming situation includes everybody. Nobody is or will be excluded. The school remains a school for everybody. The situation, which is collectively and multidimensionally molded anew again and again, proves to be an unbiased and simultaneously valuable offering of interplay life forces' interplay. The participants are able to contribute and learn in the most diverse ways. Everyone is already involved, as is the case in the integral school of life: it is a school where everybody contributes equally.

From an integral perception the MultiGradeMultiLevel-Methodology – as stated before - is an approach and at the same time essentially more than just a mere approach, more than a method. It has been found by the RIVER Team via a long road of life that has been pursued with radical consequence. The MultiGradeMultiLevel-Methodology with its own 'powers of self-transcendence' represents an integral culture of living and learning practice. It points beyond itself towards the practice of a learning life. This practice is an inherent part of the methodology. The hypothesis that the MGML-Methodology provides a pedagogical feedback tool of undivided practice of learning and living that reconnects with the learning life, the global and the universal seems justified.

3.2.3 Scientific foundations

The academic foundations of the MGML-Methodology and its Ladders of Learning in the deliberations provided in this book are oriented towards a generally integral perception of educational processes. From an etymological starting point the characterization 'integral' signifies that every life, learning and education situation takes place "whole", "completely", "forming an entity", "persisting in itself", "essentially", "soundly" and "undividedly" and "whole" (Drodsdowski 1994, 1792; Paul 2002, 501). The wholeness of all situations, that is all education that is currently taking place with possible processes of learning and education for all agents, is taken as a starting point (Rombach 1980 and 1993; also Müller 2007). Acting individually and collectively is immediately connected to the potential learning in the situation and offers further processes of education.

The academic descriptions stemming from this integral, holistic perception of situations are named 'integral education' by the authors (Girg 2007; also Müller / Girg 2007). Integral pedagogy can be identified as "as one of the youngest scientific fields that has been established within the discipline of pedagogy [...], even though according to its content it has always explicitly been inherent to all pedagogy and scientific methodology" (Müller / Girg 2007, 5).

Considering this academic perception situations are not only 'complete', but they are also always linked to the wholeness and the individual in a philosophical sense (Beierwaltes 2001). This perception and its resulting comprehension keeps the link between lived and experienced situation and the cosmic integration that transcends the individual intact. Furthermore, an educational effect is assigned to this link (Ballauff 2000).

The cosmos itself is nowadays regarded as whole that becomes reality between microcosm and macrocosm (Jantsch 1988). This whole can be thought of as 'holistic'. Here, 'holistic' intends – also in a material sense – the linkage of every individual within the wholeness, just like cell in an organ or an organ within the body. On a rational level the term 'holistic' works to clarify the inner relations between the wholeness and the individual. A holistic understanding therefore is part of a present integral culture of acting that is fulfilled concreatively according to Rombach (Haeffner 2000, 101-102; also Girg 2007, 238; Rombach 1993, 128). The integral, scientific approach at the core of this book has among others been described by Jean Gebser in his central work 1949/50 "Origin and Present" from a Western point of view for a long time (Gebser 1999). He is able to back up his remarks by referring to Eastern approaches such as the "integral yoga" by Sri Aurobindo (Aurobindo 1950). It is predominantly Gebser who is nowadays been made reference to in the respective secondary literature (Schübl 2003; Hellbusch 2003; Gottwald 2012). By now these descriptions of integral have been enhanced by further scientific approaches. For one thing these are studies about the phenomenon and the practice of awareness as the main subject. Especially the therapeutic area of studies has seen a lot of work being published (Altner 2006; Heidenreich / Michalak 2006). For another thing Ken Wilber is being recognized internationally (2001a; 2001b; 2007).

In the context of MGML-Methodology Jiddu Krishnamurti's teachings turn out to be especially relevant for the integral perception of educational situations. These are expressed by Krishnamurti's life and his oeuvre and point towards a non-dual perception of a learning life.

An integral practice of education stemming from this, forms a culture of action within science that leaves what happens situationally open. Additionally, the integral practice is aware of every situation's multiperspectivity and hence also bears the dialogue on the level of science and when generating scientific findings in mind (Bohm 2002).

3.3 Aspects of a Culture of Learning in the 21st Century

In order to somewhat grasp the immanent power of the MGML-Methodology it is mandatory and sensible to take a look on the practice of this learning culture. The first couple of chapter 2's sub-chapters focused on the complexity and interweaving of individual processes of living and learning in a global context. Living and learning are inextricably linked with each other since learning cannot be without living and learning is a permanent part of living. People are constantly part of a situation and are learning in the process. The learning processes, however, can be differentiated; learning takes place consciously and unconsciously (Göhlich / Zirfas 2007, 14), formally or informally (Meyer-Drawe 2012, 17), implicitly or explicitly, individually or collectively (Girg 2007), situationally (Rombach 1993) and throughout life (Kade / Seitter 2007). Due to this holistic complexity it is consequently not possible to reduce an understanding of learning to cognitive processes. Learning does not only take place in the brain. It is more than thinking, more than processing information in the brain. In order to comprehend the effects that the MGML-Methodology has on children, adolescents and adults, it has to be clear what the methodology has to offer for their lives and their learnings. The MGML-Methodology was extensively illustrated and illuminated in many facets in the following chapters to understand the whole range of its impact it might be helpful to read about contexts that offer reasons for its effectiveness.

As pointed out above, it is possible to describe the MGML-Methodology as a feedback tool of our life praxis. The methodology with its complex content and methodological tasks refers among others to the interweaving of educational fields with cultures of living. This shows that the MGML-Methodology is more than a method or a certain type of lesson. It is rather the foundation of life situations and learning at school for currently more than 10 million children, most of them in India, but also in Ethiopia, Nepal and Germany. These children have already begun alongside adults to shape our world and will continue to contribute their share to the world affairs – partially with much bigger responsibility than today. From the first day of school on it is their responsibility to learn for themselves and to take responsibility for others and for the world. Learning with the MGML-Methodology is complexly structured and at the same time makes good on four central criteria. According to RIVER learning should take place in small, manageable, meaningful and joyful activities. Working within the MGML-Methodology hence means working in a complex cosmos within a small space; the complex cosmos reflects the global context in the educational realm of experience.

At the core of this lies a complex understanding of learning, which will be depicted in central categories in the following. This will not be so much about describing the processes of comprehension in the brain of a human-being while learning – although these traces that are strongly characterized by the psychology of learning are obviously included in a sophisticated understanding of learning. Neuroscientific findings concerned with learning attract a lot of interest these days. (Spitzer 2006; Bauer 2006; Pöppel 2010). The explanation of learning by "a return to a material substrate" (Göhlich / Zirfas 2007, 12) opens up an interesting and new perspective. It is based on a depiction of physical and chemical processes only, thereby neglecting to look at the meaning of events (Göhlich / Zirfas 2007). From a pedagogical point of view however, it is necessary to pursue the question of meaning if one postulates the meaning as the basis of all human existence and hence human learning. At the end of the day it cannot be about an 'either – or' in any kind of way, linked with judging of any kind whatsoever concerning a better or worse understanding of learning. A comprehensive understanding of learning could rather be designed multidimensionally and try to recognize learning as an integral phenomenon. In this process constructivist basic assumptions, neuroscientific aspects as well as categories of the psychology of learning are an issue alongside performativity, mimesis and autopoiesis – to only mention a few components. A detailed list of all facets would break the mold of this chapter. Nevertheless, it is necessary to point this out in order to be able to holistically locate the foregrounded dimensions of learning with the MGML-Methodology. In drawing a picture of them two central levels are necessary: on the one hand the vast contexts of learning that are constitutive for working with the MGML-Methodology and philosophically refer back to Jiddu Krishnamurti will be laid out. Here the point will be to look at learning in the context of human life in the age of globalization. On the other hand the very specific requirements for learning with the MGML-Methodology will be detailed and referred back to the bigger dimensions.

3.3.1 Situation – Event – Experience

We always have to be aware that we are constantly in the middle of this globalization's developments and the complex challenges of our time that come along with it; we also have to remain aware that we find ourselves in a variety of life situations on a daily basis that essentially represent cosmic conditions (Girg 2007, 119). We are furthermore requested to act (Rombach 1993, 145). The uniqueness of every unparalleled and unrepeatable moment provides a cornucopia and density of potentialities (Stenger 2007, 61) from which a "punctum" (see Barthes 1989), as Roland Barthes terms it, calls out to us and seemingly seizes us out of nowhere and to which we have to specifically re-act and answer in the situation. What it actually is that makes us act and the specific way we act evades every planning and rational access. Hence it might be the case – as an example – that while we are attending a lecture that is important to us, where we are seated in the front row, we find ourselves concentrating on our throat. We are currently suffering from a sore throat and this state draws our attention to the now painful swallowing, something that would have otherwise been left unnoticed. As a result the lecture might leave a lasting impression so that in a week's time while talking about the lecture we recall our sore throat but not content discussed – although we might have planned to do so in the first place.

This example shows the eventfulness of every situation. Whatever happens in this situation has a lot of dimensions. We might be able to schedule to which of these we are going to respond, but what finally happens always remains open within the situation itself. We cannot definitely determinate to which punctum within the situation we are going to turn towards in advance. In our example we intended to attentively and intently listen to the lecture and deliberately chose a seat in the front row. What is to be seen within the situation is random. It is out of the subject's power of control, even though favorable preconditions could be arranged beforehand (Mollenhauer in Stenger 2007, 63).

The situation becomes a site of experience that we witness and on the basis of which we permanently learn. The experience occurs like a process and can be divided into a sequence of small individual components that are closely together. Stenger (2007, 62) elucidated these individual components within the process of the aesthetic experience by drawing on Mollenhauer (1990a, 1990b, 1998). What is stated for the aesthetic experience generally applies for any situation:

> "An aesthetic experience can only take place where one is successful to expose himself to the approaching within the artwork, to establish a bodily resonance and to tentatively turn to these via the sentiments released by the encounter with the artwork. However, this experience cannot be created deliberately" (Stenger 2007, 62).

It is the experiences within the event that matter. However, the experiences are neither specifically plannable nor producible. It is hence necessary to get oneself into the situation and to be open for whatever will show up, or whatever we will experience – as Wagenschein (1999, 76-77) or Westphal (2007, 53) would call it. Jiddu Krishnamurti hereby speaks of "true action" (Girg 2007, 164). We are standing within the multidimensional situation and are being spoken to. "Something involves us" as Rombach words it (1999, 154). He furthermore requests us to pay attention. In this way our relation and our relatedness to the world is shown (Bürmann 1992, 11). What appeals to us has something to do with ourselves, therefore has among others something to do with our current sensitivities, our personality and our previous experiences. The relatedness can differ in magnitude within the situations. Referring back to the lecture example, we especially felt addressed by our throat in this situation and therefore turned towards the phenomenon of pain. Our relation might change in a new situation if the person sitting next to us, who is someone we have known for a long time but seldom see, approaches us and tells us that he would like to have a chat during the next break. The arrival of a verbal message from him to us might urge us to feel curiosity or joy. The bodily impression of pain fades while a response towards the attention received from our neighbor is building up. This might lead us to reply to him: 'Yes, I would love to.'

Experience is to be understood as process-like wholeness which consists of a general openness towards the situation, the willingness to get oneself into the situation and to follow along. Subsequently the identification of the 'punctum' occurs to which we build up a response. This response causes us to act (not acting has to be regarded as acting as well).

What does this mean for the ways of learning with the MGML-Methodology? Assuming that learning takes place in situations would imply that lessons have to provide and create specific situations of learning that appeal to the pupil in such a way that he or she wants to deal with it. Therefore the materials, used by the MGML-Methodology, are thematically directly oriented on the immediate environment of the children. An example for working in language courses would be using stories that the children have already heard from their mothers and grandmothers. A child-oriented depiction by shadow-theater might succeed in reaching the child in such a way that he or she gets himself or herself into the situation of learning.

The character of the kind spirit within the shadow theater might be especially appealing; the character becomes a 'punctum' which makes the child build up a response. The child feels the power and the hope of the shadow figure and thus wants to write the story down in order to have the possibility to read it over and over again and relive that positive feeling. Linked to the theory the act of writing down the story is the action of the child stemming from the situational proposition which he or she get himself or herself into. Here the opportunity of an integrated learning experience is pivotal: learning with the brain, the heart and the hands (see Pestalozzi), or better with body and soul.

3.3.2 Bodily Learning – Performativity

The example above demonstrates what Meyer-Drawe postulates in the discourses of learning: "Strictly speaking, from a pedagogical perspective learning is experience." (Meyer-Drawe 2012, 15). She places learning and experience synonymously alongside each other in order to carve out their common features. This equalization implies a rejection of the understanding of learning as an exclusively cognitive process, of constructing a network of knowledge – as also stated by Stenger (2007, 53). Instead, the goal is to reach an "opening of entire horizons and human possibilities of existence" (Stenger 2007, 69).

This puts a special emphasis on the ever-present holistic dimension of learning. We always learn as an 'entire' human-being. We always learn within situations. Our learning performs via our body - "one cannot break away from one's body, it is always there" (Liebau 2007, 102). Therefore corporality is an important characteristic of learning, even though "solely intellectual" activities tend to be executed omitting the corporal component (Ernst 1993 in Liebau 2007, 102); it is through our corporality that we have access to the world. Liebau declares perception, invention and discovery on the one hand and incorporation and practice on the other hand as the central modi (Liebau 2007, 104). In common with Westphal (2007, 53), Liebau assumes that we learn whenever something strikes us, when we experience resistance, when we are surprised – when we are affected. He calls this starting point "crisis" (Liebau 2007, 104). Here the term crisis is not to be understood as solely negatively connoted. Crisis should be interpreted as a situation in life in which the question mentioned above 'What should I do?' emerges in a new light and prompts the learner with the task to indulge in the search of meaning within a venture (Warwitz 2001). In this situation we initially experience an inability to act. This can form into our reason to get involved with the challenge and to develop corporal dispositions in order to surpass the crisis.

Hereby, the process of learning is to be structured as such: crisis as the starting point of the process opens up the requirement towards the learner to observe a difference between what is solvable and the emerging problem that cannot be solved with skills currently possessed by the learner. Noticing this difference can create an ambition within the learner to overcome the difficulty and hence to search for feasible solutions and 'invent' them, respectively. This process of finding a solution is reached by trying and discovering the solution. In the second mode of learning the found solution can be absorbed by practice until a satisfying process is reached within the learner. This evokes a feeling of joy within the learner that is likened to the phenomenon of flow (Csikszentmihalyi, 2010). If and when this phenomenon is going to set in remains unavailable – which endorses the event character of learning with all facets used to describe this event.

The flow-experience, also known as "Montessori-Phenomenon" (Montessori / Ludwig 201) in the field of progressive education, characterizes another level of corporal or bodily learning: the learner is able to physically experience the learning success. He fells the emotions initiated by the prowess; the corporal resonance is made alive physically and can later on also be expressed on a symbolic level that encompasses thinking, cognition and ratiocination (Liebau 2007, 104).

What does this mean for when learning with the MGML-Methodology? Let us have a fresh look at our child that wants to annotate the story from within the situation. The child just turned seven and has not yet mastered the alphabet. So the child might experience a crisis within the first few lines when it realizes its inability to correctly write down an alphabetic character. In the process it first acknowledges its own inability of setting down this character. This goes along with a sense of disappointment and an emerging anger-induced gut feeling after repeated failure. However, the motivation to have access to the story at any time is so big that the child is getting involved with the challenge and searches for ways of succeeding – firstly on its own later on maybe together with others. Invention or discovery commences: the youngster is sitting at a table with two fellow pupils and asks both of them for help. The older pupils show the younger one how to note the alphabetic character by writing it down on a small blackboard. The child follows the outline of the character with its finger and gradually develops a bodily disposition to be able to write the character down on its own. The movement is repeated over and over again with the right hand – first with the finger then with the pen – until the child succeeds in legibly writing down the letter. The incorporation is executed. The child has found a solution and is able to continue writing down the story.

Corporality inhabits a central position within and for the learning process. There is a learner (Leonhardt 2006, 214) and this person determines the necessity and possibility, the explanation and the goal of learning. Learning is tied to subjects and takes place in defined "bodily situations" (Leonhardt 2006, 215). At the center of the observation is the immediate, 'functional' process of experience of the individual, the so called performance of learning and performance of the learner, respectively. Categories of the performative can be applied to this. Apart from event and corporality, situational staging as well as individual and social presence constitute further categories (Wulf / Zirfas 2004, 5-6). Learning takes place when somebody does it on his own or together with others. Learning can take place in an environment that is specifically designed for this purpose. As such, the learning situation unfolds that contains planned (that is staged) and open, (that is unplanned and unpredictable) dimensions. It is not until actually acting, learning, that these dimensions become visible and alive in their interplay. Seen as that, learning per se cannot be understood, but rather as respective, actual experienced learning situations and their respective complexity.

3.3.3 Individuality and Concreativity

The presumption of situating the act of learning and the implied coupling to one or several learners gives point to have a look at the individual and concreative components of learning. Since learning – as delineated in the above segment – is a personal process, it always initially takes place on an individual level. A learning person does so as a human-being with a unique individuality that is characterized by its corporality, emotions, thoughts, sentiments, outer appearance and character (Leonhard 2006, 214). The learning process is always to be found within a biographical context and therefore is dependent on prior experiences, prior knowledge and prior understanding (Girg 1994). In addition, cultural, regional and social contexts play a decisive role. Thus, a pupil's individuality is more than observing its performance in a certain subject or towards a certain topic. It is above all characterized by the fact of its singularity and uniqueness. No pupil, no child or adolescent is the same as the other and no child or adolescent will ever be the same as the other. School and its collective lessons constitute a meeting point of many different children and adolescents. The task is to create meaningful propositions for them within the communal experience of school. Naturally, these propositions should incorporate different types of learning, appeal to all senses (Zimmer 2012), enable action orientation and self-directed learning, in order to give the children and youth a chance to comprehensively develop their motoric, intellectual, emotional and social potential (see Meyer 2004, 97). In the vein of progressive educational postulates children and adolescents need to be given space to grow and develop freely and authentically (Lichtinger 2010, 147) – according to the principle of the Greek Pindar: "Become who you are!" (Pyth. 2, 72).

Individual learning points to the importance of the learning experience for the individual and its formation of character (personalization). Integrally applied to the individual child, the individual adolescent and the specific act of learning, the learning experience is characterized by the person's individuality, the singularity of the (learning) situation as well as the uniqueness, that is, it cannot be repeated, of the situation. The learner experiences a unique and unparalleled situation in his own specific ways that are made up of location, time, topic and the participating people. The learner forms a bodily response, construes his knowledge about that and establishes skills (Lichtinger 2010, 96). Hence, individual learning is unique, singular, mimetic and corporal.

Since educational learning feeds off of collective participation, a learning situation often also implies a collective learning experience. Acting is therefore acting within a personal relationship towards others that act in different relations and roles. The respective encounters are likewise unique and singular as are the situations in which the encounters unfold, since every person participating in the process acts differently while working with one or several other persons. For example, our seven-year old child mentioned above will learn something different when working with a female friend that is one year older, than it would when working with a boy, whom she has not spoken to before, that is three years older and just randomly happened to be sitting next to her at the table. The same applies if the girl was working with her teacher who due to her position acts differently and maybe happens to be an expert in the acquisition of written and spoken language. The learning process is collective, relational and tied to subjects that act with and for each other (Leonhard 2006, 214). The people act creatively within the cooperation and togetherness, the corporal co-presence and interaction. They concreatively take part in designing the situation and are related to everything that constitutes the situation. So collective learning is also always learning within relations and relatedness (Bürmann 1992, 11). The encounters take place between people, things, time and space. It is out of this encounter that the human-being acts and responds (Westphal 2004, 195). As a result, learning as a rule is collective, social, relational, (cor-)responsive and concreative. In which way does this learning take shape in the MGML-Methodology? We are able to relate the child's learning situation that comes to live via the encounter with the story as the subject of learning, to the various components of learning and observe their quality. Uniqueness and singularity are inherent to the individuality of the child. The child only exists this one time the way she is and with everything that she is capable of. The way she handles the task she has assigned to her herself, namely being able to write the alphabetic character down, is unique and will never happen this particular way again. Even when she is not master of this alphabetic character after an initial explanation and practice, it does not mean signify that the process repeats itself with resurfacing iterative moments. In a second step of learning the child approaches a person anew. This could be the male pupil who is three years her major and who, as the girl has found out excels in writing. He will show her the notation. This boy will choose a different way than the girl who helped the child before. He will use different words for his explanation, will use different hand movements and will maybe give her a different (maybe even more helpful) advice. On the face of it a process of explaining is being repeated. However, seen from within this process is completely different from the first one. The girl is going to act differently mimetically, comprehend different things bodily than the first time, simply because the relatedness is different this time. She is dealing with a new and different person whereby the social cooperation and togetherness forms in a new relationality. The mere fact that now the girl is working together with a boy, whom she barely knows, leads to her acting differently compared to the first situation. The (cor-)responsivity takes on different features. The concreative cooperation of both is a different one. For this reason learning is understood as an intrinsically and autonomously individual process. Its informal, implicit way always inhibits an intrinsically motivating element, something that addresses the learning person and lets it learn. The institutional, educational environment is designed to provide the possibility to learn formally and explicitly on top of informal and implicit processes of learning. The individual pupil and teacher are situated in this educational environment where learning can happen through experience. This is, as has just been shown, learning by means and within performance. This is an active, self-acting and discovering, individual and at the same time concreative act that is put into effect by experiences prepared and provided in educational opportunities of learning in school.

3.3.4 Activity and Self-Responsibility

School and education are due to their assignment always first of all staged and oriented on a schedule that follows specific steps and phases (Becker 2012). As a result an iterative momentum is immanent in lessons. In practice reasons for learning are created that unhinge singular phenomenon from their contexts, discuss them and therefore prompt the learner to learn. For the creators of the MGML-Methodology – as for all teachers in this world – the focus was and is on the key question:

How do opportunities of learning have to be and look like in order to bring a learner to want to become involved in these opportunities, to bring a learner to want to learn? The answer to this is bound to the belief that learning always takes place autonomously and is hence dependent on the learner. Learning is a process in which the learner becomes actively involved, engages with a phenomenon, poses questions and learns to look for answers. 'The Child is in the Driver's Seat' is the credo of the designers of the MGML-Methodology. This saying should have comprehensive validity for the educational opportunities of learning. An analogy to Montessori's 'Help me to do it myself' is palpable. Reasons to learn have to be provided that speak to children in such a way that they want to get involved independently and actively. At the same time these reasons have to be created with a holistic basic understanding in order to make the pupils intellectually and bodily become aware of the interweaving of individual fields of subject and work with others. Even in an educational context should learning remain an integral practice and inhabit a meaningful position in the child's stream of life. The educational process of learning ideally takes place incorporating specific material that does justice to meaningful yet simple criteria. The material should offer activities for the learner that bears the following characteristics:

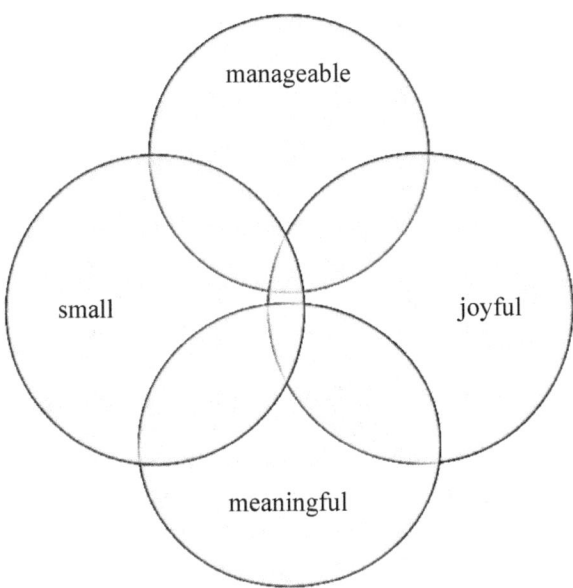

Fig. 27: Activities' characteristics

Small. Small in this context signifies that the material provided by the MGML-Methodology leads the children into time-wise manageable, self-acting processes. Thereby, the children develop the feeling to be in control of the task and to be able to solve it within an acceptable timeframe. For children in elementary school five minute phases of learning are perfect. After this time slot the task should have been solved and the child can proceed to the next one. As the children get older they are introduced to more complex challenges that inquire a longer-term timeframe but do not omit the impression of smallness. The children should always have the feeling that they are being challenged but also that the task is appropriately small considering their stage of development and size.

Manageable. Smaller tasks, in general, are tasks which are manageable. In order to be characterized as 'manageable', other aspects have to be considered. For one, children need to work on tasks which – depending on the guidelines – are resolvable alone, with a partner, or a teacher. Therefore, the task needs to be stated to that effect, so students are certain about what they have to do, without being overwhelmed by complex conceptual formulation. By means of many small manageable tasks, a sense may strengthen within them, teaching them to cope with life, step by step, in small assessable units. As they themselves will – according to Montessori's maxim – be enabled to do many small things, day by day, over the years, they also will find themselves in a position, where they have a hold on their own life and its composition. Life is manageable, is livable, is full of positive sense of achievement.

Joyful. The requirement stating that studying should be joyful and pursuing fun, also is very blatant. Initially, it contradicts the paradigm passed on in Europe over the centuries, claiming that studying means to exert oneself. It is tedious and therefore cannot be or result in fun. From notable publications in the field of neuroscience it is generally known that the context-memory is located in the hippocampus, the region of the brain in which the studying person memorizes e.g. the physical appearance of a task. Simultaneously, the amygdala provides that mechanism with an emotional evaluation – regardless of the persons willing (Kaltwasser 2010, 30). If the girl in the example, given for this history of substance-matter, likes to study, she will hence develop a positive emotional memory, which again will have a positive effect on her knowledge and on the studying situation and process as such. Simply put: if a child enjoys studying, the likelihood of it wanting to study again, is very high. It will readily pursue the next task. Incidences of studying therefore should be enriched with games and playful elements. They need to involve occasions in which laughing is allowed and wished-for. That, again, has a performative positive effect on the person itself. A school of joy is also a place full of joy, where children and teachers like to be, work, and study.

Meaningful. If the learning experience is put in direct relation to the child's or young adult's life, it may accompany an 'endowment of meaning' and simultaneously provide one's life with meaning. Therefore, the study-matter ideally is taken from the child's direct environment. Furthermore, it should orient itself on its individual interests, as well as, regional and cultural context. The stronger children's impression's get that studying enables them to design their own lives, or rather that it grants them the practical experience of modeling their private life by means of scholastic learning, the more intense they will continue that process'; move from one learning experience to the next. Hence, the tasks are connected to the living environment of the children. The stories it learns from, are regional and deeply rooted in their social groups. The children, in succession, become carriers of their own regional culture. They bring forward tradition and through that, are enabled to experience the collective identity of their society. In addition, they perceive the imminent significance of scholastic studying for their personal, non-scholastic life. They deal with regional problems and learn to do their part for the overall good of their society. By means of the core questions' important character, children and parents comprehend the significance of school itself. At the same time, school is legitimized through prolific ties to a life in society. Living and learning merge to one big picture and become an inseparable, integral field for children and young adults.

Holistic and Integral. Through the previous elaboration it becomes evident that learning may have many facets, but eludes an overall comprehension. Its inseparable connection to the human learning experience, i.e. the human as a whole, is particularly evident in the dimensions of performativity. At the same time, the depiction, which itself only ever is just a depiction or mirror-image of an all-encompassing, real and bigger phenomenon, is always incomplete. That real, bigger phenomenon may be called integral life- and learning experience: integral, whole, and all along complete. In it, everything occurs interconnected and intertwined; collaborates and interacts permanently. Hence, if learning is attributed as integral, it is acknowledged that it is a constant process, an experience. In science, one is 'only' allowed to theorize and carry out tests, in order to grasp that existing phenomenon, understand, as well as, verbalize it. Those theories, nevertheless, can only approach the 'big picture' in reality, because of their subjective and cognitive nature. They will never describe the experience in its wholeness. Accordingly, a theory of learning cannot exactly be identified as integral, but holistic at most. This differentiation of term-allocation happens due to the circumstance of emergence; the knowledge that the whole may never be thoroughly explained by the properties of its parts. The whole, the holistically real, always results in more than the sum of its pieces. It is always more than the description of integral reality (Girg 2007, 68-69; Wilber 2001b, 53-54). The depiction, which is never 'more' than a depiction of a profound, holistic whole, remains incomplete. The integral life- and learning experience occurs, although it can only be conjectured, not apprehended in its wholeness. Hence, a variety of consequences is implied for the configuration of educational didactic inducement, headed by the requirements imposed on the teacher and tutor. They are required to occupy a suppliant position and to be aware of their auxiliary purpose. Organizing and supervising classes requires a certain educational understanding, which is, as previously stated, captioned by the principle given by the experts of the MGML-Methodology: 'The Child is in the Driver's Seat'. Accordingly, if teachers want the children to drive for themselves, they are required to provide them with cars, with which they can actually attempt driving. The cars, i.e. the learning material, are chosen didactically and need to follow certain basic principles, as for example, from small to big, etc. The solid structure within the leaning material presents itself in the respective individual instructional occasion, which initially is predefined by the given material, but eventually eludes fixed designation through the learning situation of the particular child or young adult. Returning to a metaphorical language: how the child drives and which gear it uses, may be prepared in advance by a teacher, but there is always a room for situative decisions and an individual scope. The learning situation becomes a unique experience – tangible, specific, temporally singular, and for all participants individual and collective at the same time. The children cultivate a physical resonance to the encounter in the particular situation, and therefore experience the process of learning with all of their body. In doing so, the parties involved assume concrete functions and roles in the happening. If the child is at the wheel of the learning-vehicle, it will drive or apply the brake, maybe it will dismount or time and again choose new fellow-passengers or co-drivers, who assist it, or are assisted by it. By driving, braking and halting the child learns multifacetedly and multidimensionally. Contents are also cognitively being processed and categorized into the already existing network of knowledge. The actual driving, the educational action, cannot be the active creation of learning situations by the teacher (Wagenschein 1999, 36). Instead vehicles, material and giving space have to be placed at the disposal, which enables driving in such a way that something can be solidified, be established and truly gain significance within the learner. This significance is amidst the immediate stream of life. It is not only a situation of learning but also always a comprehensive situation of living. Therefore learning and living are inseparably interconnected. They are one. Learning how to drive is always already driving. It is schools' and the teachers' task to not break up this unity or split it up into 'this thing' and 'the other'. Instead it is their task is to provide these situations of learning from within the integral, to create situations that children like to attend to, situations the children want to spend time for. The things we spend time with, we give love to (Horkheimer 1978). And where there is love, we experience meaning.

3.3.5 References

Altner, N. Achtsamkeit und Gesundheit: Auf dem Weg zu einer achtsamen Pädagogik. Immenhausen bei Kassel: Prolog Verlag, 2006. Print. Reihe Bewegungslehre und Bewegungsforschung Bd. 26.

Arndt, Ch. and J. Volkert. "Amartya Sens Capability-Approach: Ein neues Konzept der deutschen Armuts- und Reichtumsberichterstattung." Vierteljahreshefte zur Wirtschaftsforschung 1 (2006): 7–29. Web. 6. May 2014. <http://ejournals.duncker-humblot.de/doi/pdf/10.3790/vjh.75.1.7>.

Aurobindo, S. Life Divine. New York: Sri Aurobindo Ashram, 1950. Print.

Ballauff, Th. Pädagogik als Bildungslehre. 4. Aufl. aus dem Nachlass. Baltmannsweiler: Schneider-Verl. Hohengehren, 2000. Print.

Bauer, J. Warum ich fühle, was du fühlst: Intuitive Kommunikation und das Geheimnis der Spiegelneurone. München: Heyne, 2006. Print. Heyne 61501.

Bauman, Z. Verworfenes Leben: Die Ausgegrenzten der Moderne. 1. Aufl. Hamburg: Hamburger Ed, 2005. Print.

---. Moderne und Ambivalenz: Das Ende der Eindeutigkeit. Neuausg. Hamburg: Hamburger Ed., 2006. Print.

Becker, G. E. Handlungsorientierte Didaktik. 10., neu ausgestattete Aufl. Weinheim (u.a.): Beltz, 2012. Print. Beltz grüne Reihe.

Behringer, L. Lebensführung als Identitätsarbeit: Der Mensch im Chaos des modernen Alltags. Frankfurt a.M., New York: Campus-Verl., 1998. Print.

Beierwaltes, W. Das wahre Selbst: Studien zu Platins Begriff des Geistes und des Einen. Frankfurt am Main: Vittorio Klostermann, 2001. Print.

Bohm, D. Der Dialog: Das offene Gespräch am Ende der Diskussionen. 5. Aufl. Stuttgart: Klett-Cotta, 2002. Print.

Bohm, D. and B. J. Hiley. The undivided universe: An ontological interpretation of quantum theory. London, New York: Routledge, 1993. Print.

Böhmer, A. and E. Fink, eds. Eugen Fink: Sozialphilosophie - Anthropologie - Kosmologie - Pädagogik - Methodik. Würzburg: Königshausen & Neumann, 2006. Print. Orbis Phaenomenologicus. Perspektiven, Neue Folge 12.

Bude, H. and A. Willisch, eds. Das Problem der Exklusion: Ausgegrenzte, Entbehrliche, Überflüssige. Hamburg: Hamburger Edition, 2006. Print.

Bürmann, J. Gestaltpädagogik und Persönlichkeitsentwicklung: Theoretische Grundlagen und praktische Ansätze eines persönlich bedeutsamen Lernens. Bad Heilbrunn/Obb: J. Klinkhardt, 1992. Print.

Castel, R. Die Metamorphosen der sozialen Frage: Eine Chronik der Lohnarbeit. 2nd ed. Konstanz: UVK-Verl.-Ges., 2000b. Print. Édition discours 44.

Csikszentmihalyi, M. Das flow-Erlebnis: Jenseits von Angst u. Langeweile: im Tun aufgehen. Stuttgart: Klett-Cotta, 2010. Print. Konzepte der Humanwissenschaften.

Dahrendorf, R. Lebenschancen: Anläufe zur sozialen und politischen Theorie. Frankfurt am Main: Suhrkamp, 1979. Print. Suhrkamp-Taschenbuch 559.

Delors, J., ed. Lernfähigkeit: Unser verborgener Reichtum : UNESCO-Bericht zur Bildung für das 21. Jahrhundert. Neuwied: Luchterhand, 1996. Print.

Drosdowski, G. Duden: Das große Wörterbuch der deutschen Sprache. Mannheim: Dudenverlag, 1994. Print. 4.

Eckert, E. Maria und Mario Montessoris Kosmische Erziehung: Vision und Konkretion. Berlin: LIT-Verl., 2001. Print. Impulse der Reformpädagogik 15.

European Commission. Gemeinsamer Bericht der Kommission und des Rates über die soziale Eingliederung. Brüssel, 2004. Print.

Fischer, F. Darstellung der Bildungskategorien im System der Wissenschaften. Ratingen, Kastellauen: Aloys Henn Verlag, 1975. Print.

Fölling-Albers, M. (2001). Veränderte Kindheit – revisited. In H. Brügelmann, M. Fölling-Albers, S. Richter, A. Speck-Hamdan (Ed.), Kindheitsforschung - Forschung zum Sachunterricht. Jahrbuch Grundschule 3. Frankfurt/Main: Grundschulverband - Arbeitskreis Grundschule.

Gebser, J. Gesamtausgabe. 2nd ed. Schaffhausen: Novalis-Verl, 1999. Print.

Girg, R. Die Bedeutung des Vorverständnisses der Schüler für den Unterricht: Eine Untersuchung zur Didaktik. Bad Heilbrunn: Verlag Julius Klinkhardt, 1994. Print.

---. Die integrale Schule des Menschen: Praxis und Horizonte der Integralpädagogik. Regensburg: Roderer, 2007. Print.

Girg, R. and Th. Müller, eds. Integralpädagogik: Wahrnehmungen im lernenden Leben. Regensburg: Roderer, 2007. Print.

Goldthorpe, J. "Globalisierung und soziale Klassen." Berliner Journal für Soziologie 3 (2003): 301–02. Web. 6. May. 2014. <http://link.springer.com/article/10.1007/BF03204672>.

Göhlich, H. D., M. and J. Zirfas. Lernen: Ein pädagogischer Grundbegriff. Stuttgart: Kohlhammer, 2007. Print. Allgemeine Pädagogik.

Gottwald, P. Integrales Bewusstsein: Wie es zur Sprache - und zur Welt - bringen? Frankfurt am Main: Peter Lang, 2012. Print.

Haeffner, G. Philosophische Anthropologie. 3rd ed. Stuttgart: Kohlhammer, 2000. Print. Kohlhammer-Urban-Taschenbücher Bd. 345.

Heidenreich, Th. and J. Michalak, eds. Achtsamkeit und Akzeptanz in der Psychotherapie: Ein Handbuch. 2nd ed. Tübingen: Dgvt-Verl, 2006. Print.

Hellbusch, K. Das integrale Bewusstsein: Jean Gebsers Konzeption der Bewusstseinsentfaltung als prima philosophia unserer Zeit. Berlin: Tenea, 2003. Print. Tenea Wissenschaft.

Horkheimer, M. "Begriff der Bildung. Immatrikulationsrede 1952/53." Bildungstheorien: Probleme u. Positionen. Ed. J. E. Pleines. Freiburg im Breisgau, Basel, Wien: Herder, 1978. 22–27. Print.

Hübinger, W.: Prekärer Wohlstand: Spaltet eine Wohlstandswelle die Gesellschaft. Politik und Zeitgeschichte. Bd. 18, 1999. Print.

Hüther, G. Die Macht der inneren Bilder: Wie Visionen das Gehirn, den Menschen und die Welt verändern. Göttingen: Vandenhoeck & Ruprecht, 2006. Print.

Jantsch, E. Die Selbstorganisation des Universums: Vom Urknall zum menschlichen Geist. 4th ed. München: Dt. Taschenbuch-Verl., 1988. Print. Dtv 4397 : dtv-Wissenschaft.

Kade, J. and W. Seitter. "Lebenslanges lernen." Pädagogische Theorien des Lernens. Ed. M. Göhlich, Ch. Wulf, and J. Zirfas. Weinheim (u.a.): Beltz, 2007. Print. Beltz Bibliothek.

Kaltwasser, V. Persönlichkeit und Präsenz: Achtsamkeit im Lehrerberuf ; (das "Achtsame-acht-Wochen"-Programm: Weniger Stress, mehr Gelassenheit!). Weinheim (u.a.): Beltz, 2010. Print. Beltz Pädagogik Praxis.

Kränzl-Nagl, R. and J. Mierendorff. "Kindheit im Wandel: Annäherungen an ein komplexes Phänomen." SWS- Rundschau 1 (2007): 3–25. Print.

Lenhart, V. "Die Globalisierung in der Sicht der Vergleichenden Erziehungswissenschaft." Zeitschrift für Pädagogik 6 (2007): 810–24. Print.

Leonhard, S. Leiblich lernen und lehren: Ein religionsdidaktischer Diskurs. Stuttgart: Kohlhammer, 2006. Print. Praktische Theologie heute 79.

Lichtinger, U. Ritual im Wandel: Zur Bedeutung von Veränderungsprozessen in schulischen Ritualen; Exemplarisch aufgezeigt am "Gewölbe-Ritual" der pädagogischen Einrichtung "Schlössli Ins", Schweiz. Regensburg: Roderer, 2010. Print. Theorie und Forschung.

Liebau, E. "Leibliches Lernen." Pädagogische Theorien des Lernens. Ed. M. Göhlich, Ch. Wulf, and J. Zirfas. Weinheim (u.a.): Beltz, 2007. Print. Beltz Bibliothek.

Ludwig, H. Montessori-Schulen und ihre Didaktik. 2th ed., revised. Baltmannsweiler: Schneider-Verl. Hohengehren, 2008. Print. Basiswissen Grundschule 15.

Meyer, H. Was ist guter Unterricht? 2nd ed. Berlin: Cornelsen Scriptor, 2004. Print.

Meyer-Drawe, K. Diskurse des Lernens. 2nd ed. Paderborn: Fink, 2012. Print.

Meyer-Wolters, H. Koexistenz und Freiheit: Eugen Finks Anthropologie und Bildungstheorie. Würzburg: Königshausen & Neumann, 1992. Print.

Mollenhauer, K. "Aesthetische Bildung zwischen Kritik und Selbstgewissheit." Zeitschrift für Pädagogik 4 (1990a): 481–94. Print.

---. "Die vergessene Dimension des Ästhetischen in der Erziehungs- und Bildungstheorie." Kunst und Pädagogik: Erziehungswissenschaft auf dem Weg zur Ästhetik? Ed. Dieter Lenzen. Darmstadt: Wissenschaftliche Buchgesellschaft, 1990b. Print.

---. "Der Leib: Bildungstheoretische Beobachtungen an ästhetischen Objekten." Interdisziplinäre Verflechtungen und intradisziplinäre Differenzierungen. Ed. Michele Borrelli and Jörg Ruhloff. Baltmannsweiler: Schneider-Verl. Hohengehren, 1998. Print. Deutsche Gegenwartspädagogik 3.

Montessori, M. and H. Ludwig. Die Entdeckung des Kindes. Freiburg (u.a.): Herder, 2010. Print. Gesammelte Werke / Maria Montessori 1.

Morin, E. and I. Brümann. Die sieben Fundamente des Wissens für eine Erziehung der Zukunft. Hamburg: Krämer, 2001. Print.

Müller, Th. "Innere Armut: Kinder und Jugendliche zwischen Mangel und Überfluss." Innere Armut (2008). Print.

---. "Die Situation als Urgrund integralpädagogischen Handelns: Wider eine Pädagogik des Bewerkstelligens und der Perspektivität." Integralpädagogik: Wahrnehmungen im lernenden Leben. Ed. Th. Müller and R. Girg. Regensburg: Roderer, 2007. Print.

Paul, H. et al. Deutsches Wörterbuch: Bedeutungsgeschichte und Aufbau unseres Wortschatzes. 10th ed. Tübingen: M. Niemeyer, 2002. Print.

Pöppel, E. Der Rahmen: Ein Blick des Gehirns auf unser Ich. München: Hanser, 2006. Print.

Precht, R. D. Wir wählen uns alle nur selbst, 2009 38. Web. 6. May 2014. <http://www.zeit.de/2009/38/Wahlkampf>.

Pyth 2. - PINDAR, Zweite Phytische Ode. (Zitiert nach Heidegger, Martin (1987): Einführung in die Metaphysik. Max Niemeyer Verlag. Tübingen. S. 77).

Rawls, J. Eine Theorie der Gerechtigkeit. 2nd ed. Frankfurt am Main: Suhrkamp, 1988. Print. Suhrkamp Taschenbuch Wissenschaft 271.

Rombach, H. Strukturanthropologie: Der menschliche Mensch. Freiburg: Alber, 1993. Print. Alber Studienausgabe.

Schulze, G. Die Erlebnisgesellschaft: Kultursoziologie der Gegenwart. Frankfurt (Main), New York: Campus, 1992. Print. Campus-Bibliothek.

Schübl, E. Jean Gebser (1905-1973): Ein Sucher und Forscher in den Grenz- und Übergangsgebieten des menschlichen Wissens und Philosophierens. Zürich: Chronos, 2003. Print.

Seitz, K. Globalisierung als pädagogisches Problem. Web. 6. May 2014. <http://doku.cac.at/kseitz.pdf>.

Sen, A. K. Ökonomie für den Menschen: Wege zu Gerechtigkeit und Solidarität in der Marktwirtschaft. 2nd ed. München (u.a.): Hanser, 2002. Print.

Spitzer, M. (2006): Lernen. Springer Verlag. Berlin und Heidelberg.

Stenger, U. "Zum Ereignischarakter in Bildungsprozessen." Pädagogik des Performativen: Theorien, Methoden, Perspektiven. Ed. Ch. Wulf and J. Zirfas. Weinheim: Beltz, 2007. Print. Pädagogische Bibliothek Beltz.

Vogel, B. "Soziale Verwundbarkeit und prekärer Wohlstand: Für ein verändertes Vokabular sozialer Ungleichheit." Das Problem der Exklusion: Ausgegrenzte, Entbehrliche, Überflüssige. Ed. H. Bude and A. Willisch. Hamburg: Hamburger Edition, 2006. Print.

Wagenschein, M. Verstehen lehren: Genetisch - sokratisch - exemplarisch. Weinheim, Basel: Beltz, 1999. Print. 22.

Warwitz, S. A. Sinnsuche im Wagnis: Leben in wachsenden Ringen ; Erklärungsmodelle für grenzüberschreitendes Verhalten. Baltmannsweiler: Schneider Verlag Hohengehren, 2001. Print.

Westphal, K. "Lernen als Ereignis. Schultheater als performative Praxis. Zur Aufführungspraxis von Theater." Pädagogik des Performativen: Theorien, Methoden, Perspektiven. Ed. Ch. Wulf and J. Zirfas. Weinheim: Beltz, 2007. Print. Pädagogische Bibliothek Beltz.

Wilber, K. Eros, Kosmos, Logos: Eine Jahrtausend-Vision. Frankfurt am Main: Fischer-Taschenbuch-Verl., 2001b. Print. Fischer 14974 : Spirit.

---. Integrale Psychologie: Geist, Bewußtsein, Psychologie, Therapie. 2nd ed. Freiamt im Schwarzwald: Arbor, 2001a. Print.

---. Integrale Spiritualität: Spirituelle Intelligenz rettet die Welt. 5th ed. München: Kösel, 2007. Print.

Wulf, Ch. and J. Zirfas, eds. Die Kultur des Rituals: Inszenierungen, Praktiken, Symbole. München: Fink, 2004. Print.

Zimmer, R. Handbuch der Sinneswahrnehmung: Grundlagen einer ganzheitlichen Bildung und Erziehung. Freiburg: Herder, 2012. Print.

4 Variations in Learning with Ladders of Learning, teaching with MGML

The MultiGradeMultiLevel-Methodology by RIVER is requested and demanded with growing momentum since the early nineties. Chapter 3 highlights these vehement inner Indian emanations as well as MGML's international variations. Today estimated 10 000 000 Indian children in 100 000 schools) are working with the methodology. Over the time variations have been established with Activity Based Learning (ABL) probably being the most prominent one. Outside India different educational efforts have taken place, too, such as Nepalese and Ethiopian projects. Through Research Team Integral MGML has also reached Europe, primarily the southern German regions around Würzburg and Regensburg. Introducing a way of "flexible learning in diverse learner groups" MGML is regarded as an educational answer to different school reforms presently taking place. The focus, however, is put on a variable and flexible use of the Methodology taking its main principles and dimensions into consideration.

4.1 Indian and International Variations

The vehement emanation of the MGML-Methodology on the teaching culture in primary schools (1-5) is currently followed up by development projects in secondary schools (6-7 and 8-10) within the Indian school system.

The Rishi Valley Institute for Educational Resources presently works on the development of lessons and first models for these grades. Developmental teams from RIVER and also the Rishi Valley School are involved. Both facilities are currently conducting testing phases. In the course of this mainly activity-oriented procedures are developed that enable experiences in research-guided science-oriented fields. Ecological issues are consciously included in these developments. Concurrently the system of Ladders of Learning for the language segment is further elaborated and varied. This is predominantly the case for the languages Hindi and English.

The MGML-Methodology by RIVER is requested and demanded with growing momentum since the early nineties. By now the possibilities of this fully individualized school have reached numerous Indian federal states, some of which actually accomplish an extensive implementation. The vehement emanation is already perceivable in the Indian federal states of Tami Nadu, Karnataka, Kerala, Rajasthan, Chhattisgarh, Andhra Pradesh and Uttar Pradesh. Currently roughly 100 000 schools are working with and 10 000 000 children are learning with the MGML-Methodology and its Indian variations!

The strongest and systematically facilitated dissemination is discernible in the Indian federal state of Tamil Nadu. There all children in primary schools are able to fully individualized learn with a variation of the MGML-Methodology called Activity Based Learning (ABL). The initiatives in Tamil Nadu were also awarded by the Indian government. All further developments within India consider the vast regional and cultural diversity within the design of the methodology.

4.1.1 Variations in Primary Education

Since the initial Ladders of Learning were created and printed and 'School in a Box' was developed in 1993, RIVER's work has emanated within India. The MGML-Methodology was initially tested and introduced in 200 schools throughout an intensive 75-day program with the support from UNICEF and the State Education Department of Andhra Pradesh. In 1994 the methodology was tested in the Mysore district in the federal state of Karnataka and the first Tamil version was developed for the Nord-Acort district in Tamil Nadu. Additionally, the MGML-Methodology was translated into a local dialect in order to educate and school the children from deprived tribes in Paperdu in the north of Andhra Pradesh. Since 1995 the MGML-Methodology is spreading all over India and has in part extensively reached the federal states of Karnataka, Kerala, Maharashtra, Uttar Pradesh, Assam, Tamil Nadu and Rajasthan. Subsequently variations in the languages Telugu, Tamil, Kannada, Malayalam and Hindi emerged over the years.

Numerous NGOs as well as teacher training teams of the state received further education and training. This development within India is exemplified based on two federal states hereafter: the development of Activity Based Learning in Tamil Nadu on the one, and the introduction of the Sneha Bala Program in RIVER's home state, Andhra Pradesh, on the other hand.

One of the most recent developments is the creation of a ladder of learning for preschoolers. These are also nurtured at the Satellite-Schools in order to not 'lose' older girls who otherwise had to look after their younger siblings. An extensive developmental work was accomplished with the help from Anette Temper and Rabea Müller from the University of Würzburg under the guidance of Thomas Müller. One ladder of learning as well as numerous associated materials for the departments of Language, Cognition, Perception and Motor skills were successfully developed, tested and implemented.

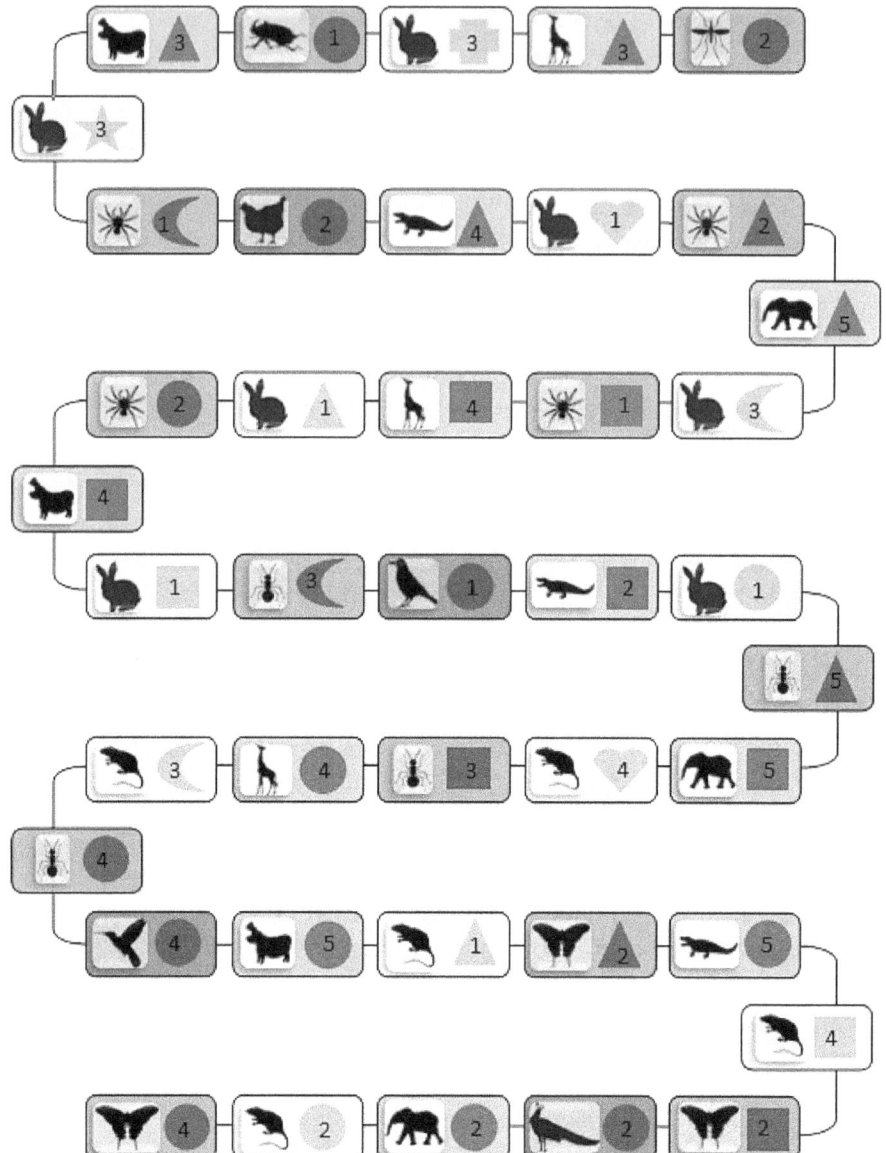

Fig. 28: The Ladder of Learning for preschool children

Activity Based Learning (ABL) in Tamil Nadu. For years the federal state of Tamil Nadu exemplified the low quality of education at school. Similar to many other Indian federal states, there was a lack of necessary infrastructure. There were too less classrooms, hardly any material, clean drinking water, no separate toilets for boys and girls as well as no possibilities for playing. Furthermore, hardly any teacher could be found in the rural areas. If some of them existed, they almost had no other option but to conduct teacher-centered lessons due their poor or non-existent education. As a result either the younger or the older pupils were neglected. The excessive demand of the few teachers combined with poor-quality equipment and low pay often enough resulted in either a no-show on behalf of the teacher, or no identification with the job, or the teacher radiating pressure and anxiety. In turn this prompted many children to stay away from school, prematurely drop out of school and leave with only rudimentary knowledge. At the end of the day this education did not suffice for learning a profession and forced many children into poverty, dependencies and menial work. Recognizing the correlations, together with the openness to execute a change in the education of teachers, adjusting the scholastic administrative apparatus and the political will as well as corresponding financial support of these processes, resulted in a radical change in schooling the children of Tamil Nadu.

The actual development of ABL started in the mid-nineties with the establishment of several schools for children who had been freed from harsh child labor. Activity-oriented material was consciously introduced in order to zero in on their attention and increase their motivation and endurance; mainly in the form of songs, games and stories. The success and the joy of this working spread like wildfire under the catchphrase of 'Joyful Learning'. Around 60 directors of schools and 7000 teachers received further training. A corresponding compendium called 'Katralil Inimai' was published with the support of UNICEF.

The first step for an extensive introduction of ABL in Tamil Nadu was undertaken by the visit of an interdisciplinary team in Rishi Valley. Results from the continued education on location were Ladders of Learning for five subjects: Tamil (language), English, Mathematics, Local History and General Knowledge as well as an artistic subject that comprised storytelling, puppet show, textile and needlework and various games. The development of these Ladders of Learning does not just constitute a variation but also a specialized expansion of the MGML-Methodology. Issues of social comparison and individual learning pace are very consciously dealt with. As a result there is a classroom with approximately 40 children spanning grades 1-4. The older children help the younger ones and the mutual support has priority instead of the social comparison.

Several millions of children from grades 1-4 learn with ABL at roughly 37.000 schools in Tamil Nadu. This work has been scientifically evaluated for the first time in 2009. Four central questions were asked:

- To which extent has ABL actually led to change in atmosphere in primary education?
- To which extent has ABL succeeded in achieving positive effects concerning the desired transformations in the village communities concerned?
- Does the inner structure of ABL actually have a positive impact on the educational level of the children?
- To which extent and how well has ABL fulfilled the intended goals concerning the scope, quality and time frame of primary education from grades 1-4?

The third question was of highest importance throughout the evaluation. All in all the positive effects of ABL could be ascertained. It became especially distinct that children from underprivileged and poverty-ridden backgrounds were able to attain equally good results as children from higher social ranks that came from public and private schools. Hence, ABL can be declared as a central key in order to bring children from socially deprived and underprivileged backgrounds and regions to the same level of education as other children. It has furthermore been determined that ABL changed the atmosphere in class from a teacher-dominated, often anxiety-inducing and scarcely activating education to a self-responsible, action-oriented and joyful learning atmosphere. This resulted last but not least in an overwhelming approval of ABL on behalf of the respective villages and communities of the children. The inner structures of ABL and its Ladders of Learning demonstrably enabled the children to develop more confidence, a heightened level of communication skills as well as intellectual flexibility.

At the same time considerable differences between individual schools were noticeable – concerning organization, learning pace and high/low classroom performance. It remains to be seen if this is due to the initial learning situation or working with ABL. At any rate did this difference entice contemplating questions concerning material for consolidation, repetition as well as broadening the scope of learning contents. The learning at one's own learning pace furthermore showed that some children had only acquired minimum fundamental skills of the 3rd grade at the end of their primary education. This can be interpreted in various ways: are these developments due to the children's level of aptitude? Do these developments come to the surface because of the work with ABL and had otherwise remained unnoticed, or are they caused by the method itself? It speaks in the quality of the evaluation's favor not to be tempted to simplistically answer these questions this way or the other. In fact it was suggested to consider them concerning slowed down learning and to observe this in correlation to individual activities on the Ladder of Learning. This has been recorded as a task for future developments. By and large the survey reaches an equally praising conclusion as the report by S. Anandalakshmy where it says: "This educational initiative could well be a forerunner for a positive change in educational standards across the country. We are now at the threshold of a silent revolution" (Anandalakshmy 2007, n.p.).

Sneha Bala in Andhra Pradesh. Compared to the development of other Indian federal states, RIVER's home state has not consequently resorted to the MGML-Methodology and its potential for the education at school for a long time. The development that was kick-started at 200 school centers by UNICEF and RIVER in 1993 did not lead to further educational development processes initially. Admittedly, in 1996 the DPEP (District Primary Education Program) was initiated which should strengthen the use of activating elements in primary education. This was followed up by the QIP (Quality Improvement Program) and the institution of lunch for all primary school children at all public schools. The government of Andhra Pradesh initiated another program called CLIP (Child

Language Improvement Program) in 2005 which tested the children in basic skills of writing, reading and the basic arithmetic operations. In 2007 CLASP (Center of Law and Social Policy) was established in order to critically evaluate CLIP. Further evaluation programs and testing procedures followed that did not change the quality of education, though. It was not until 2010 that the learning success of the children significantly increased: activity cards and Ladders of Learning were introduced for the 1st and 2nd grade under the name of Sneha Bala with the support from RIVER.

In Sneha Bala the basic structure of the MGML-Methodology is preserved. Milestones consisting of four to five learning steps are built upon each other and thus form a subject-oriented year-long Ladder of Learning. The social forms for the individual learning steps are fixed. However, Sneha Bala constitutes a shortening of the initial MGML-Methodology by not precisely differentiating the activities within a milestone. The activities for repetition as well as broadening of the educational contents were severely reduced or omitted entirely, too.

4.1.2 Variations in Secondary Education

The unusual success-story of the MGML-Methodology for primary education in India leads to developments in secondary education since 2007. The pupils that grew accustomed to being in charge of their own educational processes shall be enabled to proceed this way throughout secondary education.

The fundamental issues and challenges of an active, individual and collective learning in class in secondary education in India are similar to the ones in primary education. Secondary education is predominated by teacher-centered processes and textbook orientation, too. The accumulation of knowledge gaps has a destabilizing effect for sustainable educational processes because no corresponding opportunities of support and remedial are offered to the pupils. The teachers lack in methodical skill, an often harsh teacher-pupil relationship or also the absences of a prepared learning environment are further factors of the situation. These result in a high quota of dropouts and call for action as estimated by the RIVER-Team in its introductory descriptions for the secondary education project:

> Current scenario:
> - Learning is teacher directed and textbook based
> - The State Board textbook is content heavy but poor at developing concepts.
> - Rote learning without conceptual understanding predominates. (RIVER 2009, 1)

These factors result in a high quota of dropouts and call for action. The development of modified methodical procedures in secondary education cultures of action designed for the pupils' learning are furthered by secondary education projects that test these in corresponding model schools in Rishi Valley.

Research Team Integral had the opportunity to be on location during the past project phase and was able to gather valuable data on the design as well as the implementation via applicable field research. These findings were enhanced by multiple and extensive expert discussions with the head of the project for the development of scientific education in Rishi Valley. The following deliberations briefly delineate the principal procedures in the natural sciences. In addition to this there are also more comprehensive university thesis by teacher trainees which were initiated and supervised by Research Team Integral (Solowij 2009 and Grieb 2010).

The Rishi Valley Education Centre and the RIVER-Team work together in a project group for the advancement of the MGML-Methodology in secondary education. The project group permanently designs didactic-methodical concepts despite having few personal resources. This project group has been conceptualizing and testing activity-oriented learning arrangements for secondary school in the form of action research for more than five years. They mostly pick up on the principles of the MGML-Methodology for primary school. They consider the content-wise increased complexity of topics in class and modify the methodical arrangements for secondary education on the basis of systematized supportive analysis.

Fundamentally, an integral perception of the phenomena is taken as a starting point as well as holistically and interdisciplinary thoughts. The intended practical character in turn aims for an integral culture of action. Extensive conceptional developments and testing have already successfully been executed for the subjects of Natural Sciences, Mathematics and English.

The current valid syllabi of the respective federal states and the national curricula have to be considered for the continuation of the MGML-Methodology the same way they had to be considered for primary education. Additionally, the criteria of content related quality standards pertain in order to prepare the pupils for the final centralized examination at the end of 10th grade.

The topics for scientific classes in 'Natural Sciences' are based on the Indian standards of the 'National Curriculum Framework' from 2005 and also incorporate the quality standards of the 'State Curriculum' of the federal state of Andhra Pradesh. The concepts for grammar school seamlessly align themselves with the contents and procedures of 'Environmental Studies' (EVS) in primary school.

By way of example the following deliberations describe the developments in the scientific departments of the 6th and 7th grade. The time budget at hand encompasses 50 school weeks altogether that are listed as 30 weeks for 6th grade and 20 weeks for 7th grade. 10 lessons are schedules per week. The difference between the grades stems from the 'State Exams' that take place at the end of 7th grade. In order to prepare for these examinations additional time is needed to consolidate all contents of both grades.

The project documents of RIVER all in all describe 27 subject areas that are implemented as subject-specific topics in Chemistry, Physics, Biology and

Environmental Studies throughout the development of the project. By now the necessary MGML procedures for secondary education on the basis of the regional language Telugu were successfully tested. Almost all of the procedures are in the final design phase or are already deployed in their final design (RIVER 2009).

The materials used take subject-specific functioning, age-appropriated and proper procedures and methods into consideration. In addition the material that has been successfully implemented in primary school for years is modified and enhanced for secondary education. A list by RIVER gives an overview over the most important methods:

- Eliciting children's questions
- Pre-assessment (reviewing the child's existing knowledge in that topic)
- Information cards
- Experiments
- Data collection and field work
- Project work
- Games, stories and songs
- Glossary or dictionary
- Review material
- Assessment
- Enrichment material (River 2009, 2)

According to the topic getting started is structured by either an open dialogue that searches for questions, or experiments by the pupils, or occasions or experiences drawn from the living reality of the children and adolescents. This is often followed by multifaceted experimental situations drawn from the environment. These experiments are carried out autonomously by the pupils.

The teachers are equipped with an extensive set of round-up and support material for the highly activity-oriented procedures in scientific classes. This results in manual-like information that aims for the competence of the teachers. Special emphasis is placed on the pupils' self-agency in scientific classes, too (RIVER 2009).

The developments of the RIVER-projects have come a long way in secondary education by now. The groups of themes for scientific classes have been designed to the greatest extent. The project progression for the subjects of Mathematics and English are expedited and also supported by further interested colleagues of the Rishi Valley School.

Other project groups that are influenced by the RIVER-projects also attempt to further the changes related to the MGML-Methodology in secondary education in India.

As has been delineated in chapter 4.1.1 there is also a vehement change in primary schools related to the MGML-Methodology in the federal state Tamil Nadu that is called 'Activity Based Learning'. Project teams have introduced further developments in secondary education with the support of the comprehensive methodical-didactic skill set of the colleagues of the 'The School' of the Krishnamurti Foundation India in the context of the Indian educational initiative 'Sharva Shiksha Abhiyan, Tamil Nadu.'

In 2008 the method 'Active Learning Methodology', ALM, was developed and presented as an initial result of breaking up the teacher-centered education (www.ssa.tn.nic.in/Doku/ALM-MANUAL.pdf). It is a matter of a radically opened-up teacher-guided education that is implemented via a system of double periods. Starting from a frontal initiation of the topic, activity processes that are structured by mind maps are offered in twelve individual steps which enables the autonomous cooperation of the pupils in less than half the amount of class time. A brief participating observation on a school day at a middle school in Chennai revealed that this methodical approach innovatively breaks up the classical teacher-centered education of traditionally minded Indian colleagues and provides the pupils with activating learning processes. At the same time the teacher maintains being the general leader of the process. These results are also partially confirmed by an extensive study by Milind Brahme and Suresh Babu from the Department of Humanities and Social Sciences at the Indian Institute of Technology Madras. This study examined more than 30.000 schools in Tamil Nadu (Brahme / Babu 2011). The results allow for consequences for numerous pedagogical and organizational advancements that also refer to the general culture of action and the attitude of the teachers.

Overall the 'AML' only partially fulfills the criterions for MGML classes. However, the developments in Chennai and Tamil Nadu constitute an important step away from monotonous education and towards fully individualized educational propositions.

4.1.3 International Variations Using the Examples of Ethiopia and Nepal

The MGML-Methodology was requested by many countries all over the world. Among these are Asian as well as African and South American countries. The examples of Ethiopia and Nepal display the international importance of RIVER and the variations that stem from it.

Ethiopian Rural Education Project (EREP) Western Ethiopia has a huge demand for schools and education. Many schools were closed down or destroyed due to the Marxist regime that was in charge until the 1990s. Only about 20% of the men and far less women of the region are able to read and write.

The Ethiopian Rural Education Project is composed of a partnership between the Presbyterian Church of Susquehanna Valley in New York State, USA, and the Western Bethel Synod in Ethiopia. Prof. Thomas Scott, a participant of a mutual exchange program encouraged the establishment of a number of schools in the rural areas of Western Ethiopia.

Content-wise they went by UN Millennium Goals and kept in mind to achieve a basic literacy for boys and girls via the establishment of primary schools. Concretely all children should be able to learn at their own pace and stay in school not less than four years. Emphasis was also laid on equal treatment of the genders as well as securing economic sustainability.

A group of experts from Ethiopia developed a curriculum in cooperation with the RIVER-team in Rishi Valley in 2004 and 2006. They also created the necessary material as well as the corresponding Ladders of Learning. Two model schools were established in Western Ethiopia in 2005: one in Aleku and the other in Gaba Darbi. Both are located close to the city of Dembi Dolo. Up to that point the children of the region had no access to school education. Both schools started with a kindergarten and the 1st grade in 2006 after the developmental work with RIVER had been finished in India. From 2007 to 2009 more than 100 children visited each of the schools. Both schools were built with two classrooms that are connected via a material room in order to make the necessary material accessible for every class. All schools are equipped with their own school gardens.

A team of six men and women from RIVER ventured to Ethiopia in 2007 in order to get to know the previous developments and furthermore be able to be on hand with help and advice. A collective workshop with 21 teachers took place. Three other schools (in Dembi Dolo, Kake and Chanka) associated themselves with the EREP model. This made EREP into the trailblazer of educational developments in schools in all of Western Ethiopia. At the end of 2010 EREP's work can be stated as follows (EECMY-DASSC 2010):

1. The MGML-Methodology is implemented in two rural model schools and three further schools.
2. More than 700 children, amongst them about 200 orphans, were helped with an own AIDS program.
3. 19 wells were sunk by a water development project. About 16 000 people benefit from this.
4. A child care program was established in the communities surrounding the model schools. The program helps more than 120 orphans and affected children and supports them in their villages.
5. A hospital was established that accrues roughly 15 000 people.
6. An integrative agricultural program was started which encompasses productivity, sustainability, environment and water protection as well as the well-being of the livestock.
7. The work of EREP could be extended to the marginalized minority of the Mejengir.
8. Another primary school with now four classrooms instead of two was built.

Fig. 29: Children in Ethiopia are learning with the MGML-Methodology

'Multi-grade / Multi-class Teaching Practices' in Barabhise, Nepal. Nepal has been dealing more intensively with the question of schooling for its children of the rural mountain regions since the end of the 1980s. Likewise to many other countries with similar income and developmental structures Nepal experienced that (APEID UNESCO 1989, Aryal 2014)

- one is dealing with children that live scattered among rural regions,
- there are major differences and fluctuations in teacher training,
- many teachers are not willing to serve in remote rural areas,
- there is a major lack of teachers in the schools,
- teachers need further training in their schools on location,
- and that the educational understanding is very often not activity-oriented.

Nepal obliged to grant free and good quality access to all kinds of schooling to all children by the year. Therefore initially a number of primary schools were built in rural areas of Nepal. At the same time the engagement with the 'multi-grade/multi-class teaching' (MGT/MCT) basic arrangement, as it is called in Nepal, began. Nepal's different regions were scrutinized and analyzed in different studies according to their schooling provision, equipment, as well as applied forms of teaching by the 'Research Centre for Educational Innovation and Development' (Aryal 2014). Subsequently MGT/MCT was bit by bit introduced, practiced and implemented in schools in Nepal. As a result it became evident that the growing expansion of MGT/MCT in Nepal required to be scientifically accompanied and to be kept track of the various schools working with this approach. It became also evident that the current curriculum was oriented too much on strict subject-related content and age groups, thereby denying teaching contents at varying levels of aptitude. Hence it was decided to develop a corresponding more flexible curriculum. Furthermore it was important to lead to teachers from teacher-centered, instructional teaching to an activity-oriented teaching that would activate the pupils. This proved to be rather difficult since there was a constant lack of qualified teaching trainers and moreover since initially the teachers had issues getting to know the teaching material and realizing how to use it in a meaningful way. The induction and the emphasized autonomous energy input for the school and teaching led to the MGT/MCT not really being embraced by all teachers. In addition to that the government tried to strictly regulate applying the MGT/MCT on the basis of the current valid curriculum which led to considerable irritations and concrete problems in teaching. However, a positive development was able to be initiated with clearance of the implementation of the method according to situational circumstances.

The team from RIVER visited a region in Nepal in 2009 and initiated the deployment of MGML-Methodology in Barabhise and the surrounding area. The arisen problems that came to being throughout dealing with MGT/MCT could be overcome via a collective effort in design workshops. RIVER's cooperation with Nepal has significantly increased since 2013. Currently hundreds of schools are introduced to the MGML-Methodology and teachers are continuingly educated. Remote places and mountainous regions are especially targeted.

4.2 German Variations and the Multifaceted Quality of their Applicability

4.2.1 Developments in Primary School – selected examples

The developments in schools in Germany are currently connected to the discussion of how to deal with heterogeneity. Disregarding or neglecting heterogeneous learning groups by means of questionable forms of homogenization has by now yielded to awareness. The appreciation of the diversity and variety of the children and adolescents has intensified. Lessons are more focused on heterogeneous situations of education (Boller / Rosowski / Stroot 2007; also Bräu / Schwerth 2005; Bohl 2010).

The importance of this challenge of general educational and didactic-methodical consequences is also perceivable by looking at the regulations of the German School Award of the Robert-Bosch-Foundation by considering aspects of the "quality education" (Prenzel / Schratz / Schultebrauks-Burkhardt 2011, 9). These function as central criteria for the jury in order to assess the schools. Innovative schools are thus

- schools that found ways to productively handle their pupils different educational prerequisites, interests and performance possibilities, as well as with cultural und national heritage, gender and the educational background of the family;
- schools that effectively contribute to equating disadvantages;
- schools that continuously and methodically promote individualized learning
- schools that ensure that their pupils take the matter of learning into their own hands
- schools that enable learning that is practice-oriented and intensifies the understanding in extra-school learning spaces
- schools that continuously improve classes and the teachers' works with new knowledge (Prenzel / Schratz / Schulebrauks-Burkhardt 2011, 9)

Innovative primary schools also refer back to the extensive repertoire of the progressive educational movement in their doings. These schools thereby dynamically develop this repertoire further. Learning zones or, seen in bigger dimensions, comprehensive learning arrangements and open learning landscapes are created by learning circles and training at stations, learning mosaics, learning desks and learning workshops. Control mechanisms often come in the form of daily schedules, open or closed weekly schedules or monthly reports that guarantee the progress of the children in a systematized way.

The amount of things that schools have to implement on the level of the singular schools themselves becomes apparent when looking at the developments on the level of the general education system. Four discernible developments in primary school are attached to the preceding argumentation.

On the one hand these are the developments leading towards a 'flexible primary school' that can be perceived in the German-speaking area and also in the different federal states. At the beginning of their school education children transitioning into school from kindergarten should be allowed up to three years for taking in the content of 1st and 2nd grade. What is here requested for the initial stage of primary school is actually a necessary flexibility that needs to apply for all grades throughout the entire education, since the heterogeneity of the first two school years does not dissolve but remains an accompanying phenomenon. This flexibility over the course of five years has been granted in the MGML-Methodology for a long time.

The second prevailing task related to the education system of the primary school arises out of the so called 'small primary school'. The demoscopic change shows that especially in rural areas classes combining two grades, traditionally combining 1st and 2nd grade as well as 3rd and 4th grade, have been established. This is due to the dropping numbers of pupils. This mixing of ages which is actually encouraged by the progressive education movement, also results in different forms of learning for which the teachers require methodical-didactic support (Laging 2010).

A third issue ensues from the high level of cultural heterogeneity in classes in primary schools in urban centers. The multiculturalism in these classes strongly requires measures of fully individualized procedures in combination with community-building. Quite often more than 80 percent of the children hail from different cultural and linguistic milieus. Primary school teachers often complain that they are not able to satisfy the absolutely individual education situations of the individual children with conventional forms of teaching.

Primary school's fourth challenge is the task of an inclusive school which is to be implemented in all of Germany via a new law. A 'school for all' that should also be able to offer appropriate, competent special-needs and special educational support stretches the question of heterogeneity to its biggest dimension (Pius / Rhele 2009).

The general demand of dealing with heterogeneity and the depiction of the four current challenges of the primary school in Germany make it obvious that the MultiGradeMultiLevel-Methodology offers diverse options of action and development. These options could usefully lead to reaching the next step in quality by means of the already discovered and yet to be found forms of variations in German primary schools. The primary school in Brennberg in Upper Palatinate, Bavaria, has been having the longest experience with a self-designed variation of the MGML-Methodology. The teaching staff was inspired early on by the Indian colleagues during their first trip to Germany at an information event in 2005. However, it was decisive that a female teacher trainee was proactive. She was so inspired by her experiences in the Satellite-Schools in Rishi Valley during her study trip with Research Team Integral in 2006 that she developed a three week long sequence for Mathematics on the basis of her know-how of the MGML-Methodology and successfully tested it. This first test at a German school made it clear that the MGML-Methodology is developable and applicable in different variations. The female teacher trainee chose a learning tree as her design. She incorporated the systematized approach of the MGML-Methodology into the learning tree (Kanamüller 2006). Over the course of this thesis all materials included were meticulously developed for the practical testing and described in the following categories:

- learning and functioning objective
- description of material
- methodical information/ possibilities for variation
- possibility of control

In order to provide the children with an immediate overview over the task and also the three-week learning sequence, all materials were held available on shelves to which the children always had access. The material was organized on the shelves by a distinct and simply signaled systematization.

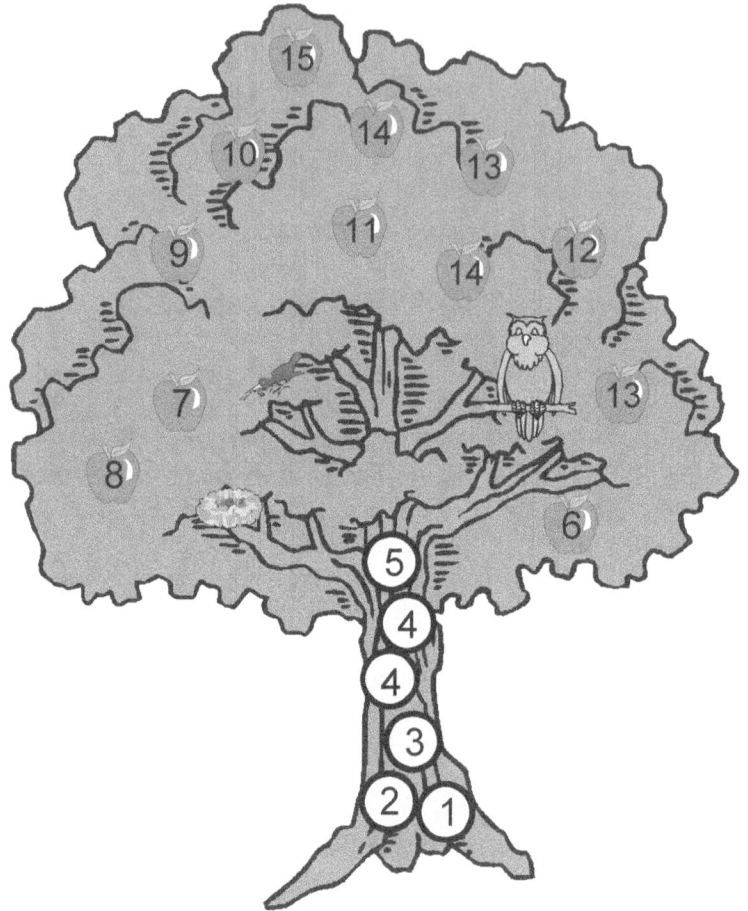

Fig. 30: First learning tree at Brennberg primary school, 2006

The colleagues at Brennberg primary school consequently picked up on the stimulus of learning trees throughout the last years and have almost entirely reorganized the education at their school according to this individualized learning by now.

Fig. 31: Material pool for the topic 'Water', 2012

Being a school experienced in sustainable teaching developments, the colleagues nowadays structure the curriculum in learning sequences of three-week to four-week units for grades 1-4. The Ladders of Learning are hereby interpreted as a succession of the learning trees. Their learning progress mostly acknowledges the systematization of the Indian milestones, though it has a more widespread layout. The learning trees serve to structure the learning processes that have to be built up throughout the year, in subject-specific sequences. The learning trees are also graphically modified into learning castles and learning snakes for the sake of variation in Brennberg. As a result arise 10-12 learning trees each that cover all educational content and skills developments designed by the syllabus.

The provision and organization of the material takes place in the classrooms. The learning arrangement is located on different shelves at the back of the classroom. It is freely accessible for everybody and systematized with symbols and furthermore serves as a prepared learning environment for the pupils. At Brennberg primary school material for individualized instruction from publishing houses, self-made material, pertinent learning games but also work and exercise books are being used. Passages that are seen as helpful are documented with their pages and continuously cited. Less useful passages of the work and exercise books are simply skipped. The steps of structure implemented in the MGML-Methodology are mostly continued in the learning trees. The setup of the learning trees considers various social forms however a systematized circulation of groups as is practice in the MGML-Methodology is not scheduled.

The children's respective work approach for an autonomous learning ensues via the overview on the learning tree where the order of possible activities in the form of compulsory tasks and enhanced optional tasks is depicted. The teacher is set free to assist and guide the learning processes of the pupils as it is the case in the original form of the MGML-Methodology in India. A big, round carpet on the floor is used as the space for an open dialogue within the class. The corresponding discussion acts for scheduling and reflection on the work and work results.

A variation of the 'Assessment Format' based on the Indian model was also used during the first implementation of the learning tree. It describes the progress of the individual children throughout the three-week testing phase of this Mathematics sequence. The teacher documents the transitions of the children from on material to another during the working processes and at a glance recognizes the overall situation within the class.

	1	2	3	4	5	6	7	8	9	10	11	12	13	14	15	🦉	🦋	☁
Alexander	20.6.	20.6.	22.6.	23.6.	23.6.	23.6.	23.6.	23.6.	29.6.	30.6.	30.6.	30.6.	4.7.	5.7.	5.7.	4.7.	23.6.	
Antonia	20.6.	20.6.	20.6.	22.6.	22.6.	22.6.	22.6.	22.6.	23.6.	23.6.	23.6.	23.6.	29.6.	30.6.	4.7.		30.6.	30.6.
Fabian	20.6.	22.6.	22.6.	23.6.	23.6.	29.6.	29.6.	29.6.	29.6.	29.6.	29.6.	29.6.	30.6.	30.6 / 4.7.	5.7.			
Iris	20.6.	22.6.	22.6.	23.6.	29.6.	30.6.	30.6.	30.6.	30.6.	30.6.	30.6.	30.6.	4.7.	5.7.	5.7.	23.6. / 7.7.	5.7.	7.7.
Jenny	20.6.	22.6.	22.6.	23.6.	23.6.	23.6.	23.6.	23.6.	23.6.	23.6.	23.6.	23.6.	29.6.	30.6.	4.7.	30.6.	30.6.	30.6.
Johanna	20.6.	22.6.	23.6.	23.6.	23.6.	29.6.	30.6.	30.6.	30.6.	30.6.	30.6.	30.6.	4.7.	4.7.	5.7.			
Julia	20.6.	20.6.	22.6.	23.6.	23.6.	23.6.	23.6.	23.6.	23.6.	23.6.	29.6.	30.6.	30.6.	4.7.	4.7. / 5.7.		4.7.	
Markus	20.6.	22.6.	22.6.	23.6.	23.6.	23.6.	23.6.	23.6.	23.6.	23.6.	23.6.	23.6.	29.6.	30.6.	5.7.			4.7.
Michael	20.6.	22.6.	22.6.	22.6.	23.6.	23.6.	23.6.	23.6.	29.6.	30.6.	30.6.	30.6.	30.6.	4.7.	5.7.	23.6. / 4.7.		
Michaela	20.6.	20.6.	22.6.	23.6.	23.6.	23.6.	23.6.	23.6.	23.6.	23.6.	23.6.	29.6.	30.6.	4.7.	4.7. / 5.7.			
Lukas	20.6.	22.6.	23.6.	23.6.	23.6.	23.6.	23.6.	29.6.	30.6.	30.6.	30.6.	30.6.	30.6.	30.6.	4.7. / 5.7.		30.6.	
Oliver	20.6.	20.6.	22.6.	22.6.	23.6.	23.6.	29.6.	29.6.	29.6.	29.6.	29.6.	29.6.	29.6.	4.7.	5.7.	4.7.	4.7.	30.6.
Sabine	20.6.	22.6.	22.6.	23.6.	23.6.	29.6.	29.6.	29.6.	30.6.	30.6.	30.6.	30.6.	5.7.	5.7.	5.7.			
Simon B.	20.6.	20.6.	22.6.	23.6.	23.6.	23.6.	29.6.	30.6.	30.6.	30.6.	4.7.	4.7.	4.7.	4.7.	5.7.			
Simon	20.6.	22.6.	22.6.	23.6.	23.6.	23.6.	29.6.	30.6.	30.6.	30.6.	30.6.	30.6.	30.6.	4.7.	5.7.		4.7.	5.7.
Tobias	20.6.	22.6.	22.6.	22.6.	23.6.	23.6.	29.6.	29.6.	29.6.	29.6.	29.6.	29.6.	29.6	30.6.	5.7.	4.7.	4.7.	4.7.

Fig. 32: Learning progress of a class in Mathematics (see Kanamüller 2006)

These processes are also documented by the children themselves when they colorize the completed stations on the available learning tree. The heterogeneity of the learning processes and the learning pace of the work process become immediately apparent via the distribution of the learning processes. Learning dynamics and also the deceleration of the learning processes become transparent for the child itself and also for the supervising teacher. The individual materials 1-15 as well as the additional tasks are cited in the following overview at the top across. The different children are cited perpendicular. The point in time of the successful handling is now stated for every child.

Unlike carried out in the MGML-Methodology at the Satellite-Schools, at Grundschule Brennberg primary school the entire learning group completes a learning tree together. The assessments necessary within the Bavarian school system are conducted after the respective learning trees are completed. Conversations with the staff at the schools conveyed that the effects of the school system become apparent since by way of grades at specific dates, normative forms of assessment have to be employed. Due to the naturally quite diverse processes of learning in the learning trees, the teachers are forced to integrate slack time for the faster working pupils and also slowing them down considering their performance dynamics. At the same time some assistance measures that are necessary for certain pupils have to be terminated as a consequence of this process of homogenization. (http://www.vs-brennberg.de/projekte/individuelles-lernen-im-mathematikunterricht)

An interesting aspect emerged in a conversation with a colleague at Brennberg primary school. Since this school deploys a weekly schedule and a learning tree simultaneously in some classes, it became evident that given free choice the children significantly preferred to work with learning trees throughout periods of individualized instruction. From this the hypothesis can be derived that children still regard weekly schedules as teacher-conducted instrument and only start to assign an ownership for themselves when working with learning trees. It is not until the learning process is executed step by step by oneself that it in terms of motivation seems to be accepted as a matter of one's own learning. This hypothesis stated here also becomes apparent in the well-tried practical situations at special-needs schools and grammar schools.

Variations of Ladders of Learning for the subject of environmental studies were first employed at Brennberg primary school in the summer of 2012. Sabine Dengler designed four milestones on the topic water covering roughly 20 lessons. These milestones were implemented in the 2nd grade as agreed with the class teacher and principal of the primary school. The topic was split up into four sub-topics, each signifying a milestone. The pupils were able to choose their starting point from three of the four. To these belonged "swimming and sinking", "our precious water" and "water as a quick-change artist". The last milestone "mixing and separating" should only be completed by the pupils after finishing the first three milestones, since the last one content-wise falls in line and builds upon the former three, respectively.

Based on the scientific centering the incorporation of appropriate experiments and research tasks constituted the biggest challenge in conceptualizing the milestones. The pupils should be introduced to working with experiments by way of working with theses milestones. They should also test the process of researching themselves: from an individually executed (small) experiment to hypothesizing to verifications and scientific clarifications. All notes were collected and documented in a 'researcher's book', a kind of process portfolio. The material necessary for the experiments and documentations were presented in a material pool at the rear of the classroom. The material pool consisted of little research boxes for every individual learning step. An introduction in how to work with the material pool preceded the work with milestones for the pupils. Important parts of the four-week long work with Ladders of Learning were round table conversations at the beginning or the end of the learning phase. In this manner the introductory conversations primarily were used for the repetition and verbalization of important phenomena and furthermore enabled the teacher to get an overview of the learning statuses of the children. The pupils were able to present manufactured products like ships in front of the plenum in the course of feedback rounds at the end of individualized instruction with the Ladders of Learning. These feedback rounds could also be used by the pupils to give feedback concerning the material and tasks, introduce improvement suggestions and further ideas or ask any remaining questions. The ritual rounded the work again and again and thus formed a framework for more open and free processes (Dengler 2012).

RIVER's directors, Padmanabha Rao and Rama Anumula, visited the Grundschule Brennberg, primary school, in 2010 and were very impressed by the developments there. Critical issues of implementing the learning trees and possible solutions for the procedures of performance assessments within the learning sequences that are structured with learning trees were discussed in conversations with the teaching staff.

The variation of learning trees is meanwhile also used at the Fromundstraße primary school in Munich. A female teacher that became experienced in the MGML-Methodology throughout a stay in Rishi Valley, India, built a wooden model in the form of a learning tree in cooperation with her colleagues at the school in Munich. The learning tree features numerous systematically aligned check marks onto which the individual symbols for the learning activities and the steps of the learning paths can be attached to. This concept of the construction of individualized learning that had been previously developed together with other colleagues at the primary school in Altenstadt offers further advantages. The children gather their next learning steps from the always new and creatively designed learning tree.

The learning tree was consciously designed with different propositions in order to provide the children a variety of different alternatives to choose from. This variation of the learning tree enables the teachers to facilitate flexible and easily modifiable learning propositions for the pupils in class. The teacher can react to a new situation on short notice and without a tremendous logistic effort and is also able to spontaneously exchange or add symbols. After some time the pupils get to know the symbols that signify the character of the learning offers and the choice of social form. Thus, it comes naturally to the pupils to structure their autonomous learning. In a conversation with Research Team Integral the female teacher stated that the children are clearly interested in being able to work with this style of education as often as possible. As it is the case in all other variations the teacher gains a surplus of time for individual support and assistance due to the autonomous working processes of the children. The variation of a learning tree which is flexibly implementable saves the teacher the time otherwise used for planning a new concept of the learning progression and enables her to immediately creatively incorporate new ideas into the learning processes.

The primary school in Loiching, Lower Bavaria, has taken to the inert logic of the MGML-Methodology with training for Mathematics and reading at an early stage, in order to more effectively implement the school's already extensive and rich material pool. There, too, it is the goal to initiate autonomous learning processes within the pupils and to make more and more systematized use of the learning material at hand. Further developmental steps were initialized via a study trip of the vice-principal to Rishi Valley. The Mathematics Ladder of Learning is currently successfully employed as 5-6 week-long sequence in the 3rd grade and is in addition tested in segments of Mathematics class in 2nd grade in the school year 2011/12. Individual working is also achieved here in connection with an open form of homework that is oriented on the respective learning and development level of the children. The stock of materials of the following Ladder of Learning is provided by already existing material for individualized instruction on the one hand and by using the school's work and text books on the other hand. The figure of the Ladder of Learning 'numbers to 1000' clearly designates goals and materials. Furthermore, the symbols for social forms and various fields of activity are used. The ascending Ladder of Learning lists 24 individual activities. The depicted plan is printed out in an eye-pleasing A3-format and then handed to the children who color and write on it while working with it. The teachers confirm the successful process with a signature in the boxes with lines.

Even the mathematics festivity, the idea of the Metric Mela, was seized on at Loiching Primary School. Mathematical learning stations were set up in the school building and in the school garden, with a special emphasis on considering all senses, in order to celebrate and playfully experience mathematics.

The reading education at Loiching Primary School has been under development for quite some time. It is kept more open within its systematics and outline, and is also oriented towards open reading periods. Here, the pupils are guided by provided work folders that include exercise sequences as has been described in a student's small study. The pupils are furthermore introduced to using a so called reading cart, which allocates the usable learning material at different spots in the school building (Siewert 2008).

The changes in the teaching culture are integrated into a systematic school development process at the primary school in Loiching, too. The school's interior design is accommodated with the teaching development and implemented as an open learning space concept. A stacked learning auditorium offers systematized mathematics material. The open library and reading space, which is arranged according to subjects, complements this arrangement. Additionally, there is a reading tree house with freely accessible computers. The school's inner learning space is extended by a newly designed exterior. Thus, the Loiching Primary School features an innovative overall concept that consciously promotes individual learning processes of children.

A high level of flexible MGML-usage becomes visible at Ilztalschule near Passau that was founded in 2010. Ilztalschule is conceptualized with progressive teaching. The small 'school for everyone' works across age groups and inclusively. The MGML-Methodology's know-how is conclusively merged with Montessori pedagogy and its learning materials. One of the two founders is a former student with Research Team Integral. She was the first to work with MGML trees of learning at Brennberg Primary School.

The school is spatially structured according to a principle of subject-specific learning rooms. These rooms are used for free working by the children at different phases of the day. There is a mathematics room, a language room and a room for cosmic education at hand.

Fig. 33: Language room of the Ilztalschule with fully systematized material pool

The material available is completely systematized in taking Montessori and MGML principles into account. Corresponding labels on the accurately organized material provide information on the systematics in all rooms. It becomes clearly perceptible that the contents of the primary school curriculum are interpreted with attractive learning provisions and are offered as an immensely competent and clearly designed prepared learning environment. However, the children work without Ladders of Learning at the Ilztalschule. Instead, it is an entirely open and free process to which the children can turn to. It is not until the teachers' post-documentation of the children's workings that the simultaneously existing linearity of the learning progress becomes clear. This makes it a deconstructed variation of the MGML-Methodology that comes into existence via the type of the prepared learning environment and the children's open processes. To have an overview of the existing material and its structures, the two principals have designed so-called learning maps. The latter shows possible learning sequences and their relatedness to others in form of nets.

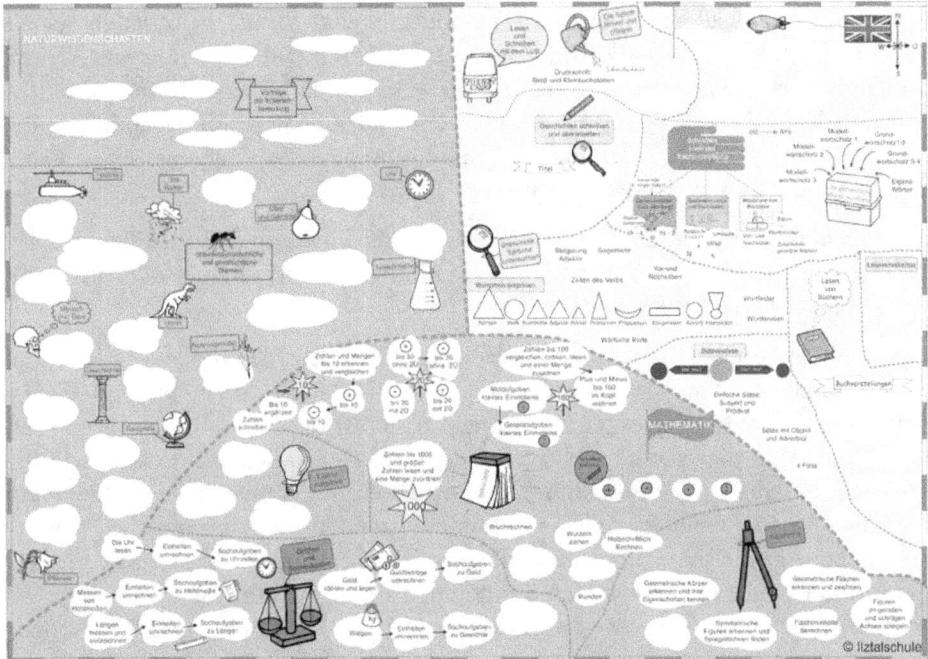

Fig. 34: A learning map at Ilztalschule

The high quality of the educational processes at this school is known in the entire region by now. Students of the Universities of Regensburg and Passau come to sit in classes, offer compact courses for the university and support students in understanding flexible learning. It is also remarkable that the principal of a public primary school has asked for all of her colleagues to sit in on classes for one day each, in order to become encouraged to accompany the children's autonomous learning by means of appropriate learning arrangements.

Meanwhile numerous subject areas have been quintessentially processes by the conception of individual milestones. This has been done with teachers through the workshops with teacher trainees and the students' theses. The subject areas include German, Mathematics as well as Local History and General Knowledge, Art, Music and Science. In the process the students work together in subject teams in order to support each other while conceptualizing the milestones. Thereby, they make use of their team's immense creative potential. Even second-semester students succeed in conceptualizing fully individualized learning arrangements and skillfully create the necessary material for that.

Thus, attractively designed conceptions for language acquisition were created. The year-long Ladder of Learning was hereby represented by an oversized sunflower. The individual petals and their segments provide the milestones in accord with the MGML-Methodology.

The material is consequently distinguished by color according to its categories. Symbols continue the furthermore differentiated organization of the tasks and explain activity characteristics and meaningful social forms. In order to secure the learning results, evaluations are included in small and large intervals. These evaluations also consequently continue the RIVER-Team's essential requirement to make the tasks small, joyful, meaningful and manageable. In addition, the working and exercising elements consider multi-sensory reading and enable creative processes via constructive tasks.

In the meantime more than 25 academic theses have been written for the primary level in which teacher trainees engaged in certain topics of primary education and also extensively documented the process.

The practical concepts, documentations and testing lead to the conclusion, that teacher trainees and student teachers are actually able to implement the MGML-Methodology of high-quality in primary schools on the basis of the valid curriculum, after they have been thoroughly and systematically introduced to the MGML-Methodology. In assisting the teacher trainees' theses, Research Team Integral was also able to draw more conclusions for the training of teacher trainees concerning the conduct, and dealing with heterogeneous learning groups. These findings are nowadays already included in the introductory workshops on the MGML-Methodology. Research Team Integral thus actively follows their Indian colleagues' principle of 'Action Research' in its own project process and in doings so creates a learning process in which students, teachers and academics form a learning community in order to sustainably and concreatively construct and map out the developmental process in primary schools.

4.2.2 Developments in Secondary Education – selected examples

The sector of secondary education also displays multifaceted interpretations and variations of working with Ladders of Learning. Currently there are comprehensive practical experiences for the department of middle and high schools. These documented experiences are in the following presented in detail.

Experiences in Middle School. Colleagues at the Winthirplatz middle school in Munich provided experiences that are consequently oriented towards the traditional structure of Ladders of Learning as it is set by RIVER. Ladders of Learning for working with multicultural learning groups could be implemented in secondary education level I via several German-Indian advanced education measures by an interested group of teachers. The learning process in the linguistically and culturally challenging heterogeneity of language learning assistance classes is successfully structured by a design of Ladders of Learning.

An already existent language course was therefore transformed into a linear milestone. Linked to that, the existent course was also deconstructed into individual activities – according to the learning steps on a Ladder of Learning. The appropriate material for the learning activities of the course were geared to the learning activities as well as pragmatically and quickly applicable designed. The classroom was rearranged by the teacher into working areas with learning stations and decentralized learning areas for the usage of different social forms, while considering multimedia support systems. A motivated learning attitude can quickly be achieved in this learning group which features extremely different levels of learning and performance. Every adolescent is able to find a learning activity that corresponds to his level and that is at his currently possible learning pace, which will increase later on (http://www.kompetenz-interkulturell.de/userfiles/Sprachfoerderung/Lernleiter-HS_Winthirplatz.pdf.).

Several further elements of RIVER's work are successfully offered at the middle school in addition to the testing in the department of German as a second language. Among other things, there is also a mathematics gala that is regularly held. There the pupils measure people and objects, document measurements and weights and work on complex reality-linked calculations. All this fittingly takes place during Christmastime and according to the rules and regulations of a Metric Mela. The definite implementation of this gala at Winthirplatz Middle School is described in an individual passage in more detail.

Experiences in High School. An increased level of heterogeneity has not only become common at primary and middle schools, but also at high schools. The pupils' diversity concerning performance levels has been negated at high schools for a long time. Pupils were simply selected away to other schools. Declining numbers of pupils as well as a reinforced emphasis onto the orientation on the child are gradually leading to a more open form and interpretation of education and lessons.

Here the MGML-Methodology offers ideal opportunities. Differentiated learning propositions within the milestones open up the possibility to adjust the learning options regarding the learning pace, level of requirements or the type of learning. Every pupil embarks on his own path in the process within the milestone. He can decide for himself when he needs a break and is thus able to follow his individual rhythm of concentration and relaxation phases. The same could also be possible for the choice of the working place, if the tasks left room for several options or allowed for the working place to be freely selectable. The Werner-von-Siemens-Gymnasium in Regensburg regards the establishment of sequences of individualized instruction as the focal point of its educational and pedagogical endeavors. For this reason the high school established an individualized instruction project in the school year of 2010/11. The project took place in selected classes of the 5th grade and targeted periods of open education in the subjects German, Mathematics and English for at least on 45 minute long lesson per week. This practice was continued in the school year 2011/12 and furthermore expanded with four new classes of 5th graders.

The initial extensive work with Ladders of Learning took place in 6th class during the first quarter of the school year 2011/12. At first, parts of the first units of the text book were reinterpreted into a milestone. In the following the entire second unit was designed and implemented as a four-week long learning sequence. This took place in the context of a thesis that was simultaneously crafted by Grimm (2012).

Whereas the curriculum for five school years has been systematized in India the teachers at Werner-von-Siemens-Gymnasium aim at combining individualized and teacher-centered forms of education. A teacher wanted to transform a longer teaching sequence into working with milestones with a class of 6th graders mentioned above. Therefore the second unit, which is laid out for 16 periods, was divided into three differently colored or usable milestones. These were called 'Around Town', 'Ghost Stories' and 'Past Progressive'.

The topic 'talking about buildings /institutions' is at the center of the milestone 'Around Town' (Grimm 2012, 71-130). Apart from the content this also aims at improving the pupils' communication skills in the oral department. As shown in the overview, the milestone's design was chosen in order to initially let the pupils acquire the necessary vocabulary, practice the pronunciation and apply it in context via a linear learning sequence including several introductory steps and tasks. In order to keep the respective tasks small and manageable, the introductory tasks are divided into meaningful sub-areas and are initially individually handled before a complex combination ensues. The learning success is then reviewed by means of an evaluation, before a freely selectable proposition of assistance or extension, respectively, can be treated.

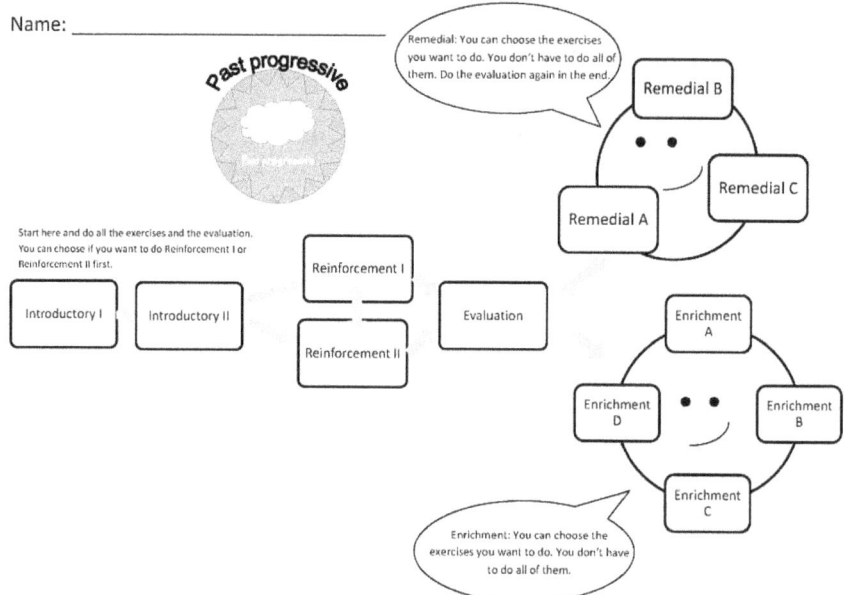

Fig. 35: Milestone 'Past Progressive'

This set-up slightly differs from the one that was just described above: the two introductory subcategories within Introduction I and II are only then followed up by a period of working out and enlarging upon which actually provides a choice concerning the order of handling the tasks. The set-up for the amplification and assistance, respectively, is the same as in the milestone 'Around Town'.

The third milestone called 'Ghost Stories' arose out of the need for a subject area that is open enough to cover the upcoming featured vocabulary of the unit as well as the structure of 'would like sth./ would like to do sth.'. Here the emphasis is on vocabulary work and listening-comprehension exercises for the pupils (Grimm 2012, 42). The higher volume of remaining words results in a larger amount of introductory tasks and a multi-path structure, respectively. This structure supports the smooth process of working with Ladders of Learning due to offering a variety of possibilities for starting points for the pupils as well as rendering the process easily manageable and able to differentiate. Jams or periods of waiting at the material pool and the supply of quantities of duplicate copies of the material, respectively, are generally sidestepped in this way. Moreover, the pupils are conveyed the feeling that it is more often their choice decision to make. This usually has a motivating effect and trains their scheduling skills at the same time.

The selection of types of tasks was done according to criteria set by the teacher. The selection represents didactic deliberations and hence preferably ideally initiates and accompanies the children's learning processes. Concerning the vocabulary work, for example, a specific emphasis was put on considering different types of learning as well as including all senses. Speech and writing should be established and the word should appear in context. The characteristic of joyful learning should materialize in manifold ways within the exercises.

Besides the conception of the milestones as well as the elaboration of the material, the presentation of the material proposal and an adequate configuration of the learning space had to be reflected about. A unique spatial concept was developed for the activity with Ladders of Learning and the pupils were prepared for the changeover prior to the beginning and for the recurrence at the end. Purposeful and free, comfortable working that is supported by rules and rituals can only happen with high-quality in a decentralized arrangement of working possibilities, a selected place for the teacher and a clear presentation of the materials. Intense working at the same time requires the possibility of occasional relaxation. Therefore a small retreat and relaxation area has been installed in the learning room.

The initial skepticism if such an extensive rearrangement of the classroom at the beginning of every period of individualized instruction was not too time consuming could be rapidly dissipated in the field. It becomes apparent that it is only possible to work at a high level and with corresponding concentration in a learning environment if it takes the various social forms like individual work, working with a partner and in group into account and makes good on all methodical requirements. The entire rearrangement process took less than a minute since the pupils were explicitly instructed in the matter and so every pupil swiftly knew which piece of furniture had to be transported to its new location by whom.

Referring to the Indian model, a support system has also been integrated into the Ladder of Learning project which on the one hand serves to relieve the teacher, on the other poses an incentive to work for the pupils and also provides an opportunity for learning by teaching. In order to identify the King of Learners the title 'King of the Day' as well as a button with the logo of the current phase of the lesson's milestone is awarded after a final look at the performance throughout the milestone.

The paradigm shift was initiated for the teacher by the conscious establishment of a 'new place' within the learning events (Grimm 2012, 66). It becomes easier to restrain oneself and become an unobtrusive companion if the place and the obligation that comes with it is being defined prior to the new kind of lessons. During this learning unit the new perception of the role should initially manifest itself with the teacher not roaming the classroom controlling the pupils, but getting information about the pupils' processes and constantly offering them her help. She dedicates more responsibility for their working to the pupils and remains seated at her table, that is, not without keeping bright eyes on the events and documenting anything remarkable for a later feedback phase. Thus, it is on the pupils to learn to realize when they need help and getting that help from the teacher at her table. The high probability that individual pupils will not be able to immediately implement the new rules concerning the way of working and will use their 'newly found' liberties for different purposes, or will go about things the 'wrong' way, is willingly accepted. These way pupils learn by experience but are also confronted about their behavior at a later stage and are asked to comment on it in a one-on-one conversation or a full assembly. This can be perceived as patronizing but is absolutely necessary for two reasons. Firstly, it becomes transparent that the children are responsible for their actions and they have to justify them. Secondly, it conveys that the teacher is interested in working during individualized instruction and also consequently demands this. The seriousness of open learning is further emphasized.

The establishment of circuit phases has stood the test for working with Ladders of Learning as well as all forms of open learning. Thus shorter or longer conversations in the full assembly or a circle can take place at the beginning or the end of a working period, in which all are gathered looking eye to eye. This acts an element that strengthens the group but also offers the opportunity to address a variety of things that should be coordinated, organized or acknowledged. During the introduction stage of working with Ladders of Learning the morning circle has the essential function to serve as a space and slot for the introduction of the method and all its relevant aspects of its procedure.

The circle provides for this to happen step by step. Here rules and rituals are established just like symbols or the structures of processes are.

Circles at the beginning and the end assume motivational roles throughout the course of the learning unit. Individual pupils can be asked at the start of the activity what they plan to do for the respective lesson and report at the end how they succeeded and discuss with the other pupils why this was not the case simultaneously. The observational aspects from individualized instruction may help the teacher to specifically choose pupils for that. It can be pupils that present 'best practice' to the others or pupils that can be supported in their further development by learning groups.

Contemplative circles in the form of circles at the end are further used a disciplinary elements with the teacher signalizing which processes she has witnessed in the classroom and how she estimates these.

Furthermore, these conservations provide an excellent opportunity to receive feedback from the pupils on topics, conceptions and the work climate. This way the pupils are being taken seriously and instantly involved in optimization process. Experience has shown that the pupils contribute a lot of good ideas that considerably enhance the quality of the material. Moreover, this also implicitly and explicitly addresses the deeper motivations for open learning and everybody gets to identify with it.

The provided achievements in the open form of working with Ladders of Learning can be evaluated and estimated on several levels. The associated steps can be fanned out into a diagnosis of the learning level and procedures of assessment and performance evaluation (Grimm 2012, 69).

The evaluation, in the sense of a validation of the learning level, that ensues after the enrichment phase can be conceptualized as a small test or game in which the pupils assess their performances themselves and are able to close gaps themselves by means of additional material. The pupils' current learning progress is documented on the available interpretation of the Ladders of Learning by coloring the respective task boxes on the overviews of the milestones that are handed out to every child as a worksheet. These three sheets are filed away by the children in their individualized instruction folders which remain openly accessible in the classroom. The folders offer the teacher the possibility to regularly inspect the progresses. Since the pupils are only then handed an overview of the milestone by the teacher when they actually start to work with it, an approximate view of the heterogeneous processes of the pupils is revealed. In addition to that opportunities for an unsystematic validation of the level of knowledge unfold again and again throughout the working progress in the context of teacher-pupil conversations that come about when the child approaches the teacher's table for handling certain tasks. The exact path of learning taken becomes comprehensible for the teacher, at the latest, at the completion of the milestone since the individualized instruction folder is reviewed and all tasks are briefly discussed together during the presentation of the 'King of the Day' title.

After finishing the learning sequence a test for the whole class is also possible and imaginable. Alternatively the opportunity arises to get the material collected and arranged in portfolios by the pupils. These can be judged upon previously set criteria. For this specific example at first a class test was used and in the following milestone the validation of the portfolios was deployed to a huge success.

The pupils were overall very satisfied with working with Ladders of Learning and throughout valued this form of working positively. They predominantly referred to the workflow being easily comprehensible due to its well-structured nature. Furthermore, the pupils mentioned that the new spatial concept considerably facilitates and supports the process of tasks.

It will be interesting to observe how working with Ladders of Learning is pursued at the school. Among other things, working with Ladders of Learning in Mathematics concerning fractions for a 6th grade class was provided and tested in the context a thesis in the school year of 2012/13.

Metric Mela. The idea to organize a mathematics gala themselves came about after parts of the teaching staff from Winthirplatz Middle School, Munich, had been on a study trip to Rishi Valley. Since 2008 the German Metric Mela has become a staple of school life and is annually held around Christmastime. The integrated primary school also participates and the school's doors are also opened for parents and visitors. In 2012 there will be jubilee mathematics gala in celebration of the centennial of the school's existence because that year also marks the 5th year since the German Metric Mela was launched.

The mathematics gala is run and organized for 500 schoolmates by 9th graders. Tasks around mathematics are presented in a Christmas context at stations. The gala takes place in the gymnasium. Due to the size of the hall and the amount of participants every 45 minutes three new classes pass through the stations together. Teams of 9th graders are responsible for running one station each. Participating pupils and teachers are handed a control slip at the entrance of the mathematics gala for an overview of the various stations. These feature everyday life issues such as guessing weights and sizes, respectively, while using the human body as a tool for measurement etc. Goals for the mathematics gala are:

- promoting taking delight in mathematics
- enticing all senses
- making everyday life issues tangible
- playfully presenting learning content
- strengthening the school spirit
- experiencing individual learning in an action-oriented way

The teaching staff coordinates and oversees the progress of the project. The Metric Mela held in southern India provided the blueprint that has been developed into an own logistics and structure of procedure. Meanwhile the mathematics gala has also taken place at different schools in Munich and is even getting more popular with schools all over Bavaria. These schools appreciate the joyful way of encountering mathematics with fun and in a celebratory fashion. The colleagues in Munich share their knowledge in continued educations to make sure that this event will also be successful. Even the newspaper Süddeutsche Zeitung published a report on the mathematics gala and the Institute for the Quality of Schools and Educational Research included it into its guide to intercultural learning called 'Kompetenz Interkulturell' (http://www.kompetenz-interkulturell.de/index.php?Seite=434).

4.2.3 Developments in Special-needs Schools – selected examples

Variations of the MGML-Methodology have been deployed in different special-needs schools in Bavaria since 2007. In some special-needs the methodology is used in primary education for children with the special-needs emphasis on the subjects German and Mathematics. The actual difference is that here variations are developed and deployed that rely more on worksheets instead of the material pool. Existent special-needs material is usefully included. Corresponding workings are also happening at St. Vincent-Schule – a school for children with behavioral disorders. This is a school for educational support that is located in Regensburg. It teaches German and Mathematics for grades 1-4 according to the curriculum for primary education in Bavaria.

Fig. 36: A pupil learning with her Ladder of Learning at St. Vincent-Schule, school for children with behavioral disorders

Some topics from the subject EVS have also been arranged in the form of Ladders of Learning. Existent text and work books were cut up and its contents were rearranged in folders in a sensible way. These now make up the pool which the children use to work with individually differentiated Ladders of Learning. The implementation of the MGML-Methodology was also tested at a special-needs center for intellectual development – mainly in art.

Further Master theses within in the context of disability and the MGML-Methodology have been written since 2011. Especially the challenges brought to the forefront by the UN-Convention on the Rights of Persons with Disabilities and the inherent task to realize an inclusive school system led to an increased demand of the MGML-Methodology. Several counties in the federal state of Bavaria have indicated their interest. Furthermore, several hundred teachers for children with special educational needs were introduced to and further educated in the MGML-Methodology during basic workshops by Dr. Thomas Müller at the University of Würzburg. A variety of special-needs schools are currently testing variations of the MGML-Methodology in Language and Mathematics, especially in the special-needs department of learning.

On studying the development in individual special-needs schools it becomes possible to make out various positive effects that are especially frequent and impressive with children that are slacking, frustrated with school and are displaying behavioral problems (Müller 2012a; 2012b; Schnur / Müller 2013): The linear structure of Ladders of Learning, whose artwork allows the children to detect a direction, creates security and orientation – something that truly caters to children displaying behavioral problems who are ambivalent or insecurely bound. However, also children with learning impairments strongly profit from this structure. At the same time the possibility to work at one's own pace and not be forced to go along with the allegedly uniform pace of the class is consciously kept open. Certainly, other forms of open learning and education like weekly schedules, for example, display similar structural elements. As distinguished from that working with Ladders of Learning not only depicts the assigned tasks on a map but (1) it renders the learning content discernible as a purposeful learning process for the children through its immanent analytical structure in a didactically sensible sequence of steps. Moreover, (2) the children experience all tasks in a larger (school year-long) context. It should be added that it is not about a schedule that, although autonomously, has to be handled within a certain amount of time, but (3) that every step can be taken in one's own learning pace. Ladders of Learning are predominantly graphically presented. The feature a direction and a goal and thus create an idea as well as an outline for one's own development. 'I am actually progressing forward' is the central fundamental experience at that, which is especially undergone and expressed by children who have experienced failure at school and biographically and therefore display signs of frustration and behavioral problems: the visualization of one's own learning trajectory positively opposes the multiple experiences of termination and failure within the family and in mainstream schools. The Ladders of Learning clearly show that they are actually progressing. Especially children that display learning impairments due to social neglect and ambivalent bonding experiences, experience the positive demand of responsibility as well as the appreciation of their own development via the autonomous progress on the Ladders of Learning. This is an experience that many of these children were yet to make in their learning biography.

In India the children are able to gather not only the content and the corresponding learning activity but also the connection with the social form from every step on the Ladder of Learning. As a result, they learn to work together with other children in different situations of support and further receive the assistance that they individually require or that the learning content demands. A rotation via various social support systems like this is not possible in the department of special-needs schools or has not been materialized up to now. Merely partner work has been incorporated as a social form. On the one hand the sizes of the classes are too small in order to work with four to six social forms. On the other hand the social challenge would be too much for many children and hence push them to their limits or come into conflict with them. By the same token working with Ladders of Learning without a system of rotation does not exclude social learning. Children are able to learn that everyone in the community of the class has his or her own task. This results in a comparative but not competitive behavior. For many children with special-needs this constitutes liberation from a biographical fundamental experience of competition in which they often had to assert themselves in their families and in school. Not having to competitively assert themselves in class essentially contributes to the children's easing as well as experiencing relief by working at one's own learning pace. In addition to that systems of experts were numerously established in which individual pupils, figuring as so-called 'supporter children', are at the other children's command. The success at that is remarkable.

For the mostly rural situation in India the Ladders of Learning were designed in a way that the children who cannot attend class due to harvest season, religious holidays or other occasions, can pick up their learning process wherever they had to discontinue it. This way it cannot happen that the children miss the continuity of the class since they generally proceed at their own pace. Thus a high rate of drop-outs among pupils could be eradicated. In regard to working with children with special-needs this structure has the effect that the children are able to 're-embark' in the case of conflicts and crises after these were resolved and handled. This furthermore provides that remedial pedagogical work for the individual child's personal and social development can materialize beyond the classroom and during class since neither the teacher nor the pupil has to fear that the affected child might miss the connection.

Within the MGML-Methodology the instruction to work on a task comes from the graphical form of the Ladder of Learning. The pupils locate themselves and via the structure of symbols autonomously gather which task has to be worked on with which material and which social form. Ultimately the pupils instruct themselves to commence with the upcoming task. Several years of experience in the department of special-needs schools have shown that even children who display refusing of school and performance are very eager to work with Ladders of Learning. What is more: they outright demand this type of work. This exceptional strong dynamic is for one thing certainly attributable to the case that children are able to perceive themselves within their own learning development. For another thing they are responsible for controlling their learning processes. Especially children displaying behavioral problems often had very ambivalent or traumatic experiences with adults. Therefore it can be assumed that it will pose difficulties for them again and again to receive education instructions by adults. They might experience themselves at it at the mercy of the adults on an emotional level and hence react warily. This might lead to a refusing demeanor or other conflicts. Instructions that can be given to children displaying behavioral problems by themselves and that also impartially speak from the matter are thus exceedingly effective.

4.3 The MGML-Methodology's flexibility in its International Importance

Ladders of Learning and the MGML-Methodology have been consciously used for classes not only in India but also beyond that for several years now. For one thing, this emphasizes the methodology's global importance. For another thing, the methodology turns out to be a flexible and versatile form of teaching classes for heterogeneous learning groups that ideally takes individual and concreative learning into consideration. In passing on the MGML-Methodology it has always been important for RIVER to regard the methodology as a recommendation and leave space for an adaption concerning the specific regional and cultural, national and international necessities. The required 'ownership' of the users is only permitted with such an approach. By appropriating and interpreting and being able to modify the methodology a strong personal connection is originated, which in turn only now enables a successful establishment in the long run.

A look at the existing variations offers a vast range of variations. One of Research Team Integral's research tasks is currently to collect and document the various versions. These are also individually analyzed concerning their basic principles, and ordered according to their different structures. Prior to describing the specific variations of Ladders of Learning in detail there will be an overview of the existing fundamental forms and variations that have emerged and developed in the examples thus far.

4.3.1 Best-Practice-Examples

Ladders of Learning are being used in urban as well as in rural contexts at public and private schools; the extent of the usage ranges from a complete educational form up to a methodical implementation in partial sequences. Due to their

148

conception Ladders of Learning are especially suitable for multi-grade and across-ages learning groups; however, Ladders of Learning also decisively alter working in more homogeneous classes since they individually consider all learning peculiarities immediately and at all times. So far Best-Practice-Examples could have been documented

- at public schools on preschool and primary level
- at the level of secondary education (grades 5-10)
- at special-needs schools for children with learning difficulties, behavioral disorders, children from difficult social contexts or children with developmental delay
- in cooperation classes and inclusive learning groups
- as learning sequences for German as a foreign language or German as a second language beginners' and advanced level
- as a structuring support element at progressive schools (e.g. Montessori schools)
- within the transformation to pedagogy for 'street children'

4.3.2 A Change in Approach: From Teaching to Learning

The essence of working with Ladders of Learning is the conscious paradigm change: departing from teaching and imparting and moving towards enabling and allowing learning. For this to happen, the processes of the learners, the children and adolescents, have to be the main focus of the education. Therefore learning propositions in small steps and action-oriented learning material is needed. Conventional text books and exercises that usually depict the curriculum can be used for this however new functions in new contexts are assigned to them. This constitutes a fundamental change of their usage in classes. The contents of text books have to be disassembled in partial units according to the conception of a Ladder of Learning, and reassembled according to the structure of the milestone. In the process these contents are categorized, analogous to the learning steps for the milestone, as material for the introduction, reinforcement, evaluation, remedial or enrichment. In terms of content the learning goal stays the same. By contrast, lessons are provided differentiated, activity-oriented and fitted for pupils' individual learning process.

4.3.3 Types of Ladders of Learning

A pivotal research finding from screening and systematizing the existing Ladders of Learning has been the documentation and abstraction of the concrete examples at hand into various types of Ladders of Learning and variations in combination. The Indian original version initially features two types of Ladders of Learning: on the one hand there is the linear arrangement of the curriculum's content for the subjects Mathematics and Mother Tongue. Here it is the child's task to follow the serial guidance through the material – at its own pace.

Fig. 37: Basic layout of a linear Ladder of Learning

The Ladder of Learning is thematically centered and systematically laid out for the departments of natural and social sciences (Local and General Knowledge and Biology and History respectively). This provides a multitude of content-related starting points and options on the topic for the child. This pursues two goals: for one thing the high degree of decontrolling should enable a joyful, meaningful and manageable learning with material for the children; for another thing the learning arrangement represents various views on the topic. This facilitates the buildup of a complex network of knowledge of action, instead of isolated segments.

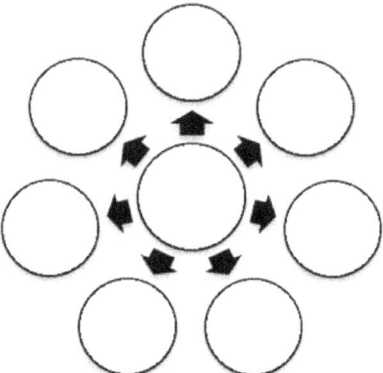

Fig. 38: Basic layout of a systemic Ladder of Learning

The two completely different structures of Ladders of Learning can naturally be combined and elaborated in linear Ladders of Learning with systemic branching, for example. A strictly linear beginning in the introduction and an ensuing diversified systemic reinforcement is also possible. In the example concerning creative approaches to dealing with poems this is followed by a linear evaluation and a systemic branching into remedial and enrichment.

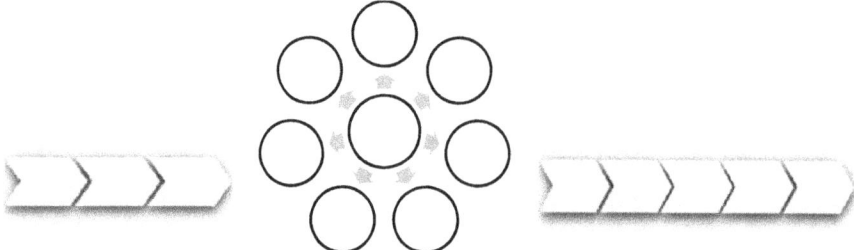

Fig. 39: Two possible combinations within the basic layout

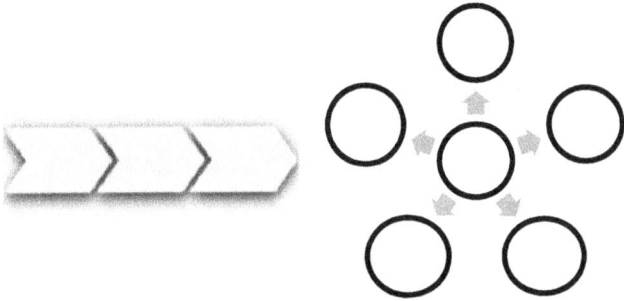

Fig. 40: A linear Ladder of Learning with parallel segments

4.3.4 Components for the Preparation of Material

Ladders of Learning can not only be distinguished concerning their typology but also concerning the provided material. Thereto three main elements can be identified at first. These can in turn be used individually or in various combinations.

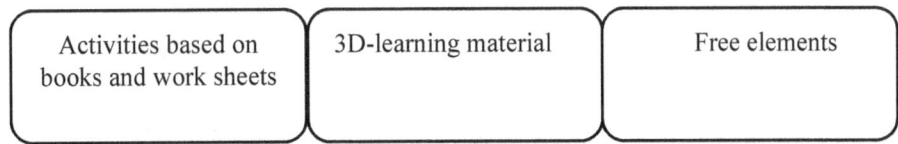

Activities based on books and work sheets | 3D-learning material | Free elements

Fig. 41: Exemplary components for the preparation of material

Activities based on books or worksheets. As a stimulus text books and teaching guides can serve as idea generators and didactic fund of material for the conception of Ladders of Learning. For this to happen the text books and teaching guides have to be deconstructed and incorporated into the Ladder of Learning as components. Like this, for example, reading and working with a passage from the corresponding workbook may constitute a learning step within the milestone. Old text books are also cut up and newly rearranged into components in India. This way they become part of the learning proposition within plentitude different activities that are combinable with each other. Worksheets often support phases of exercising or are used to substantiate the learning content during reinforcement.

151

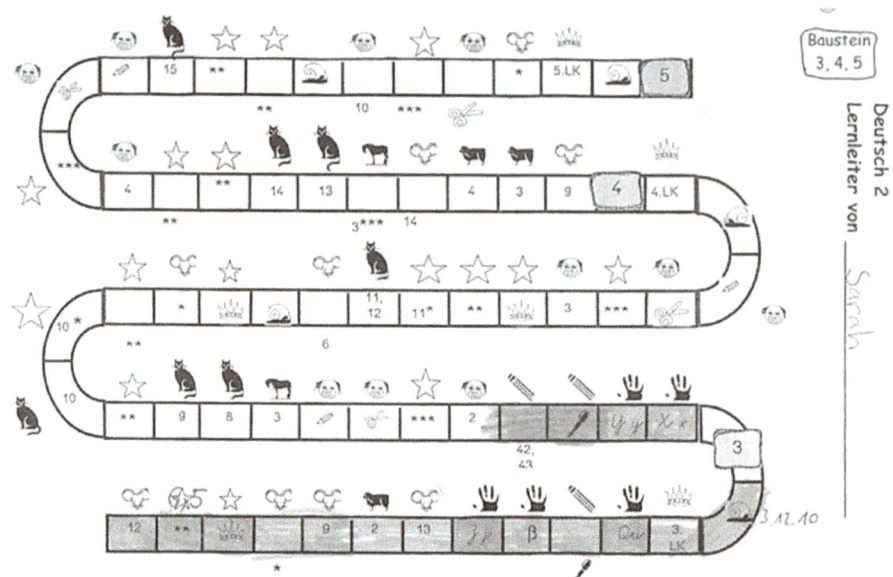

Fig. 42: The symbols represent textbooks and workbooks as well as worksheets

This 2-D material is often used for getting started with working with Ladders of Learning in order to provide an initial, easy and quickly manageable version of a Ladder of Learning for the deployment. These materials are - due to the material criteria 'joyful' and 'meaningful' – as quickly as possible substituted or enhanced with material that appeals to different sensory channels and is more activity-oriented. It is usually not until then that the regional, cultural and personal context of the school is being considered within the learning material.

Three-dimensional learning and working material. Today there is a huge variety of three-dimensional learning and working material that stems from the long experience of progressive pedagogy – especially from the stimuli of Maria Montessori. This material is designed in order to guide and assist the children in their individual learning processes and constructions of knowledge. Especially Montessori-material offers a broad range of aesthetic, clearly structured, solution-intrinsic working material for Mathematics, Mother Tongue and Cosmic Education. Due to their high level of action-orientation and training of the senses, the already systematized propositions with its attractive, durable material that is easy to handle, can serve as a real asset to working with Ladders of Learning. Past experiences show that it is very easy to integrate these propositions into the system of the MGML-Methodology and that they make joyful learning available for the children.

Open elements / open Ladders of Learning. Beyond any form of materialization Ladders of Learning may also contain open components that are filled with fitting content by the children and adolescents themselves. Thereby the children and adolescents can choose the fitting content from a selection, or even absolutely freely. This way Ladders of Learning endorse individual processes of scheduling and step by step help the pupils to organize their work themselves, in order to be able to act and learn completely on their own responsibility as young adults. The process of passing on the responsibility is gradually designed and ultimately goes from pre-structured phases by the teacher to the transfer to the pupil, who is able to use the Ladder of Learning as a year-long logbook or learning diary or open year-long work schedule. Therewith his workings are regularly documented over the course of the school year and can be contemplated and modified, if necessary, with the teachers and tutors.

On primary level the individual blank spaces that leave room for content freely chosen by the pupil can be precursors for this. Here the pupil picks something from a learning counter and fills the learning step with content himself. Alternatively, pupils can also use the structure of Ladders of Learning for planning and preparing, in terms of content, a trip, an excursion, or a small project. It is also on the cards that the pupils, especially on the level of secondary education, thematically fill the structure of one or several milestones of the Ladder of Learning. The material can stem from a material pool or from the pupil's own research. This is conceivable up to weekly, monthly and ultimately entire school year schedules. Then the year-long ladder functions as a plan of structure for the learning path of the individual pupil. Here the pupils autonomously fill the learning path step by step themselves while the teacher provides advice and counseling. The learning path can be contemplated and evaluated as a documentation of the learning at the end of the year.

The design of the Ladders of Learning is very flexibly and individually interpretable considering the components in terms of content, as well as the possibilities of material. Three-dimensional material can be combined with worksheets and open elements within one Ladder of Learning – depending on the demand in the class and the teacher's creativeness.

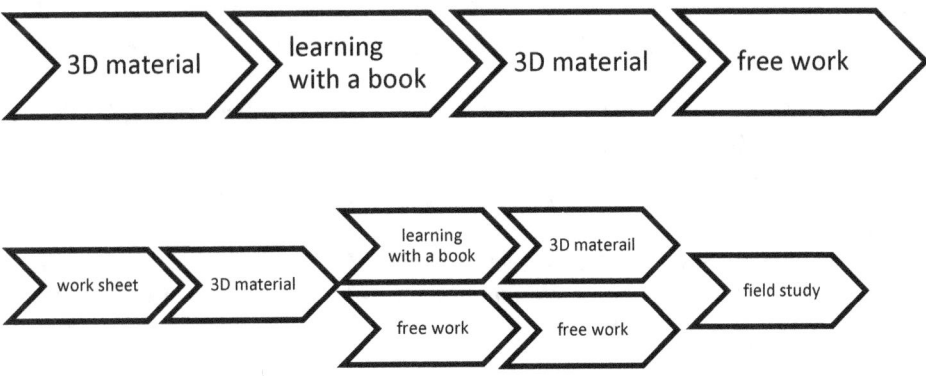

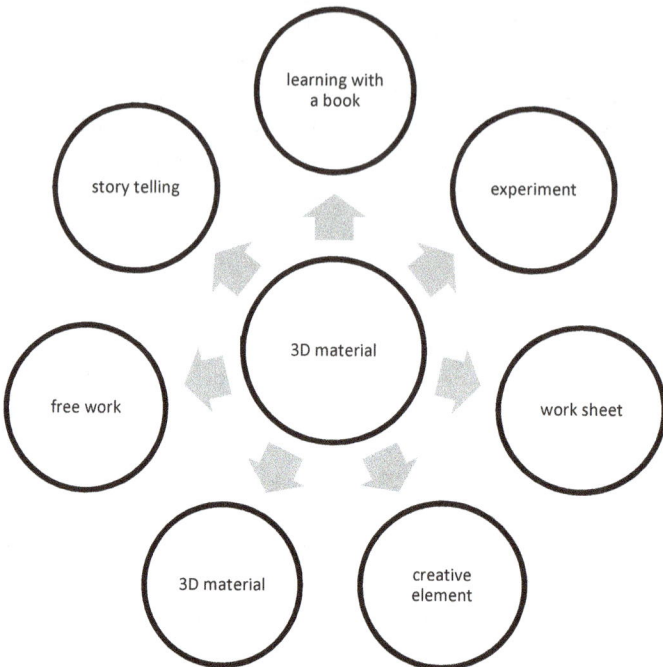

Fig. 43: Three different variations for the preparation of material

4.3.5 References

Abhiyan, S. S. (2009). Active Learning Methodology. http://www.ssa.tn.nic.in/docu/alm-manual.pdf. Accessed 6. May 2014.

Anandalakshmy, S. (2007). Activity Based Learning: A Report on an Innovative Method in Tamil Nadu. http://www.ssa.tn.nic.in/docu/abl-report-by-dr.anandhalakshmi.pdf. Accessed 6. May 2014.

Birch, I. & Lally, M. (1995). Multi-Grade Teaching in Single Primary Schools. UNESCO. http://bvirtual.proeibandes.org/bvirtual/docs/multigradeteachingprimaryschools.pdf. Accessed 6. May 2014.

Bohl, T., & Kucharz, D. (2010). *Offener Unterricht heute: Konzeptionelle und didaktische Weiterentwicklung*. Weinheim: Beltz.

Boller, S., Rosowski, E., & Stroot, T. (Eds.) (2007). *Heterogenität in Schule und Unterricht: Handlungsansätze zum pädagogischen Umgang mit Vielfalt*. Weinheim: Beltz.

Brahme, M., & Babu, S. (2011). *Active Learning Methodology: A Review: A Study of the Middle School Pedagogical Intervention of SSA Tamil Nadu*. Unpublished manuscript.

Bräu, K., & Schwerdt, U. (Eds.) (2005). *Heterogenität als Chance: Vom produktiven Umgang mit Gleichheit und Differenz in der Schule*. Paderborner Beiträge zur Unterrichtsforschung und Lehrerbildung 9. Münster: Lit.

Dengler, S. (2012). *Arbeiten mit Lernleitern im Sachunterricht der Grundschule: Konzeptentwurf und Erprobung der Methodik für den HSU-Unterricht in der 2. Klasse der Grundschule Brennberg zum Thema „Wasser"*. Unpublished manuscript.

Grieb, J. (2010). *Handlungsorientierter Physikunterricht am Beispiel der Mittelschulentwicklung in Rishi Valley*. Unpublished manuscript.

Grimm, M. (2012). *Individualisierter Englischunterricht mit Lernleitern.* Unpublished manuscript.

Kanamüller, L. (2006). *Indische Satellite-Schools als Grundlage der Entwicklung und Konstruktion von Lernleitern.* Unpublished manuscript.

Laging, R. (Ed.) (2010). *Altersgemischtes Lernen in der Schule: (Grundlagen, Schulmodelle, Unterrichtspraxis)* (4th ed). Grundlagen der Schulpädagogik 28. Baltmannsweiler: Schneider-Verlag Hohengehren.

Müller, Th. (2012b). Erfahrungen mit dem konkreten Einsatz der Lernleiterarbeit in der Grundschulstufe der St. Vincent-Schule. *Fördermagazin*, 3, 53-54.

---. (2012a). Mit mir geht was weiter…: Zur Arbeit mit der MultiGradeMultiLevel-Methodology und ihren Lernleitern an der St. Vincent-Schule. *Fördermagazin*, 3, 49-52.

Pius, T., & Rehle, C. (Eds.) (2009). *Inklusive Schule: Leben und Lernen mittendrin.* Bad Heilbrunn: Klinkhardt.

Prenzel, M., Schratz, M., & Schultebrauks-Burkhart, G. (Eds.) (2011). *Was für Schulen! Schule der Zukunft in gesellschaftlicher Verantwortung ; der Deutsche Schulpreis 2011.* Seelze: Kallmeyer.

Rishi Valley Institute for Educational Resources (RIVER) (2009). *Science curriculum for REC Middle School: An Overview.* Chennai: Krishnamurti Foundation India.

Schnur, S., & Müller, Th. (2013). *Elemente der MultiGradeMultiLevel-Methodology: Möglichkeiten und Grenzen für den Unterricht mit verhaltensauffälligen Schülern.* Schriften des Instituts für Sonderpädagogik der Julius-Maximilians-Universität Würzburg. Würzburg: freisleben.

Siewert, N. Individuelle Förderung von Lesekompetenz in der Grundschule – Theoretische Überlegungen und Darstellung des Praxisbeispiels der Volksschule Loiching. Regensburg: unpublished, 2008. Print.

Solowij, T. (2009). *Zur Bedeutung von Schülerexperimenten als Beitrag für einen aktivitätsorientierten Unterricht – aufgezeigt an der Mittelschulentwicklung der RIVER-Projekte.* Unpublished manuscript.

5 Consequences and Perspectives

MGML in theory and practice lead to outlining consequences and introducing existing projects in chapter 5. Spheres of action are teacher training, evaluation of MGML practice and research as well as bearing MGML's global significance in mind. From the experiences of the Indian RIVER-Team, as well as from the viewpoint of the currently documented developments in Germany it becomes clear that several developmental steps are helpful in the training. Creating milestones, testing and evaluating them support the learner's belief in MGML's manageability at school. Research work of Research Team Integral adds reflected factors for success. Additionally, particular variations of MGML such as developed for street children education answer specific life and learning tasks and lead together with international cooperation at university level to a wide and deep understanding of MGML's impact.

5.1 Building Skills for the MGML-Methodology in Teacher Training

As clearly shown in the deliberations on the RIVER-Team's measures of teacher training, measures of teacher training and further teacher training are essential for the introduction of the MGML-Methodology in order to guarantee successful working during the implementation.

The following deliberations make use of the comprehensive experiences in further education of the Indian colleagues as well as the experiences gained by Research Team Integral throughout its seminars and workshops at the universities of Regensburg and Würzburg from 2008 to 2014. The perspectives could also be incorporated into the training of practicing teachers via continued teacher trainings as well as counseling for teachers on the introduction of the MGML-Methodology. Interesting strategies of initial training for the introduction of the MGML-Methodology and its Ladders of Learning have meanwhile also emerged for the German-speaking countries. These strategies were largely derived from the already occurred seminars and the continually further refined processes. The longstanding German-Indian cooperation with the RIVER-Team and the solid contacts made it possible that the first workshops in Germany were held and conducted with RIVER's directors Padmanabha Rao and Rama Anumula.

Fig. 44: The University of Regensburg's first workshop in German-Indian cooperation

Drawing on previous experiences, the introductory processes can be structured into eight steps. All of these contain further, smaller sub steps. The eight steps for a learner of MGML are:

I. Acquiring a preliminary school-educational and integral-pedagogical horizon for the initial training in the MGML-Methodology
II. Informing in detail on the MGML-Methodology
III. Conceptualizing and developing an exemplary milestone on the basis of a freely chosen topic from the syllabus in a team
IV. Critically and constructively contemplating and reflecting on the milestone as well as further developing the draft with an ensuing production of material
V. Testing the milestone with a pilot group as a simulated preset test with an ensuing repeated revision and subsequent implementation in an actual lesson
VI. Compiling and testing of a sequence for a subject or a (half-) year-long Ladder of Learning in actual lessons for a class or a learning group at a school
VII. Compiling and testing of milestones from a group of colleagues in several subjects at a school
VIII. The usage of variations of the MGML-Methodology as a daily practice at a school

Steps I - IV have been successfully implemented with numerous teams of teacher trainees over the course of the previous workshops. In addition, the strategies and potential structures of the processes were refined step by step within these phases. Further steps V and VI were implemented by teacher trainees throughout practical phases and also delineated in academic studies as theses. These steps have also been repeatedly processed by teachers in the last three years. The corresponding scientifically documented experiences provide further insights for the induction (e.g. Grimm 2012). Steps VII and VIII are successfully and regularly applied in various subjects, classes, grades and types of schools by colleagues from the schools described in the preceding passages.

These eight steps that are outlined here aim at extrapolating the extensive methodical-didactic potential of the MGML-Methodology of the RIVER-Team in an open learning process as well as seizing and using the subject-specific, didactic-methodical or also creative competence of the individual participants for the measures of training.

The entire group of participants and also the executing lecturers or academic directors consider themselves as a learning community. New forms of a fully individualized education are conceptualized and prepared in the course of this synergy. The systematized process depicted here is also necessary for the reason that potential threats of a reduction of the MGML-Methodology might set in, such as

- the reduction of the Ladders of Learning to a guiding system without setting the pupils free concerning the time schedule
- the proposition of boring, not fully elaborated material
- the lack of activity-oriented learning opportunities
- the insufficient deconstruction of work and text books
- too little time for joyful learning
- too few options in the milestones or Ladders of Learning
- maintaining the pressure to perform and performance comparison within the class
- interfering with the children's and adolescents' own pace of learning by prematurely slowing down the processes of learning at a faster pace
- the reduced process of group formation and the absence of the supporter system
- the usage of MGML as a trivialized teaching method

Training Step I: The tendencies of reduction cited above that might come along with seizing the MGML-Methodology and elaborating potential variations have led Research Team Integral to establish a reform-oriented, educational horizon in the first module of the training. This process is at first unattached to the MGML-Methodology. Working with teacher trainees and experienced teachers alike has shown that it makes sense for all participants to first consciously become aware of their individual subjective theory of school and teaching. The respective team meetings offer an opportunity to critically contemplate and scrutinize the difference in perspectives of the individual participants and also the degree of innovation of one's own idea of teaching concerning a new culture of learning, in an open dialogue. At the same time the learning group functions as a mutual potential of motivation and natural corrective.

After this phase, the participants are offered to discuss the fundamental question of individualization, dealing with heterogeneity and the possibilities of the various variations of open education by using all kinds of material. This serves to extrapolate the fundamental intentions of the progressive teaching and reform-oriented thinking and panoply, as well as to recognize the many-faceted variations of acting for instructional and educational processes of design.

An important further step is appreciating and quintessentially getting to know the currently manifesting 'best practice' in the German-speaking area. The schools that are awarded by the German Schools Award, as well as the list of criteria for the quality of schools, provide a growing fund and corresponding changes of perspectives. In addition to this the renowned network 'Blick über den Zaun' is able to provide insights and reveal new possibilities of design of an innovative school via its "Standards for reform-oriented schools". (http://schulpreis.bosch-stiftung.de/content/language1/html/index.asp; http://www.blickueberdenzaun.de) Sitting in on classes at two reform-oriented schools is recommended in addition to the predominantly theoretical initial training. Immediately leaving for an altered practice and being perceptive therein triggers a profound mental and likewise bodily experience of being-with and understanding. These experiences help to render the previously individual subjective theory liquid. Sitting in on classes also promotes the willingness to get oneself into new things, like the

RIVER-Team's MGML-Methodology. All these preparatory measures, as well as further ones that are not listed here, for a training in the MGML-Methodology are complemented by the studying of basic skills that are necessary for an innovative development of teaching and schools.

Training Step II: Acquiring general information on the MGML-Methodology prior to the start of the training is the second multi-layered activity and task of the participants. Basic information on the components of the methodology are as important as their genesis via the development of a 'School in a Box.' The participants can use the homepage of the RIVER-project for this, as well as publications by RTI and as required reading this present comprehensive work on the MGML-Methodology. In order to realize that the MGML-Methodology is not merely a method but rather an example of a methodical securing of an integral culture of acting, the participants are asked to delve to corresponding secondary literature. It is only then that the essentiality of the MGML-Methodology and its variations as well as its global importance can be appreciated. Thus the induction into the methodology requires knowledge of the philosophical background texts by the Indian educational philosopher Jiddu Krishnamurti, on whom the pedagogues in Rishi Valley refer to (see Chapter 2.1). Further knowledge is required on integral-educational cultures of acting that are incorporated with various pedagogical and philosophical movements and Research Team Integral's own thoughts (Girg 2007; Müller / Girg 2007).

The by now abundant fund of theses to consult, as well as expert discussions with teacher trainees that have already participated in MGML-workshops and have conducted MGML-testing, furthermore provide opening perspectives in the induction.

Supplementary it is recommended to watch the movie *A Freedom to Learn* that was shot for RIVER by a Mexican film team. The movie enables educational insights into the daily teaching processes at the Satellite-Schools, contains interviews with practicing teachers and also shows the history of origin as well as regional cultural contexts.

In this phase of private study all participants are asked to bring the questions that arose during the preparatory phase, to the workshop or course.

Training Step III: The third training step targets the practically applicable skill of the participants concerning the MGML-Methodology. The intention is for the teacher trainees or teachers to conceptualize a milestone for fully individualized learning in a subject of their choice and regarding a concrete topic of choice. The topic has to be taken from the current valid curriculum and the teacher trainees or teachers also have to design and create all materials necessary. This also requires a precursory professional skill and an extensive pool of material for potential future activities in the milestones. This phase is always organized in teams of at least two but preferably three or four participants.

Throughout the course of the subsequent phases of training step III it is commenced to again reflect on and visually provide all aspects, characteristics and criteria of design for activities from preparatory steps I and II. The flip chart sketches that emerge from this interactive dialogue show all effective principles of construction in a way that is condensed cross-linked and centered on the individual learning activity. These sketches also serve in the following for reflecting on the quality of the developed milestones and support the processes of revision.

Based on this information, the team commences its differentiated process of construction that is initially modestly accompanied by the lecturers. Based on our experience with teacher trainees the proceeding developmental processes for the conception and creation of the milestones take up the time of about three half working days, which is roughly twelve working hours. By the same token the training takes place in rooms in accordance with the criteria of a prepared learning environment.

Critical phases in the developmental process become apparent again and again in the workings of the teams. Most times these phases are related to the duration of the milestones, their structural forms and the creative finding process of even more activity-oriented learning. However, from RTI's standpoint these tough working phases are necessary in order to achieve more profound, more ambitious developmental processes. The teams are intensely assisted and accompanied in these situations. All proposals for activities that should be offered for the learning of children and adolescents should at the end of the day be approved off and regarded as of high quality by all members of the team and also all lecturers. Subject-specific principles, multi-sensory learning or other general principles of scheduling classes are thereby all equally considered. The criteria for individualized instruction material are applied for all creations of material. The already mentioned characteristics for the introduction into the MGML-Methodology, which were termed 'small', 'manageable', 'meaningful' and 'joyful' 'activities' by the RIVER-Team, serve particularly as quality criteria for the emerging milestones. The consideration of social forms as well as the usage of logical guiding systems of symbols is contemplated in the same manner. Training step III closes with a presentable milestone that contains all systematized and elaborated materials and is presented on tables in step IV. Here it is discernible that the criteria for grading, for the usage of various social forms and the symbols were considered for the implementation of the chosen topic. A key clarifies the meaning of the symbols. The choice of alternative learning paths and learning propositions is incorporated at two points in the milestones, thus enabling a more differentiated working. Aesthetic components like the choice of color have a guiding as well as orienting character. The criterion to offer joyful activities and learning with all senses is realized by corresponding design elements.

Training Step IV: All created milestones of the various teams are presented in training step IV. Every presentation takes place in three phases. At first, the members of the team delineate the process of development and present the created milestones in their fundamental construction and in all individual activities. The milestones are analyzed in a discussion. The options of solution are presented in detail and also discussed. This provides further enticing variations in structure and material design for all participants of the workshop.

In the second phase the other teams give the participants differentiated feedback. Again, this results in new insights for the team concerning their own and the others' milestones. Here the participants learn in detail to deal with various variations of learning progressions and get to know the pros and cons of the different solutions.

In the third phase the teachers dwell on the strengths of the respective milestone for every team in a differentiated way. They furthermore give constructive advices for further development concerning parts that are not yet totally successfully elaborated.

The presentation and the discussion last for about half an hour. The process of presenting achieves another level of competence of the participants that is brought in via the convergent collective competence of the entire learning community of a workshop. The participants recognize by way of these various solutions in different subjects, on different topics and for different grades, what abundant variations of workings the MGML-Methodology gives rise to. They furthermore gather how flexibly the methodology is applicable and thus makes it possible for already designed milestones to once more increase their quality. Since documentations and picture material is created for all milestones, this developmental step results in a large pool of suggestions for new introductions, workshops and training courses.

The introductory steps I – IV can easily be conducted with students during their teacher training at the universities. Both the University of Regensburg and the University of Würzburg hold corresponding reflective experiences.

Training Step V: In terms of practical application the milestones have to be considered in the contexts of actual happening lessons with a corresponding class or learning group. The phase of conceptualizing is thus followed up by the elaboration of a longer sequence. A subject-specific testing phase should be scheduled for roughly 8 to 15 periods. The children's and adolescents' learning is structured via 3-5 milestones within this time budget.

The practical application itself is preceded by a simulated practical phase with a pilot group. The so called MGML-pretest serves to test the viability of the individual learning activities, to detect potential problems in understanding concerning tasks or descriptions of material and alter these in advance. Additionally, the entire process of the milestone is once more examined concerning its inner logic. The experiences gained from pretests undertaken by

Research Team Integral reveal that an individual or a small planning team cannot always simultaneously keep an eye on all relevant aspects of construction. The involvement of a group in the pilot situation enables detailed analyses on arisen qualities of material, still existing ambiguities concerning the tasks as well as weak spots in the overall arrangement of the MGML-construction. Furthermore, the pretest offers the first 'real' implementation of the planned conception and thus offers a first teaching experience with the milestone and its materials. Now things are planned are among other things with the number of pupils in the testing class, the necessary changes of the room for the various social forms, the provision of the material and the expected time schedules.

This phase is conducted by Research Team Integral while working with students in a small peer-group, lecturers involved. Mostly these are students that have already been introduced to phases I - IV and that have already conceptualized a milestone. In this phase they take on the role of the pupils and work through all the elements of the milestones themselves, while writing down occurring difficulties in handling and constructive suggestions on notepads.

A longer conversation ensues at the end of the pilot phase. This talk provides room to collectively revise all critical parts and suggestions for solutions and results in further modification.

Training Step VI: The testing of a subject sequence now requires the production of the materials, all tasks as well as the overview of the milestones with the final design. Here also aesthetic aspects like coloring, shaping and the form of the setup of the small resulting material pool are considered.

The procedures are beforehand discussed in circle conversations and the used symbols are explained, in order to prepare the pupils for the deployment of the milestones or the Ladder of Learning. It is also pointed out that they are about to engage with an altered role of the teacher and that their self-responsibility is continuously demanded.

The now created sequence for autonomous learning in about 3 – 5 milestones is set up immediately before its use in a learning arrangement that is fitting for the classroom. The room structure is changed accordingly. The realizing teachers correspondingly prepare themselves for the changed teacher's tasks of accompanying and supervising, advising or also working with a small group. The examples for the deployment in secondary education in sub-chapter 2.2.4 make some of the essential phases of this training step concretely comprehensible. For one thing the phase of the first practical testing also features the documentation of the pupils' learning success via possible assessment variations. For another thing the partial and overall evaluations also provide conclusions on the development of the pupils' performance.

It is also important that the realizing teacher are also trained in forms of reflection – especially in handling circle conversations and feedback sessions, for them to be able to learn to assess the altered practice and its effects, strengths and weaknesses, as well as creating a forum to appreciate the works of the children and adolescents. The teachers can transition into a regular practice in working with Ladders of Learning after a successful testing. The pace of broader range usage of working with Ladders of Learning with the MGML-Methodology depends on how fast the necessary materials can be created or how fast further colleagues can be found that want to participate in this development of a fully individualized learning within a learning community.

Training Steps VII and VIII: Training steps VII and VIII extend the previously described introductory work to further colleagues, subjects and grades, respectively. These phases of the training already touch upon the central questions of a more comprehensive systematic school development at a singular school since strategies shown here intervene in an innovative way with the development of lessons by way of personnel progress and also entail changes on the level of organizational development. According to Research Team Integral, the following steps are important for training step VII:

1. developing model examples in different professional or team groups
2. surpassing the 'critical mass' in a professional group at a school
3. conducting in-school further education seminars in professional groups
4. choosing interdisciplinary topics and learning sequences
5. conducting testing in real-life situations in subjects at the schools
6. training of in-school experts on consulting the process
7. giving continuous support from the school administration

Schools with a broad range of experience in systematic and sustainable school development are able to take on these steps on the mentioned and also varying paths. In-school further education for teachers becomes absolutely necessary in this phase in order to secure the sustainability of the deployment within the teaching staff. The staffs of the schools that cooperate with Research Team Integral can be encouraged by various ways of impulses of school development. This way they can successfully find variations of the MGML-Methodology and incorporate them in their culture of teaching and their school concept. Training step VIII is clearly located on that school level that can be labeled as the buildup of a complete model. While considering the necessary processes of school development, for this hitherto the following is needed:

1. establishing an interdisciplinary competence team on the MGML-Methodology
2. supporting processes with a systematized school development
3. developing further material for various subjects to apply practically
4. supporting colleagues in the development, recognizing
5. realizing necessary changes in the school's time structure
6. undertaking processes of change in the spatial conception of the classes
7. developing conceptions for the classrooms and the whole school's space allocation plan

From the experiences of the Indian RIVER-Team, as well as from the viewpoint of the currently documented developments in Germany it becomes clear that working practical examples are extremely helpful for the training in the MGML-Methodology. Every example has entailed interested teacher trainees and colleagues. Expert talks at the university with representatives of the various practicing schools in the context of bigger events for students and teachers have shown just how much this encourages others to embark themselves. Fully individualized schools are no longer perceived as a utopia, but as a practical variation of a contemporary school in the 21st century.

5.1.1 Research on the MGML-Methodology

The conditions and implications of learning with Ladders of Learning are researched in various grades and types of schools within the related research projects.

The research team examines the processes of developing expertise of the teacher trainees or teachers, the planning processes of the learning sequences, as well as the processes of implementing and carrying out working with Ladders of Learning and milestones, respectively. The focus is on quality and the characteristics of the individually and collectively occurring learning processes in the learning group. Four questions are central for this:

1. Which processes are significant for teacher trainees and teachers when developing expertise for the MGML-Methodology, and how is the transformation of one's own development of expertise being experienced?
2. Which elements conduce to success of working with the MGML-Methodology and Ladders of Learning? Which factors are crucial for a successful process? What are obstructing and hampering factors?
3. In which ways do the tasks and methods of the pupils change? Which learning processes becoming apparent individually and in the learning community?
4. Which effects does working with the MGML-Methodology and Ladders of Learning have on the participating pupils, teacher trainees and teachers?

The goal of the research project is to work out those factors of the processes and the necessary elements of design in the course of a participatory action research (PAR), which are fundamental for a success of the MGML-Methodology in day-to-day teaching. By focusing on the processes in working with the MGML-Methodology, we see a chance to name generalizable factors of the process and elements of design that are specific for a certain situation.

These can serve as further marks of orientation for the teachers. Gained insights can become useful in combination with integral opportunities for action in new situations. They offer an option for designing a lesson with the MGML-Methodology and accompany learning with Ladders of Learning.

At the same time, the analysis of the planning processes and practical tests of the MGML-Methodology and its examples of Ladders of Learning increases our own understanding of the factors that are necessary for a successful teacher training and working with the MGML-Methodology. The analysis can be very helpful in guiding and counseling teacher trainees for these reasons.

The academic research work in the university education and training of teachers, in the continuing education of teachers, as well as in the field of practical teaching, needs a sensitive interaction on a par with the partners at the universities and schools. Therefore, we understand research – just as all pedagogical situations and processes – as an integral practice that is founded on specific fundamental cultures, that is developed carefully and is cautiously revised over and over again. We wish for all participants to acknowledge the integral basic dimensions, to be aware of the interior and exterior dynamics of the processes and to be interested in a successful work alliance.

The cooperation of scientists, teachers, students and pupils – a foundation of participatory action research – primarily requires building trust on all sides. This is linked to a transparent communication and disclosure of goals and interests. The sounding of chances and limitations within the process is to be conducted in meta-interactions just as facets in the content-related cooperation and social interaction. The research project aims at tracing the educational practice when teaching with the MGML-Methodology and learning with ladders of laddering, as well as perceiving, describing and discursively contemplating its connected and vivid multidimensionality. The cooperation of all actors is diversely and vividly expressed and concreatively designed. It is integral research's task to describe and interpret the ever-changing educational process that is constantly and immediately happening for everybody – even for the researcher (Girg 2007, 38). The findings are based on the perception of individual situations and actors. A collective effort to interpret takes places during dialogues and cooperative processes of exchange. Here, every participant assumes a specific task that is important for the development of insights. The specific task ensues from the participant's role and activities in the field. The subjective conceptions of the immediately acting participants in the field are perceived and taken serious at it. The scientist assumes an important role due to his "double membership in two worlds and a privileged situation of being relieved from daily pressures in the research field" (Breuer 2010, 51). He contemplates the practical action while especially considering scientific theories and models and thus incorporates further options of interpretation into the process of understanding. Researchers and the people being researched are inextricably connected in the results.

A broader definition of data is assumed for the data collection in the researches on the MGML-Methodology (Glaser 2007, 57: "All is data."). The data collection takes on various forms and at first includes all known – and if necessary also unknown – possibilities in the sense of a docta ignorantia in the research process (Girg 2007, 53). This is, among other things, important for the reason that has been found out. It states that for researches following the principles of 'action research', the choice of methods should maintain dynamic in order to adjust to the circumstances on location (Noffke 2013, 14). Out of this understanding a variety of different forms of data collection and sources are incorporated into the process of interpretation.

Research work in the preparatory phase of working with Ladders of Learning in class. In order to be able to make assertions concerning the factors necessary for a successful MGML, the precursory conceptual, personal and interactive processes of the teachers or students, as well as supervisors and companions are considered when collecting the data. The actors are asked to document their developments in journals, as far as possible, and to provide these for the phases of evaluation. Another foundation of data are the statuses of material in earlier or later steps of the preparation, as well as the documentation of special events that are relevant for the testing. Tools for collecting data in this phase are:

- overall concept plus activities and their revision
- journals and/ or individual notes of the actors
- chronological listings of situations of consulting and advising plus pretests
- reports of quintessential situations of consulting and advising plus pretests
- chronological listings of special activities, if necessary recollection reports

Research work in concrete testings with the pupils. A triangulated data collection is also targeted in the interactions of the testing (Flick 2011). Particular attention is brought to atmospheres in the descriptions. These atmospheres can also be reflected in the emotions of the researchers. Thus, the researchers are asked to document their responses via contact with the field and its participants. In terms of research strategy, clarifying conversations with participants can be helpful to timely and collectively contemplate and adapt to classification in categories (Mayring 2008, 74-76). Photographs are included into the interpretation as captured moments. Their iconography and iconology can enhance and substantiate observations – always while specifically bearing in mind their form as "secondary subject" (Panofsky 1955, 37). Tools for this phase are:

- journals of field studies from various researchers
- photographs of individual situations in class
- spatial sketches or sketches concerning the spatial movement of singular pupils
- material, also pupils' results
- conversations with pupils, teachers and further people involved

Research work on developing expertise and in contemplations of teacher trainees and teachers. In addition to that, not only all researchers, but all adults involved in the events are asked to document their processes of learning, development and experience. This can be done in the form of journal entries.

They are also asked to deliver a statement and an interpretation via a written interview on special aspects that were proven to be relevant in the preliminary phase of the research process and on further possibly emerging elements. The completed written interviews provide a further opportunity for triangulation by way of the different perspectives that were brought in.

The students' written term papers purvey additional interesting and relevant hints for the research process. Being complex amounts of data that depict and reflect the various phases, these papers constitute a fund of meaningful information – especially considering feedback and contemplation.

Consequently it is paid attention to preferably register all levels of the event within the documentation of data. That is to say that not only are elements on the factual level being considered in the reports and journals, but also the relationship level and intrapersonal processes. These processes are an essential part of a complete, integral situation that should not be underestimated. For compiling field study journals it is recommended to not only note descriptive recollections of the processes and situations, but consciously consider one's own emotions, associations or phantasies. These might be of huge importance for the upcoming evaluation when contemplated in the group afterwards (Breuer 2010, 61). Some of the tools are:

- field journals
- questionnaires
- feedback material (among others in academic term papers)

The phase of evaluation is characterized by communicative validation. Identified factors for success are examined considering their normative quality in expert discussions. However, insights derived from case studies are always at first set in relation to the individual case – analogous to the procedure in casuistry (Dörr 2012, 13). The possibility for a transfer or general validity is checked in dialogue and the assignment to further testing. When these preconditions are fulfilled, the factors for success that stood the test are included into the design process in form of recommendations.

Due to the chosen research design the research results are subject to a continuing developmental process. Thus far factors for success in learning with Ladders of Learning and teaching with the MultiGradeMultiLevel-Methodology are:

- 'ownership' of the teacher in the sense of a real interest in implementing MGML as well as own commitment of learning and development
- systematized application of all training elements of the MGML-Methodology in teacher training and continuing education of teachers
- conceptions of material according to the regulations of RIVER with a special emphasis on the possibilities of variations in the sense of ownership by the teacher
- pretest of the material in a small group
- development and stringent implementation of an inherent symbol system within the material

- spatial arrangement with special emphasis on working areas that are specifically defined according to the social form
- appropriate provision of material and presentation of all necessary information and overviews
- usage of expedient elements of the product and process documentation (usually portfolio)
- regular plenary sessions with different functions (introductory sessions, feedback sessions, etc.)
- implementation and usage of supportive rituals
- individual possibilities of variation in the structures of Ladders of Learning and milestones, respectively

5.2 International and Global perspectives

5.2.1 Pedagogy for street children education and MGML-Methodology

An important field of the MGML-Methodology that is emerging on a global scale is working with street children. From a German perspective this might seem unusual due to street children hardly playing a role in the educational awareness of rich European countries. However, in actual fact children and adolescents are also living on the streets and do not participate in schooling in these countries. Millions of children and adolescents live on and off the streets worldwide. They do not have access to schools or have lost the access. Concerning this matter there are two fundamental developments in Germany: for one thing the master's program 'street children pedagogy' of the Pedagogical College Heidelberg, for another thing the Street School in Mannheim.

Although generally different from the rural situation in India, there are similar manifold and diverse initial conditions for the educational work with children and adolescents living on the streets (Müller 2009a). Street children bring along very different experiences of education and preconditions of performance: as much as living on the streets connects and unites them with other children and adolescents, they otherwise differ as much concerning these aspects. This is added by specific difficulties. Living on the streets, being without a home and without strong structures lead to massive problems for many children. Additionally, the streets as a working and living environment unfurls its own unique dynamics and follows its own rules. As arduous and burdensome life in the milieu of 'the streets' might be, it is equally seductive and attractive. Living on the streets also always promises apparent liberties and the fulfillment of rather 'difficult' needs. School's engagement and obligation, taking place at strictly regulated hours with fixed contents at fixed locations, can become an ambivalent experience: either a place of desire beyond the unconditional life on the streets or the epitome of the constraint of a life in the liberty of the streets, places and cities. At first, a couple of essential aspects are worked out in order to clarify working with the MGML-Methodology in this pedagogical area.

Living in the streets as a habitat? From an architectural point of view space does not emerge by keeping free of or omitting development, but rather by adding shaping elements. A space is a shaped, designed area that gains its effect by added elements. Just think of St. Peter's Square in Rome: what would it be without its colonnades, without its obelisks and without its fountain and spouts? What would the Place Vendôme in Paris be without its Arc de Triomphe or the Plaza Mayor in Salamanca without its harmony of enclosing facades? A space can only become one if there are streets that lead to and away from it.

Aside from architecture space is also sometimes referred to as so called habitat. One's own place in life also emerges via forms of design from which life is able to fully unfold and freedom and meaning can arise. One's own place in life is not found or acquired by avoiding shaping it, by omitting existential dimensions of life or relinquishing personally essential aspects of life.

The arrangement and order of the individual elements and the dimensioning of architectural spaces like habitats are a perpetual task of formation. Having a place in life does decidedly not mean to go with the flow of the streets and possibly losing oneself in the course of that. It actually means to experience orientation that can arise from individual and collective formation and can result in feelings and certainties of safety, support and stability.

Living on and with the streets is not a habitat at first since the streets are one-sidedly limited and simultaneously absolutely open and unlimited. The streets are hardly or not at all shapeable since they lack moments of rest due to their flowing and vectored character, while forms or dimensional life movements threaten to take over on the personal side of things. He who talks about having his place in living on the streets might certainly be right – when observed specifically. However, this statement contains an intrinsic, existential contradiction.

The streets are space between movement and stagnation. The streets as a habitat are hardly or only very narrowly shapeable. At the same time they embody, among other things, a stress ratio of movement and stagnation, though. The streets seem untenable in the sense of a boundless movement and hardly ending continuation. Streets rarely 'end' and only seemingly serve as means of orientation for children and adolescents, even if they lead in a certain direction according to their functionality – that is getting from A to B.

However, the streets can also be a place of refuge. Hence, there is a movement towards or into them. As a place of refuge they can indeed provide shelter, relief and escape due to the anonymity they offer. But every refuge contains a flight: the flight from everything that is beyond the refuge. The streets as a refuge, as the epitome of flight, are due to its anonymity rather a space that suppresses and excludes questions of identity that does not allow them or brings them up in the first place. Places are identity-establishing by nature, though, the architectural and the existential ones. They provide a formative character for a city, a country, but also for the life of every individual human-being and the tasks that come with it.

Whoever has not fled to the streets has possibly been exiled to it: has been expelled from his own home, his own identity, from the existential rest of a habitat – into the movement of the streets, into its fragile stress ration of closeness and distance, of refuge as well as imposition in and by anonymity. Whoever has been exiled to the streets experiences them also as a space of stagnation, as a final destination where the existence is ultimately far less of a dynamic adventure than a constant struggle to survive. The streets rarely enable the positive dynamic of an identity-establishing formation and thus they stand for stagnation and not personal development or even growth. The streets are a space of identity-expelling, of identity flight, of the search for identity, of in-between and transitional identities. However, they are also a space of resistance, a space of personal and societal objection. In these cases the streets are consciously sought or at least accepted (see parts of the punk scene, for example). This being the case, and this is pedagogically important, the streets actually do implicitly contain the potential to have an identity-establishing effect. The streets are more of a spot than a place. Spots are geometric, standardized and objectified spaces with a certain function. Spots resemble passages in terms of their functionality: mostly public, brightly lit, random, made for the masses. You do not settle down on spots, you can only use or pass them by. Places, on the other hand, are spaces where one can settle down. Places are private and intimate. They cannot be found on maps and continuously reemerge as the basis of human living and experience. Mostly places only become places when they become separated places.

The human-being of modern times is threatened with losing with places altogether, though (see Chapter 3.1). He is always on the move, only passing by streets and occupying spots only temporarily on his way. The streets are the architectural epitome of spot-ness and at the same time the job description of the modern human-being: fleeting and fluid, like Bauman describes it. It is characteristic of the modern human-being to have more non-places than places, to record more loss than acquisition of identity. Streets seem to signal departure, movement, freedom and dynamic and resemble an infinite loop of life for children and adolescents that live in and with the streets as much as for the modern human-being in general. This infinite loop has no goal, is always moving and yet only permanently repeating itself without creating anything new. However, pedagogy is at first never really concerned with streets but with paths. It is about paths that are found, sought, accompanied, offered or questioned. Educators accompany paths in the most diverse forms, whichever profession they actually occupy. Hence, in this context the question is how

- to turn streets of life into paths of life with help from pedagogy
- to turn spots and passages into places and habitats
- and how forms of accompanying children and adolescents in the streets could look like?

170

The streets between public and private, between inside and outside. Streets more and more become public spaces, spaces of passages and permeability. It is rare that they become living environments at selective points like street cafés, street theaters or play streets, for example. Streets as spaces of communication, of dialogue, of encountering, of being-seen, of perceiving and being-perceived, as well as the people coming together are rare in the modern forms of society at the beginning of the 21st century. Whoever lives on the streets is living publicly and yet anonymously. He loses his privacy: he loses the moments of secrecy, of enclosedness, of distinctiveness and of what needs to be preserved. He also mostly does not gain any new connections or commitments despite the large amount of people on the streets. On the other hand this non-binding nature also offers temptations: one can choose the direction of where to go oneself. One can chose to walk, run, linger, or stand still, to beg or just to look on. The streets are the epitome of self-determination: at least they suggest this.

In this context a reference to the opposition of 'inside' and 'outside' has to be made: inside is home, outside is freedom, as known from many teamsters and their respective truck. The streets have the same meaning for some people. However, the opposite might also be the case: freedom is inside and home is outside. Just think about the homeless that would love to settle down again or people that were exiled onto the streets but do not feel at home there. These two poles sometimes blur into indistinguishability for the children and adolescents living in the streets. Here also lie pedagogical tasks: collectively looking at and questioning the inside and the outside and then bringing it into initial forms of formation.

Educational miniatures for a street children education. The aspects mentioned above reveal which profound and existential questions pedagogy for street children is dealing with. These questions were seized by students from Germany, Southern America and Russia in the workings of the module of methodology during the university course 'Street Children Education' at the Pedagogical College Heidelberg in 2009 (Müller 2009b).

Dealing with these existential topics of children and adolescents living on the streets initially resulted in questioning the current educational understanding of common contents in Mathematics, Language and other subjects. Meaningful educational miniatures, for the streets, in the sense of von Elschenbroich's educational miniatures as written down in her publication for "Weltwissen der Siebenjährigen" (2001), were compiled and written down.

It was a matter of shelter, weather, survival, fear, truth, trust, freedom, business acumen, disappointment, addiction, criminality, loneliness, independence, hunger / food, abuse, sexuality, depression, hierarchy, wishes / dreams, belonging, humor, work, identity, influence, belief / superstition, inventiveness, creativity, family, homesickness / home, orientation, restlessness, adults, age, retreat / privacy, property, memories, relationships, ties, hygiene, religion, death, animals, bravery and language. These topics were described in their relation to street children. Meaningful goals of learning and education were then deduced and formulated from these descriptions. As an example, the educational miniatures for the topics 'Survival and Fear' are depicted below:

One is frightened if something uncontrollable, unnatural or life-threatening is heading one's way. The fears can be evoked in human-beings by things, people, situations, noises, odors etc. The fear materializes in various ways that are externally visible or internally palpable. Either one freezes in fear or runs away in panic trying to escape the perilous situation. Either way, the emotion of fear is tight-knit with the desire to survive. By contrast surviving does not exclusively mean being frightened.

Surviving means satisfying external and internal needs, taking care of oneself or being protected by someone that cares for you. Trust, adapting, flexibility and a strong will are amongst the concepts that secure survival. Hence fear and survival are tight-knit. You call someone suicidal if he or she seems to be fearless and does life-threatening things despite all objections and fears by others. However, there are also some situations where fear needs to be overcome in order to survive. For example, jumping out of a burning house (vertigo), or overcoming one's fear of going to school. By achieving this, a feeling of being strong and elevated ensues. Life is characterized by the interplay of holding one's own and losing.

Fear as a natural protective reaction of survival plays a role in every society. Children are afraid of things that are big, loud, and uncontrollable and especially of things that are invisible. They are furthermore especially afraid of things that were declared as threatening or forbidden by their parents, grandparents or society. We are afraid of dying because we do not know what will happen afterwards. We want to survive because life on earth in a situation that we know is familiar to us. It is under our control and within our sight. Street children live in constant fear of not being able to survive, of not living another day, of not having enough to eat, of not being able to escape a street fight or the police, of not having a safe place to sleep. The desire to have something to hold on to amidst the confusion of violence, fugacity, distrust and lack of orientation is as big as the fear to let go of these things. The fear of not surviving is paralleled by the fear of leaving this perilous existence.

- Every street child should experience overcoming fear.
- Every street child should know a remedy for fear.
- Every street child should experience which effects and power over fellow human-beings it has by frightening them.
- Every street child should have experienced that it is worth to survive.
- Every street child should have experienced the strength to win the fight to survive.

Fig. 45: Example of an educational miniature

The Ladder of Learning of the existential. A Ladder of Learning with existential fundamental topics for street children was compiled from the drafted educational miniatures. The topics were organized into milestones and brought into a possible sequence of dealing with and working on:

realisation	habitation	freetime	stile of living	goals	sucess
					a own family
character attitude	me self	7 dreams desires	Occupation	abilities	dreams
membership					
religion believes	creativity	secrets	6 identity soul	sexualty love	abuse
					realtions spearations
criminality	vulnerabilities	duties rules	5 sexuality / realtions	privacy	trust distrust
age					
work	addicitions	HIV	diseases	hygieny	nutrition
					body
lonleyness	dolor depression	death	faith	joy	4 me and others
fears					
3 fears lease on live	freedom	orientation aims	ideas plans	independence bindings	2 freedom development
					language
1 origin family	birth	family	home homeness	parents adults	memories

Fig. 46: Ladder of Learning with existential fields

This variation of a Ladder of Learning does not contain an immanent didactic structure anymore. The focus was on topics that are able to be worked on at school, topics that are relevant for children and adolescents living on the streets and are thus topics that could be perceived as appealing, meaningful and worthwhile. Various materials of dealing with it at school or forms of expression via theater, dance, art and writing were compiled or conceived for every single field in the process. As in Rishi Valley, the basis of this Ladder of Learning forms a loop of basic abilities and skills. In the case of street children and adolescents these abilities and skills refer to simple basic school skills and exercises on concentration and communication. It is also possible that the children and adolescents do not only work with the Ladder of Learning from bottom to top but also from top to bottom. They could also single out individual fields or milestones that especially appeal to them. This variation prevents dropping out the same way the Ladders of Learning of the MGML-Methodology by RIVER do. The same way some children in India do not attend school because they have to help with the harvest or are celebrating a festivity for several days, children and adolescents living on the streets also vanish for days and weeks until they show up again at a project of support or schooling. Hence, the Ladder of Learning enables them to re-enter their workings at school at every time.

This variation of working with the Ladder of Learning strongly acknowledges the existential life experiences of children and adolescents in the streets. By now it has been applied in the townships of South Africa as well as in an industrial city in Siberia.

5.2.2 International Cooperation on the Variations of the MGML-Methodology

The MGML-Methodology has been radiating all over the world for some time, as addressed in chapter 4.1. The worldwide importance of the MGML-Methodology has been realized by the integral-pedagogical experience of Research Team Integral at an early stage.

The German-Indian cooperation of Research Team Integral at the Chair of Education of the University of Regensburg was expanded to a second academic platform with expertise in special education in the winter term of 2011, namely the Chair of Pedagogy for Behavioral Disorders at the University of Würzburg due to the effort of Thomas Müller. Intensive international horizons and lasting international project outlines, especially considering the connection of the question how to realize inclusive educational systems have also emerged at the University of Würzburg.

By now and by way of the DAAD (German Academic Exchange Service) a long-term supported and considerably expanded German-Indian cooperation exists owing to the team at the University of Würzburg. Partners are, on the one hand, the highly renowned Indian Institute of Technology Madras (IITM Chennai) located in southern India, and, on the other hand, the Rishi Valley Institute for Educational Resources (RIVER) in Rishi Valley. Study trips and conferences are organized and short-term guest lectureships are mutually enabled via the program A New Passage to India both on the level of student exchanges and on the level of lecturers in cooperation with Milind Brahme and Suresh Babu at IITM Chennai. This German-Indian cooperation was secured via a MoU (Memorandum of Understanding) beforehand. The DAAD-project that is promoted by the Federal Ministry of Education and Research is successfully executed and will be maintained until 2017.

In terms of content the focuses include, next to the cooperation on the MGML-Methodology, enhanced questions concerning special and supporting education as well as the fields of application of the UN convention of Disability Law on inclusion. Comprehensive scientific views on inclusion and pedagogical options of acting in inclusive learning groups were presented by a panel of experts at an international workshop at the University IITM Chennai in February 2013. These views were also examined from German and Indian perspectives. The conference enabled the participating students from the universities of Würzburg, Regensburg and Chennai to further educate them with high-quality academic reasoning on inclusion at an international level.

The development of the projects already successfully shows to which extent the variations of the MGML-Methodology are able to accomplish a flexible and diversely modifiable contribution to specific and individualized education. The supporting-specific competence contained therein has a special significance. The necessary scientific questions and their study are of corresponding importance. A first publication, from the University of Würzburg is already available (Schnur / Müller 2013).

The majority of the project participants are teacher trainees with a major in special education at the University of Würzburg. However, also students from other disciplines were able to conduct field research in the context of this DAAD-project in and around Rishi Valley. This study trips had a musicological or cultural studies emphasis.

Besides, there are more lines of development in Europe and in Germany. Connections to the MGML-Methodology with the psychological faculty at the University of Lorraine Metz/ Nancy, France, and the 'Pedagogical Café', a group of teachers in Metz, were established by respectively making contact from 2012 to 2014. During the same period, Research Team Integral was approached by the Chair of Primary School Education at Charles-University in Prague, Czech Republic. A corresponding cooperation was established subsequently. Contacts to the Edith-Stein Hogeschool in the Netherlands were also cultivated during this period. Research Team Integral introduced the French and Czech partners to the fundamental principles of the MGML-Methodology on several occasions during the period from 2012 to 2014. This was helped by the academic program for mobility of lecturers promoted by ERASMUS. Both the Czech and the French partners participated in international introductory workshops at the University of Regensburg. Lecturers and also individual students and interested teachers were able to obtain the first levels of the MGML-competence. For November 2015 an exploration workshop is planned with teachers and headmasters in Bressanone, Italy. In adult education a cooperation project has been launched between Research Team Integral and Technische Hochschule Deggendorf. The college is about to design degree programs (Bachelor and Master) based on the structures of Ladders of Learning and employing the main principles of MGML. Research Team Integral has taken over coaching and supervising tasks in this 6 year project (2014 – 2020).

On the student level the students from the University of Regensburg were able to contribute to the growth of MGML in France and the Czech Republic – for example via a semester abroad. By now, Research Team Integral has launched a new project. They also received inquiries for advice concerning the development of MGML-oriented schools in Nepal via a German NGO. Flexible learning in learning communities shall be established with German support of teachers on location at these schools.

The scope of the international project developments cannot yet be conclusively delineated. However, Research Team Integral at the University of Regensburg clearly sees this in the context of the emerging development of a 'Universal Resource Centre', which will take on these international tasks in the long run. Central school-educational goals are important for all internal projects. The involved MGML-experts both at the University of Regensburg and at the University of Würzburg consciously face the challenges of education of the 21st century, as they were set out by the UNESCO early on. These organically connect with the integral cultures of acting described in this book. The MGML-Methodology opens up a culture of acting that is to be described as comprehensive, holistic and integral (see Chapter 3) in accordance with the worldwide decade of 'Education for Lasting Development' that ends in 2014. Furthermore, the MGML-Methodology also opens up possibilities for the implementation of the follow-up program 'Global Action Program for Education for Sustainable Development' that offers guidelines from 2015 on.

These measures provide a basis for the application of the MGML-Methodology, but also take up the goals of the UNESCO as they are set out in the world education report of 2013/2014 Teaching and Learning. Achievement for all!

What is central in terms of content is the global task to deal with diversity and the appreciation of the singularity of every child in its unique living and learning situations, which can manifest themselves in totally different societal and cultural field of the respective countries. The point is to create sensitivity. Furthermore, this is essential for learning communities and designing flexible learning arrangements and to accompany and materialize the activities of learning and the interaction of the learning group in manifold ways. This is also obviously guided and regulated by the rights of children as they are written down in the Convention of the Rights of the Child. These also provide international orientation for further developments. The comprehensive, cultural and ecological orientation of the MGML-Methodology, as laid out in of this book, additionally opens up the connecting-ability to all questions of sustainability that is demanded in the international programs.

Hence, it is necessary to exhibit proof of the applicability of the MGML-Methodology in various European and further international contexts and settings. For this to happen, pilot teams are formed in the respective practical projects. These pilot teams consist of project partners and interested people from the school department. The national teams internationally interchange and collectively develop expedient strategies for the elaboration of new, culturally adaptable variations of the MGML-Methodology and also corresponding modules of training, which are evaluated over the course of the project, too. On the other hand, exemplary characteristics at schools and educational institutions of the different countries arise in the course of the project processes, as well as expert teams for the training on university and school level. These expert teams are also on hand for interested people and developments in other countries. The modules that need to be elaborated are generated, described in a nuanced way, and step by step tested by an international consortium in an open, concreative process of the project partners employing their respective expertise. These modules are afterwards further developed over the course of the project and can be made available via nationally and internationally applicable sets of material, if an adequate guarantee of resources is provided. Apart from finding variations of the MGML-Methodology, especially the question of cultural adaption, which already played a major part for the developments within India, as well as the question of 'ownership'. 'Ownership' hereby means the acceptance of active personal responsibility for all project steps.

The following results can be expected over the course of the commenced international cooperation:

- the establishment of systematized, flexibly applicable training modules for the development and usage of European and worldwide possible variations of the MGML-Methodology
- exemplary models at schools in various societal and cultural settings
- existence of 'resource packs' with strategies and manifold material for the establishment of national and international variations of the MGML-Methodology
- national and international competence teams
- strategical papers for the participation of further internal partners

'Resource Packs' are diversely expandable training packages with systematized progressions and strategies. These packages are furthermore equipped with corresponding material and also advices for distance learning. The objective and goals are richly varied applicable for the different European and international fields and the various cultural and country specific educational contexts. Photography and film documentations shall be created in the process of the development. These should make it easier to break in to find variations of the MGML-Methodology.

All processes and international cooperation of development are scientifically accompanied in form of the 'Participatory Action Research'. This is the case in order secure quality and generates factors for success for the international horizon, as well as to examine and prove MGML's available 'Global Significance' of the MGML-Methodology from various cultural perspectives in concrete examples.

5.2.3 MGML-Methodology: Global Education and Global Significance

Measures by the European Union have been targeting the transcending horizon of a global understanding of education for a couple of years. They are nurtured, amongst others, by the concepts of the UNESCO and their education-related targets of the Millennium Development Goals as well as the EU's projects on 'Global Development Education' and 'Global Education'.

The Lisbon based 'North South Centre – European Centre for Global Education and Solidarity' of the European Union with its Global Education Program is responsible for 'Global Education.'

177

Interesting first developments and connecting lines between 'Global Education' and the MGML-Methodology were drawn through a conference of the so-called Visegrad-countries, on 'Global Development Education'. Representatives of more than 20 different nationally and internationally operating NGOs from the Czech Republic, Slovakia, Poland and Hungary came together for a several days long conference in Prague in the spring of 2011.

The director of the Rishi Valley Institute for Educational Resources, RIVER, Padmanabha Rao, and a member of Research Team Integral at the University of Regensburg, Dr. Ralf Girg, were invited as experts for the MGML-Methodology. The MGML-Methodology could be presented to an international group of participants throughout a two day workshop. These several hours of interactive presentations and works examined the general and contentual arrangement of the MGML-Methodology in terms of to which extent it contributes to global action and thought, to 'Civic Education' and 'Global Education', and to ecological long-term learning. The extensive dialogues during the conference showed just how much the MGML-Methodology actually pursues the central goals of the most diverse aspects of 'Global Education' with its numerous holistically connected individual aspects.

The following compilation on learning with Ladders of Learning and teaching with MGML of Research Team Integral was created over the course of the last couple of years and was internationally presented in Prague for the first time. It depicts the global importance of this methodology through the characteristics of the MGML-Methodology, reacts to noticeable learning successes and the thereof resulting effects in the societal context. The known demand to think global and act local is hereby operationalized via the concrete measures of this holistic methodology and is lived with lasting effects in the educational sector.

Characteristics of MGML-Methodology	Learning outcome	Expected effects
systematised free processes of learning	Stable individual progress	Providing the essential stability without compromising free progress
Ladder of Learning	Self-responsibility; taking ones learning in one's own hands, following long term targets; awareness of ones position on the learning map	Creating a step by step learner centred environment; support an individualized progression towards a long term goal; to change the role of the teacher in the learning process towards facilitation and co-learning
Ladders of Learning in linear and systemic systematisation	Becoming familiar with diverse ways of constructing knowledge and understanding; to be aware of the wholeness of themes, discovery of perspectives and the links between them	Preserve the individual characters of different disciplines or subject; taking care of interdisciplinary connections,
Milestone construction with	Stable construction of	Content broken up into self-

introduction, practice exercises, evaluation, reinforcement and enrichment	knowledge and understanding; sense of direction, contentment and a sense achievement arising from a meaningful and needful engagement and	constructible portions; Systematised optimises learning; continuous engagement with the learning process; giving a clear guidance to the learner
Material pool with tasks and activities of different kinds,	Developing different competences and skills like information processing, experimentation, documentation, presentation, productions	all aspects of individuality are included; involving the use of senses; catering to individual learning styles; drawing form social biographic background;
Culture specific and situation oriented texts and themes touching the daily life of the children	More sense in learning, motivating, feeling of inclusion of oneself, understanding the own role in the community as well as in the world at large	Rootedness in the own culture and connection to the actual living situation
The curriculum and the corresponding activities are targeted towards preservation and development of the local culture	Healthy acceptance and pride in their own heritage; competence to accept progressive elements of rapid change in the global environment; simultaneously maintaining the native cultural wisdom	Maintain the richness and diversity of local cultures and traditions,
Integrated evaluation of the learning processes in the Ladder of Learning in the form of short and long term tests	Self-reflection about the learning process; Identification of subject specific areas that the child needs to work on	Feedback for the child; realistic review of the sustainability of the constructed knowledge, skills and competences
Continues orientation and documentation of the learners progression	Daily resolution of issues and renewal of guidance strategies; parental involvement in the child's progress	Record keeping for the purpose of reflection of the teacher, communication with the parents
Natural mixed age groups through living and changing grouping system with different helping systems	Self-acceptance and discovering one's own role in the community; more self-confidence; learning sharing, cooperation and supporting	Individualised learning pace; non-competitive environment; coeducational issues addressed; natural tapping of children's abilities to build up a mutual exchange and support environment both individual and community oriented
Free field studies, extending the learning space to the surrounding and the community	Motivated and joyful learning, developing of scientific attitudes; understanding the practical use of knowledge and understanding	Creating an undivided, real, context-friendly and rich learning space , discovery and enquiry oriented learning
involving parents especially women in educational processes	Identification of roles and active involvement in process of change in the community	Women emancipation; appreciation for the role of education in the upliftment of the community

Fig. 47: MGML's characteristics

Further topics related to the MGML-Methodology were addressed during the conference. The NGOs were especially interested in the question which factors lead to a success of the RIVER-projects. The deliberations of RIVER's director and the scientific comments from the viewpoint of Research Team Integral led to special insights that can be applicable in future national and international projects. The following factors could be discerned and named:

- cooperation with all interested groups like teachers, headmasters, school administration, curriculum developers, artist, persons responsible within the education system
- establishment of a first pilot team of teachers/ experts
- the teachers' sense for being a creative part of the collective development (ownership)
- establishment of innovative fields of practice with a linked 'Resource Centre'
- establishment of model schools
- situation-oriented, integral culture of acting during the project processes
- participants' self-active taking part, active acceptance of 'ownership'
- working from different perspectives within the project
- cooperation with alternative schools/ educational institutions and their impulses

The conference's closing report of the provided workshops reveals that it has been also acknowledged on this European level how important a contribution for the field of 'Global Education' hails from an integral culture of acting that can be provided by the MGML-Methodology and its variations (Visegrad, Workshop 1). The developments depicted in chapter 2 and 4 impressively show the international potential impact of the MGML-Methodology. They furthermore grant it an outstanding relevance for further instructional and educational developments within the international education sector. In its further dynamic unfolding of potential, the unambiguously discernible 'Global Significance' of the MGML-Methodology is going to enable flexible learning in heterogeneous learning communities for children, adolescents and teachers on a worldwide scale.

5.2.4 References

Breuer, F. (2010): Reflexive Grounded Theory. Verlag für Sozialwissenschaften. Wiesbaden.

Elschenbroich, D. (2001). *Weltwissen der Siebenjährigen: Wie Kinder die Welt entdecken können*. München: Goldmann.

Girg, R. (2007). *Die integrale Schule des Menschen: Praxis und Horizonte der Integralpädagogik*. Regensburg: Roderer.

Girg, R., & Rao. P. (2011). Freedom to Learn – Multilevel Perspectives from RIVER (education towards global citizenship at community level). *Visegrad Regional Seminar*. Prague.

Glaser, B. (2007): The Grounded Theory Review. Volume 6. Issue 3. Sociology Press. Mill Valley.

Grimm, M. (2012). *Individualisierter Englischunterricht mit Lernleitern*. Unpublished manuscript.

Mayring, P. (2008*). Qualitative Inhaltsanalyse: Grundlagen und Techniken.* Weinheim: Beltz.

Müller, Th. (2009a). Straßenkinderreport: Zur Lage der Kinder in der Welt. http://www.strassenkinderreport.de/index.php?goto=206&user_name=. Accessed 6. May 2014.

---. (2009b). *Lernen über, mit und von Straßenkindern: Methoden der Straßenkinderpädagogik.* Unpublished manuscript.

Müller, Th., & Girg, R. (Eds.) (2007). *Integralpädagogik: Wahrnehmungen im lernenden Leben.* Regensburg: Roderer.

Noffke, S. (2013): "Revisiting the Professional, Personal and Political Dimensions of Action Research." In: Noffke, S./Somekh, Bridget: Educational Action Research.Sage Publication. London.

Panofsky, E. (1955): "Ikonographie und Ikonologie." In: Ders. (2006): Ikonographie & Ikonologie. DuMont Literatur und Kunst Verlag. Köln.

Schnur, S., & Müller, Th. (2013). *Elemente der MultiGradeMultiLevel-Methodology: Möglichkeiten und Grenzen für den Unterricht mit verhaltensauffälligen Schülern.* Schriften des Instituts für Sonderpädagogik der Julius-Maximilians-Universität Würzburg. Würzburg: freisleben.

6 Growing and Flowering with the MGML-Methodology

Chapter 6, the last chapter, sums up the book's main issues once again creating a synoptic overview of the central effective powers of the MGML-Methodology. It highlights MGML's value on the different levels of teaching in the classroom, school development and life disclosing MGML's potentials of growth and flowering.

Thirty years have passed since the young couple, Padmanabha Rao and Anumula Rama, started carrying their orange cloth bag from village to village through the barren country of Southern India.

Thirty years in which the cloth bag has evolved into small boxes that are stored on shelves at the wall; or experimental boxes that contain the most diverse objects for research tasks, a wall hanging from which learning games for English classes can be gathered; educational miniatures that can be stimuli of learning for existential topics, or vivid learning spaces with circling learning groups.

Thirty years, in which the 50 children from the first village school have become more than 10.000.000 children at more than 100.000 schools!

Thirty years in which the MGML-Methodology has not only reached India, but also Nepal, Ethiopia, South Africa, Namibia, Kenya, Siberia, France, the Czech Republic, Northern Italy and Germany.

The development taking place puts us in a cheerful and confident mood: there is change within the schools.

But why has precisely the MGML-Methodology developed such a power? Why has precisely the MGML-Methodology been able to grow that much beyond a method and become a complex concept of educational reform that works worldwide?

Why has the MGML-Methodology lastingly changed the Indian school landscape over the course of the last thirty years?

Why is it now also exuding in Europe where diverse approaches of open education have already been known for a long time?

The preceding chapters may have shown that the MGML-Methodology is much more than an educational method – even though it offers and conceptualizes teaching with a method and a clear-cut structure. It might be helpful to once again create a synoptic overview of the central effective powers of the MGML-Methodology, as well as to portray its potentials on the various levels of education and school in a summarizing and condensed way.

On the micro level the MGML-Methodology can be understood as a teaching method: it transforms the yearly state curricula into learning schedules for children and adolescents and designs small, manageable, meaningful and joyful learning activities corresponding to the principles of a complex and holistically understood didactic triangle. All dimensions of planning and opening are considered thereby and also match the respective needs and requirements. The often mentioned maxim 'The Child is in the Driver's Seat' is thus accounted for. Hence, heterogeneity is not an obstacle in the process of creating lessons, but rather the actual, real situation of 'multigrade' and 'multilevel' that can be easily and meaningfully designed via adequate teaching provisions. The teaching experiences show us that it is almost time for a new maxim for learning with Ladders of Learning and teaching with the MultiGradeMultiLevel-Methodology: the bigger the level of heterogeneity among the children, the better it is to design learning with Ladders of Learning. The abundance of diversity is purposefully utilized in the methodology in order to make the children aware of their diversity in a positive way. The MGML-Methodology enables flexible learning in heterogeneous learning communities.

The multiple variations that are by now internationally available are also interesting. They all follow the fundamental structural principle via the five learning steps; the characteristics of the learning activities and the further criteria of design, but can always be newly differentiated and interpreted. The options vary from simple linear or systemic models of Ladders of Learning to linked variations or existential forms to the deconstruction of the Ladder of Learning, respectively to empty Ladders of Learning that can be filled by the pupils themselves, or that pre-structure the materials for easier handling. At the same time, the possibilities of MGML-practice give rise to vital, interconnected learning spaces with flexible time structures.

Moreover, the MGML-Methodology acts on the meso-level of school development. The concept allows for a complete change of school within the shortest amount of time, while simultaneously maintaining an optimal usage of all resources at hand. The teachers work out all materials required for the classes in professionally instructed workshops within few weeks and immediately implement their results in practice. Teaching and personnel progress are left as a unity in the process. This way, the further education of the teachers immediately affects the quality of the classes and vice versa. The central motif of 'ownership' opens up the clear structure of the MGML-Methodology for the own contentual formation by the teachers. It leaves creative room for the people involved in the process and awards them the feeling of creating and forming something new and idiosyncratic. By seizing regional, cultural peculiarities, the moment of identity is extended onto the entire school family. Parents and the community become aware of the 'ownership' in their respective individual form.

Ultimately, the MGML-Methodology is resonant to the macro-level of life. Already the choice of material for working with the MGML-Methodology shows the conscious effort of being close to real life. The stories of the grandmothers, the traditional shadow play, songs or dances are consciously incorporated by the Indian colleagues. All of these are contents of the school, or the daily school routine of the children that continue and promote their cultural identity. The children advance through them and discover their hidden richness. At the same time, they learn how to manage and deal with uncertainties, crises and change. For the children – and also for the teacher – the small learning step opens up the learning situation, which is always new and into which they are allowed to get themselves into tentative, corporally perceivable, sensually seizing, bodily experiencing and intellectually comprehending ways.

However, every learning step is not only consciously planned and designed while being close to real life and focused on the pupils. It also demonstrates a special attitude and culture of acting. What occurs in the daily routine at school, what occurs in the encounters and occasions of communal and individual acting and forming, is a part of the big learning and living process of the individual child within and with the particular community. The provisions of the MGML-Methodology become reasons of the way of life, become biographical beads that link up to form chains, become threads of life that weave into a network. They are metaphoric of integral life praxis. Within this praxis every framing and planning takes a back seat. The actual happens – unique, singular and distinctive. For this reason the MGML-Methodology is also a non-method.

The doings of the young married couple might have been derided at first when they embarked on their journey thirty years ago. It might have been thought that dry land will always be dry land and will never become green pastures. But exactly that is what has happened. The poorest of children were given the opportunity to blossom and grow. Padmanabha Rao and Anumula Rama overcame many obstacles along the way. They were not deterred or discouraged and rose above themselves again and again. And all over the world the number of those grows that likewise have embarked on that journey and are embarking on it.

The vivid example of the two teachers from Southern India and the diverse developments, especially in Europe, are able give helpful stimuli.

Wherever it is succeeds to acknowledge and appreciate the integral interweaving and cosmic importance, there school will change. In cases where framing leads to freedom and awareness presides over the encounter with children, adolescents and adults, learning will change.

What might yet blossom out of this?

7 Works Cited

Abhiyan, S. S. (2009). Active Learning Methodology. http://www.ssa.tn.nic.in/docu/alm-manual.pdf. Accessed 6. May 2014.

Akila, R. (2009). A Trigger for Change in Primary Education: An Evaluation of ABL in Tamil Nadu. http://www.ssa.tn.nic.in/Docu/Coverpage.pdf. Accessed 6. May 2014.

Altner, N. (2006). *Achtsamkeit und Gesundheit: Auf dem Weg zu einer achtsamen Pädagogik*. Bewegungslehre und Bewegungsforschung Vol. 26. Immenhausen: Prolog Verlag.

---. (2007). Achtsamkeit und die Freude am Lernen. In T. Müller, & R. Girg (Eds.) *Integralpädagogik: Wahrnehmungen im lernenden Leben* (pp. 173-92). Regensburg: Roderer.

Anandalakshmy, S. (2007). Activity Based Learning: A Report on an Innovative Method in Tamil Nadu. http://www.ssa.tn.nic.in/docu/abl-report-by-dr.anandhalakshmi.pdf. Accessed 6. May. 2014.

Birch, I. Lally, M. (1995). Multi-Grade Teaching in Single Primary Schools. UNESCO. http://bvirtual.proeibandes.org/bvirtual/docs/multigradeteachingprimaryschools.pdf. Accessed 6. May 2014.

Arndt, C., Volkert, J. (2006). Amartya Sens Capability-Approach: Ein neues Konzept der deutschen Armuts- und Reichtumsberichterstattung. *Vierteljahreshefte zur Wirtschaftsforschung, 75.1*, 7–29 (2006). doi:10.3790/vjh.75.1.7.

Arnold, K.-H., & Sandfuchs, U., & Wiechmann, J. (Eds.) (2006). *Handbuch Unterricht*. Bad Heilbrunn: Klinkhardt.

Aryal, P. N. A Study on Multi-grade/Multi-class Teaching: Status and Issues. http://www.cerid.org/?s=formative&a=download&id=16a39404a3b807ad6a0f1ca0a89225f0. Accessed 6. May 2014.

Aurobindo, S. (1950). *Life Divine*. New York: Sri Aurobindo Ashram.

Ballauff, T. (2000). *Pädagogik als Bildungslehre* (4th ed). Baltmannsweiler: Schneider-Verlag Hohengehren,

Barthes, R. (1989). *Die helle Kammer: Bemerkung zur Photographie*. Frankfurt: Suhrkamp.

Bauer, J. (2006). *Warum ich fühle, was du fühlst: Intuitive Kommunikation und das Geheimnis der Spiegelneurone*. München: Heyne.

Bauman, Z. (2005). *Verworfenes Leben: Die Ausgegrenzten der Moderne*. Hamburg: Hamburger Edition.

---. (2006). *Moderne und Ambivalenz: Das Ende der Eindeutigkeit*. Hamburg: Hamburger Edition.

Becker, G. E. (2012). *Handlungsorientierte Didaktik* (10th ed). Weinheim: Beltz.

Behringer, L. (1998). *Lebensführung als Identitätsarbeit: Der Mensch im Chaos des modernen Alltags*. Frankfurt/Main: Campus.

Beierwaltes, W. (2001). *Das wahre Selbst: Studien zu Platons Begriff des Geistes und des Einen*. Frankfurt/Main: Vittorio Klostermann.

Benner, D., & Oelkers, J. (Eds.) (2004). *Historisches Wörterbuch der Pädagogik*. Weinheim: Beltz.

Bohl, T., & Kucharz, D. (2010). *Offener Unterricht heute: Konzeptionelle und didaktische Weiterentwicklung*. Weinheim: Beltz.

Bohm, D. (2002). *Der Dialog: Das offene Gespräch am Ende der Diskussionen* (5th ed). Stuttgart: Klett-Cotta.

Bohm, D. & Hiley, B. J. (1993). *The undivided universe: An ontological interpretation of quantum theory.* London/ New York: Routledge.

Böhmer, A., & Fink. E. (Eds.) (2006). *Sozialphilosophie - Anthropologie - Kosmologie - Pädagogik - Methodik.* Perspektiven Vol. 12. Würzburg: Königshausen & Neumann.

Boller, S., Rosowski, E., & Stroot, T. (Eds.) (2007). *Heterogenität in Schule und Unterricht: Handlungsansätze zum pädagogischen Umgang mit Vielfalt.* Weinheim: Beltz.

Bönsch, M., & Moegling, K. (Eds.) (2012). *Binnendifferenzierung.* Theorie und Praxis der Schulpädagogik 17-18. Immenhausen: Prolog.

Borrelli, M., & Ruhloff, J. (Eds.) (1998). *Interdisziplinäre Verflechtungen und intradisziplinäre Differenzierungen.* Deutsche Gegenwartspädagogik Vol. 3. Baltmannsweiler: Schneider-Verlag Hohengehren.

Brahme, M., & Babu, S. (2011). *Active Learning Methodology: A Review: A Study of the Middle School Pedagogical Intervention of SSA Tamil Nadu.* Unpublished manuscript.

Bräu, K., & Schwerdt, U. (Eds.) (2005). *Heterogenität als Chance: Vom produktiven Umgang mit Gleichheit und Differenz in der Schule.* Paderborner Beiträge zur Unterrichtsforschung und Lehrerbildung 9. Münster: Lit.

Buddensiek, W. (2001). *Zukunftsfähiges Leben in Häusern des Lernens: Szenarien, Projekte, Baupläne, Lernmaterialien; Theoriebausteine, Multimediaclip.* Göttingen: Die Werkstatt.

Bude, H., & Willisch, A. (Eds.) (2006). *Das Problem der Exklusion: Ausgegrenzte, Entbehrliche, Überflüssige.* Hamburg: Hamburger Edition.

Bürmann, J. (1992). *Gestaltpädagogik und Persönlichkeitsentwicklung: Theoretische Grundlagen und praktische Ansätze eines persönlich bedeutsamen Lernens.* Bad Heilbrunn: Klinkhardt.

Castel, R. (2000a). Die Fallstricke des Exklusionsbegriffs. *Mittelweg, 36,* 11–25.

---. (2000b). *Die Metamorphosen der sozialen Frage: Eine Chronik der Lohnarbeit* (2nd ed.). Édition discours 44. Konstanz: UVK.

Copei, F. (1969). *Der fruchtbare Moment im Bildungsprozess* (9th ed.). Heidelberg: Quelle & Meyer.

Csikszentmihalyi, M. (2010). *Das flow-Erlebnis: Jenseits von Angst und Langeweile: im Tun aufgehen.* Konzepte der Humanwissenschaften. Stuttgart: Klett-Cotta.

Dahrendorf, R. (1979). *Lebenschancen: Anläufe zur sozialen und politischen Theorie.* Frankfurt/ Main: Suhrkamp.

Danner, H., & Lippitz, W. (Eds.) (1984). *Beschreiben, Verstehen, Handeln: Phänomenologische Forschungen in der Pädagogik.* München: Röttger.

Delors, J. (Ed.) (1996). *Lernfähigkeit: Unser verborgener Reichtum: UNESCO-Bericht zur Bildung für das 21. Jahrhundert.* Neuwied: Luchterhand.

Dengler, S. (2012). *Arbeiten mit Lernleitern im Sachunterricht der Grundschule: Konzeptentwurf und Erprobung der Methodik für den HSU-Unterricht in der 2. Klasse der Grundschule Brennberg zum Thema „Wasser".* Unpublished manuscript.

Dörr, M., & Müller, B. (Eds.) (2012). *Nähe und Distanz: Ein Spannungsfeld pädagogischer Professionalität* (3rd ed.). Weinheim: Beltz.

Drosdowski, G. (1994). *Duden: Das große Wörterbuch der deutschen Sprache.* Mannheim: Dudenverlag.

Dühlmeier, B. (Ed.) (2008). *Mehr Außerschulische Lernorte in der Grundschule: Neun Beispiele für den fachübergreifenden Sachunterricht.* Baltmannsweiler: Schneider Verlag Hohengehren.

Eckert, E. (2001). *Maria und Mario Montessoris Kosmische Erziehung: Vision und Konkretion*. Impulse der Reformpädagogik 15. Berlin: LIT-Verlag.

EECMY-DASSC. (2010). Western Wollega Bethel Synod Development and Social Service Commission: Annual Progress Report. http://www.erep-schools.net/development/reports.html Accessed 6. May 2014.

Elschenbroich, D. (2001). *Weltwissen der Siebenjährigen: Wie Kinder die Welt entdecken können*. München: Goldmann.

European Commission. (2004). Gemeinsamer Bericht der Kommission und des Rates über die soziale Eingliederung. Brüssel. http://europa.eu/legislation_summaries/employment_and_social_policy/situation_in_e urope/c10616_de.htm. Accessed 25 March 2015.

Fischer, F. (1975). *Darstellung der Bildungskategorien im System der Wissenschaften*. Ratingen: Aloys Henn Verlag.

Fölling-Albers, M. (2001). Veränderte Kindheit – revisited. In H. Brügelmann, M. Fölling-Albers, S. Richter, A. Speck-Hamdan (Ed.), *Kindheitsforschung - Forschung zum Sachunterricht*. Jahrbuch Grundschule 3. Frankfurt/Main: Grundschulverband - Arbeitskreis Grundschule.

Fuhr, R., & Dauber, H. (Eds.) (2002). *Praxisentwicklung im Bildungsbereich - ein integraler Forschungsansatz*. Schriftenreihe zur humanistischen Pädagogik und Psychologie. Bad Heilbrunn: Klinkhardt.

Gebser, J. (1999). Gesamtausgabe (2nd ed.). Schaffhausen: Novalis.

Giddens, A. (1995). *Konsequenzen der Moderne*. Frankfurt am Main: Suhrkamp.

Gilber, E. (2007). *Kindern Wege öffnen: Beschreibung, Kritik, Weiterentwicklung: Das Bildungsprogramm AIE zur Eingliederung von ‚Out of School Children' in Indien*. Unpublished manuscript.

Girg, R. (1994). *Die Bedeutung des Vorverständnisses der Schüler für den Unterricht: Eine Untersuchung zur Didaktik*. Bad Heilbrunn: Klinkhardt.

---. (2007). *Die integrale Schule des Menschen: Praxis und Horizonte der Integralpädagogik*. Regensburg: Roderer.

Girg, R., Lichtinger, U., & Müller, T. (2011). *The MultiGradeMultiLevel-Methodology and its global significance: Ladders of Learning, variations, scientific horizons; a report*. Regensburg: Roderer.

---. (2010). *Die MultiGradeMultiLevel-Methodology und ihre Lernleitern*. Regensburg: Roderer.

Girg, R., & Rao. P. (2011). Freedom to Learn – Multilevel Perspectives from RIVER (education towards global citizenship at community level). Visegrad Regional Seminar. Prague.

Göhlich, M., Wulf, C., & Zirfas, J. (Eds.) (2007). *Pädagogische Theorien des Lernens*. Weinheim: Beltz.

Göhlich, H. D. M., & Zirfas, J. (2007). *Lernen: Ein pädagogischer Grundbegriff*. Allgemeine Pädagogik. Stuttgart: Kohlhammer.

Goldthorpe, J. (2003). Globalisierung und soziale Klassen. *Berliner Journal für Soziologie*, 3, 301–02. Accessed 6. May 2014. <http://download.springer.com/static/pdf/224/art%253A10.1007%252FBF03204672. pdf?auth66=1427297468_81c48e51720a74a9b260f6c393744e48&ext=.pdf>.

Gottwald, P. (2012). *Integrales Bewusstsein: Wie es zur Sprache - und zur Welt - bringen?*. Frankfurt/Main: Peter Lang.

Götz, M. (2014). *Lernen mit Lernleitern im Musikunterricht der Grundschule*. Unpublished manuscript.

187

Grieb, J. (2010). *Handlungsorientierter Physikunterricht am Beispiel der Mittelschulentwicklung in Rishi Valley.* Unpublished manuscript.

Grimm, M. (2012). *Individualisierter Englischunterricht mit Lernleitern.* Unpublished manuscript.

Gruber, H. (2006). Situiertes Lernen. In K.-H. Arnold, U. Sandfuchs, & J. Wiechmann (Eds.), *Handbuch Unterricht.* Bad Heilbrunn: Klinkhardt. pp. 331 – 34.

de Haan, G. (1996). *Die Zeit in der Pädagogik: Vermittlungen zwischen der Fülle der Welt und der Kürze des Lebens.* Weinheim: Beltz.

Haeffner, G. (1996). *In der Gegenwart leben: Auf den Spuren eines Urphänomens.* Stuttgart: Kohlhammer.

---. (2000). *Philosophische Anthropologie* (3rd ed.). Stuttgart: Kohlhammer.

Heidenreich, T., & Michalak, J. (Eds.) (2006). *Achtsamkeit und Akzeptanz in der Psychotherapie: Ein Handbuch* (2nd ed.). Tübingen: dgvt-Verlag.

Hellbusch, K. (2003). *Das integrale Bewusstsein: Jean Gebsers Konzeption der Bewusstseinsentfaltung als prima philosophia unserer Zeit.* Berlin: Tenea.

Horkheimer, M. (1978). Begriff der Bildung. Immatrikulationsrede 1952/53. In J. E. Pleines (Ed.), *Bildungstheorien: Probleme u. Positionen* (pp. 22-27). Freiburg: Herder.

Hosang, M. (2000). *Der integrale Mensch: Homo sapiens integralis.* Gladenbach: Hinder + Deelmann.

Hübinger, W. (1999). Prekärer Wohlstand: Spaltet eine Wohlstandswelle die Gesellschaft. *Politik und Zeitgeschichte,*18, 18-26.

Hüther, G. (2006). *Die Macht der inneren Bilder: Wie Visionen das Gehirn, den Menschen und die Welt verändern.* Göttingen: Vandenhoeck & Ruprecht.

Jäger, R. S. (2007). *Beobachten, beurteilen und fördern! Lehrbuch für die Aus-, Fort- und Weiterbildung.* Erziehungswissenschaft 21. Landau: Verlag Empirische Pädagogik.

Jantsch, E. (1988). *Die Selbstorganisation des Universums: Vom Urknall zum menschlichen Geist* (4th ed). München: dtv-Wissenschaft.

Kade, J., & Seitter, W. (2007). Lebenslanges Lernen. In M. Göhlich, C. Wulf, & J. Zirfas (Eds.), *Pädagogische Theorien des Lernens.* Weinheim: Beltz.

Kaltwasser, V. (2010). *Persönlichkeit und Präsenz: Achtsamkeit im Lehrerberuf.* Weinheim: Beltz.

Kanamüller, L. (2006). *Indische Satellite-Schools als Grundlage der Entwicklung und Konstruktion von Lernleitern.* Unpublished manuscript.

Kaplan, Robert D. (1996). *The ends of the earth: From Togo to Turkmenistan, from Iran to Cambodia - a journey to the frontiers of anarchy.* York: Vintage Books.

Kränzl-Nagl, R., Mierendorff, J. (2007). Kindheit im Wandel: Annäherungen an ein komplexes Phänomen. *SWS- Rundschau,* 1, 3–25.

Krishnamurti, J. (1953/1981). *Education and the significance of life.* San Francisco: Harper & Row.

---. (1991). *The second Krishnamurti Reader.* London: Penguin Books.

---. (2004). *Krishnamurti's notebook.* Ojai: Krishnamurti Publications of America.

---. (1981/2006b). *Letters to the Schools, Vol. 1.* Chennai: Krishnamurti Foundation India.

---. (1974/2006a). *On Education.* Chennai: Krishnamurti Foundation India.

---. (2005). *This light in oneself: True meditation.* Boston: Shambhala.

---. (n.d.). The Intent of the Krishnamurti Schools. https://www.brockwood.org.uk/intentions.html. Accessed 9 December 2014.

Krishnamurti, J., & McCoy, R. (2006). *The whole movement of life is learning: J. Krishnamurti's letters to his schools.* Bramdean. Krishnamurti Foundation India.

Krishnamurti Foundation India. (2011). Rishi Valley School: 80 years. Chennai: Krishnamurti Foundation India.

Laging, R. (Ed.) (2010). *Altersgemischtes Lernen in der Schule: (Grundlagen, Schulmodelle, Unterrichtspraxis)* (4th ed). Grundlagen der Schulpädagogik 28. Baltmannsweiler: Schneider-Verlag Hohengehren.

Lenhart, V. (2007). Die Globalisierung in der Sicht der Vergleichenden Erziehungswissenschaft. *Zeitschrift für Pädagogik, 6,* 810–24.

Lenzen, D. (Ed.) (1990). *Kunst und Pädagogik: Erziehungswissenschaft auf dem Weg zur Ästhetik?* Darmstadt: Wissenschaftliche Buchgesellschaft.

Leonhard, S. (2006). *Leiblich lernen und lehren: Ein religionsdidaktischer Diskurs.* Praktische Theologie heute 79. Stuttgart: Kohlhammer.

Lichtinger, U. (2010). *Ritual im Wandel: Zur Bedeutung von Veränderungsprozessen in schulischen Ritualen; Exemplarisch aufgezeigt am "Gewölbe-Ritual" der pädagogischen Einrichtung "Schlössli Ins", Schweiz.* Regensburg: Roderer.

Lichtinger, U. (2014). Schule – Ort der Begegnung, Stätte des Menschseins? In J. Fetzer, N. Fischer, & C. Tillack, *Beziehungen in Schule und Unterricht.* Kassel: Prolog.

Lichtinger, U., Th. Müller, and R. Girg. "Individuelles Lernen mit Lernleitern." Binnendifferenzierung. Ed. M. Bönsch and K. Moegling. Immenhausen: Prolog, 2012. Print. Theorie und Praxis der Schulpädagogik Bd.17-18.

Liebau, E. (2007). Leibliches Lernen. In M. Göhlich, C. Wulf, & J. Zirfas, *Pädagogische Theorien des Lernens.* Weinheim: Beltz.

Ludwig, H. (2008). *Montessori-Schulen und ihre Didaktik* (2nd ed.). Basiswissen Grundschule 15. Baltmannsweiler: Schneider-Verlag Hohengehren.

Mayring, P. (2008*). Qualitative Inhaltsanalyse: Grundlagen und Techniken.* Weinheim: Beltz.

Meyer, H. (2004). *Was ist guter Unterricht?* (2nd ed.). Berlin: Cornelsen Scriptor.

Meyer-Drawe, K. (1984). Der fruchtbare Moment im Bildungsprozess: Zu Copeis phänomenologischen Ansatz pädagogischer Theoriebildung. In H. Danner, & W. Lippitz, *Beschreiben, Verstehen, Handeln: Phänomenologische Forschungen in der Pädagogik* (pp. 91-106). Munich: Rottger.

---. *Diskurse des Lernens* (2nd ed.). Paderborn: Fink.

Meyer-Wolters, H. (1992). *Koexistenz und Freiheit: Eugen Finks Anthropologie und Bildungstheorie.* Würzburg: Königshausen & Neumann.

Milerova, J. (2011). Visegrad Regional Seminar on Global Development: Final Report. http://www.fors.cz/user_files/visegradseminar_finalreport.pdf. Accessed 6. May 2014.

Miller, A., & Wulf, C. (Eds.) (1999). *Transformation der Zeit: Wie der Zeitenwandel die Menschen und die Welt verändert.* Darmstadt: Synergia.

Mollenhauer, K. (1990a). Aesthetische Bildung zwischen Kritik und Selbstgewissheit. *Zeitschrift für Pädagogik, 4,* 481–94.

---. (1990b). Die vergessene Dimension des Ästhetischen in der Erziehungs- und Bildungstheorie. In D. Lenzen, *Kunst und Pädagogik: Erziehungswissenschaft auf dem Weg zur Ästhetik?* Darmstadt: Wissenschaftliche Buchgesellschaft.

---. (1998). Der Leib: Bildungstheoretische Beobachtungen an ästhetischen Objekten. In M. Borrelli, & J. Ruhloff, *Interdisziplinäre Verflechtungen und intradisziplinäre Differenzierungen.* Deutsche Gegenwartspädagogik 3. Baltmannsweiler: Schneider-Verlag Hohengehren.

Montessori, M., & Ludwig, H. (2010). *Die Entdeckung des Kindes.* Gesammelte Werke / Maria Montessori 1. Freiburg: Herder.

Morin, E. (2001). *Die sieben Fundamente des Wissens für eine Erziehung der Zukunft.* Hamburg: Krämer.

Müller, Th. (2012b). Erfahrungen mit dem konkreten Einsatz der Lernleiterarbeit in der Grundschulstufe der St. Vincent-Schule. *Fördermagazin*, 3, 53-54.

---. (2009b). *Lernen über, mit und von Straßenkindern: Methoden der Straßenkinderpädagogik.* Unpublished manuscript.

---. (2012a). Mit mir geht was weiter...: Zur Arbeit mit der MultiGradeMultiLevel-Methodology und ihren Lernleitern an der St. Vincent-Schule. *Fördermagazin*, 3, 49-52.

---. (2009a). Straßenkinderreport: Zur Lage der Kinder in der Welt. http://www.strassenkinderreport.de/index.php?goto=206&user_name=. Accessed 6. May 2014.

---. (2007). Die Situation als Urgrund integralpädagogischen Handelns: Wider eine Pädagogik des Bewerkstelligens und der Perspektivität. In R. Girg, & T. Müller, *Integralpädagogik: Wahrnehmungen im lernenden Leben.* Regensburg: Roderer.

---. (2008). *Innere Armut: Kinder und Jugendliche zwischen Mangel und Überfluss.* Wiesbaden: VS-Verlag.

Müller, T., & Girg, R. (Eds.) (2007). *Integralpädagogik: Wahrnehmungen im lernenden Leben.* Regensburg: Roderer.

Nassehi, A. (2006). Die paradoxe Einheit von Inklusion und Exklusion: Ein systemtheoretischer Blick auf die ‚Phänomene'. In H. Bude, & A. Willisch, *Das Problem der Exklusion: Ausgegrenzte, Entbehrliche, Überflüssige.* Hamburg: Hamburger Edition.

North-South Centre - European Centre for Global Interdependence and Solidarity (n.d.). Education: Strategies and Capacity Building for Global Education. http://www.coe.int/t/dg4/nscentre/GE_en.asp. Accessed 6. May 2014.

---. (n.d.). Global education guidelines: A handbook for educators to understand and implement global education. http://www.coe.int/t/dg4/nscentre/GE/GE-Guidelines/GEguidelines-web.pdf. Accessed 6. May 2014.

Otto, R. (1978). *Das Heilige: Über das Irrationale in der Idee des Göttlichen und sein Verhältnis zum Rationalen.* München: Beck.

Partho (Ed.). *Integral Education: A Foundation for the Future.* Pondicherry: Ubs Publishers' Distributors (p) Ltd.

Paul, H., et al. (2002). *Deutsches Wörterbuch: Bedeutungsgeschichte und Aufbau unseres Wortschatzes* (10th ed.). Tübingen: M. Niemeyer.

Pius, T., &Rehle, C. (Eds.) (2009). *Inklusive Schule: Leben und Lernen mittendrin.* Bad Heilbrunn: Klinkhardt.

Pleines, J. E. (Ed.) (1978). *Bildungstheorien: Probleme und Positionen.* Freiburg: Herder.

Pöppel, E. (2006). *Der Rahmen: Ein Blick des Gehirns auf unser Ich.* München: Hanser.

Precht, R. D. (2009). Wir wählen uns alle nur selbst. Zeit online. http://www.zeit.de/2009/38/Wahlkampf. Accessed 6. May 2014.

Prenzel, M., Schratz, M., & Schultebrauks-Burkhart, G. (Eds.) (2011). *Was für Schulen! Schule der Zukunft in gesellschaftlicher Verantwortung ; der Deutsche Schulpreis 2011.* Seelze: Kallmeyer.

Rawls, J. (1988). *Eine Theorie der Gerechtigkeit* (2nd ed.). Suhrkamp Taschenbuch Wissenschaft 271. Frankfurt/Main: Suhrkamp.

Riedmeier, V. (2014). *Buchstabeneinführung mit Lernleitern: Praktische Erprobung in einer ersten Klasse.* Regensburg: Unpublished manuscript.

Rilke, R. M. (1988). Samskola– Wie Schule sein könnte. In D. Lenzen, & R. Winkel, *Pädagogische Epochen: Von der Antike bis zur Gegenwart*. Düsseldorf: Schwann.

Rishi Valley Education Center. Brochure Study Centre. Unpublished document.

Rishi Valley Institute for Educational Resources (RIVER). (2003). *A multigrade trainers's resource pack: Background document-I*. Chennai: Krishnamurti Foundation India.

---. (n.d.). A multigrade trainer's resource pack: A trainer's module- II. Krishnamurti Foundation India.

---. (n.d.). A multigrade trainer's resource pack: Background document- II. Krishnamurti Foundation India.

---. (n.d.). *Redesigning the Elementary School: MultiLevel Perspectives from Rishi Valley*.

---. (2009). Science curriculum for REC Middle School: An Overview.

Rodrigues, H., & Krishnamurti, J. (2001). Krishnamurti's insight: An examination of his teachings on the nature of mind and religion. Varanasi, India: Pilgrims Publishing.

Rombach, H. (1980). *Phänomenologie des gegenwärtigen Bewusstseins*. Freiburg: Alber.

---. (1993). *Strukturanthropologie: Der menschliche Mensch*. Freiburg: Alber.

Roth, H. (1976). Die „originale Begegnung" als methodisches Prinzip. In H. Roth, *Pädagogische Psychologie des Lehrens und Lernens*. Hannover: Schroedel.

Schleicher, K. (2009). *Lernen im Leben und für das Leben: Informelles Lernen als Zukunftsaufgabe*. Hamburg: Krämer.

Schnur, S., & Müller, Th. (2013). *Elemente der MultiGradeMultiLevel-Methodology: Möglichkeiten und Grenzen für den Unterricht mit verhaltensauffälligen Schülern*. Schriften des Instituts für Sonderpädagogik der Julius-Maximilians-Universität Würzburg. Würzburg: freisleben.

Schromek, A. (2012). *MultiGradeMultiLevel-Methodology in der Oberstufe am Beispiel des Deutsch als Fremdsprache Unterrichts in Namibia*. Unpublished manuscript.

Schübl, E. (2003). *Jean Gebser (1905-1973): Ein Sucher und Forscher in den Grenz- und Übergangsgebieten des menschlichen Wissens und Philosophierens*. Zürich: Chronos.

Schulze, G. (1992). *Die Erlebnisgesellschaft: Kultursoziologie der Gegenwart*. Frankfurt/Main: Campus.

Seitz, K. (2002). Globalisierung als pädagogisches Problem. http://doku.cac.at/kseitz.pdf. Accessed 6. May 2014.

Sen, A. K. (2002). *Ökonomie für den Menschen: Wege zu Gerechtigkeit und Solidarität in der Marktwirtschaft* (2nd ed.). München: Hanser.

Sequeira, A. R. (1996). *Die Philosophien Indiens*. Indische Philosophie 1. Aachen: Ein-Fach-Verlag.

Siewert, N. (2008). *Individuelle Förderung von Lesekompetenz in der Grundschule – Theoretische Überlegungen und Darstellung des Praxisbeispiels der Volksschule Loiching*. Unpublished manuscript.

Solowij, T. (2009). *Zur Bedeutung von Schülerexperimenten als Beitrag für einen aktivitätsorientierten Unterricht – aufgezeigt an der Mittelschulentwicklung der RIVER-Projekte*. Unpublished manuscript.

Stenger, U. (2007). Zum Ereignischarakter in Bildungsprozessen. In C. Wulf, & J. Zirfas (Ed.), *Pädagogik des Performativen: Theorien, Methoden, Perspektiven*. Weinheim: Beltz.

Sting, S. (1999). Zeit für sich selbst: Zur Zeitdimension von Selbstbildungsprozessen. In A. Miller, & C. Wulf (Ed.), *Transformation der Zeit: Wie der Zeitenwandel die Menschen und die Welt verändert*. Darmstadt: Synergia.

Thapan, M. (2001). J. Krishnamurti: (1895-1986). *Prospects: the quarterly review of comparative education*, 31(2), 273-86.

---. (2006). *Life at school: An ethnographic study* (2nd ed.). New Delhi: Oxford University Press.

Thich, N. H. (2004). *Das Herz von Buddhas Lehre: Leiden verwandeln - die Praxis des glücklichen Lebens*. Freiburg: Herder.

Vogel, B. (2006). Soziale Verwundbarkeit und prekärer Wohlstand: Für ein verändertes Vokabular sozialer Ungleichheit. In H. Bude, & A. Willisch (Ed.), *Das Problem der Exklusion: Ausgegrenzte, Entbehrliche, Überflüssige*. Hamburg: Hamburger Edition.

Wagenschein, M. (1999). *Verstehen lehren: Genetisch - sokratisch - exemplarisch*. Weinheim: Beltz.

Warwitz, S. A. (2001). *Sinnsuche im Wagnis: Leben in wachsenden Ringen; Erklärungsmodelle für grenzüberschreitendes Verhalten*. Baltmannsweiler: Schneider Verlag Hohengehren.

Watschinger, J., & Kühebacher, J. (Eds.) (2007). *Schularchitektur und neue Lernkultur: Neues Lernen - neue Räume*. Bern: hep Verlag.

Westphal, K. (2007). Lernen als Ereignis. Schultheater als performative Praxis. Zur Aufführungspraxis von Theater. In C. Wulf, & J. Zirfas, *Pädagogik des Performativen: Theorien, Methoden, Perspektiven*. Weinheim: Beltz.

Wiater, W. (2012). *Unterrichtsprinzipien* (3rd ed.). Prüfungswissen - Basiswissen Schulpädagogik. Donauwörth: Auer.

Wilber, K. (2001b). *Eros, Kosmos, Logos: Eine Jahrtausend-Vision*. Frankfurt/Main: Fischer.

---. (2001a). Integrale Psychologie: Geist, Bewußtsein, Psychologie, Therapie (2nd ed.). Freiamt (Schwarzwald): Arbor.

---. (2007). Integrale Spiritualität: Spirituelle Intelligenz rettet die Welt (5th ed.). München: Kösel.

Winkel, R., & Lenzen, D. (Eds.) (1988). *Pädagogische Epochen: Von der Antike bis zur Gegenwart*. Düsseldorf: Schwann.

Wulf, C., & Zirfas, J. (Eds.) (2004). *Die Kultur des Rituals: Inszenierungen, Praktiken, Symbole*. München: Fink.

---. (2007). *Pädagogik des Performativen: Theorien, Methoden, Perspektiven*. Weinheim: Beltz.

Zimmer, R. (2012). Handbuch der Sinneswahrnehmung: Grundlagen einer ganzheitlichen Bildung und Erziehung. Freiburg: Herder.

GPSR Authorized Representative: Easy Access System Europe, Mustamäe tee 50, 10621 Tallinn, Estonia, gpsr.requests@easproject.com